A NAMELESS BODY

The woman's nude body was lying a few feet from a large tree in a grassy area covered with leaves on the right side of the dirt road just over a steep rise. She was lying on her back with her arms extended up from her body. Her legs were slightly apart and extended, but it didn't appear her body had been "posed." There was a black-and-tan striped shoelace or bootlace around her neck. Police couldn't figure out if there were two laces or one lace that had been wrapped around her neck twice. There were leaves on the left side of her head and maggot eggs on her face, genitals, and the other openings on her body.

Police also found empty shopping bags and facial tissues near the woman's body, which they collected as evidence. About a hundred feet away from her body in the shoulder-length grass next to the road and near a bean field, police found a white tennis shoe with blue striping on it. A short distance away, police discovered the other tennis shoe in a thicket. It appeared that someone had tossed each shoe separately into the brush from the road because police didn't find any evidence that anyone had trampled on the scrub in the area.

The woman's body was sealed and photographed, then recovered by employees of a local funeral parlor. Detectives finished up a little after two-thirty in the morning. They went back to the Peoria Police Department (PPD) to try to identify the body. They looked through missing persons reports to try to figure out who she was.

D1132787

BONE CRUSHER

LINDA ROSENCRANCE

PINNACLE BOOKS
Kensington Publishing Corp.
http://www.kensingtonbooks.com

PINNACLE BOOKS are published by

Kensington Publishing Corp.
119 West 40th Street
New York, NY 10018

All Kensington Titles, Imprints, and Distributed Lines are available at special quantity discounts for bulk purchases for sales promotions, premiums, fund-raising, and educational or institutional use. Special book excerpts or customized printings can also be created to fit specific needs. For details, write or phone the office of the Kensington Special Sales Manager: Kensington Publishing Corp., 119 West 40th Street, New York, NY 10018, attn: Special Sales Department, Phone: 1-800-221-2647.

Pinnacle and the P logo Reg. U.S. Pat. & TM Off.

ISBN-13: 978-0-7860-2214-4
ISBN-10: 0-7860-2214-0

First Printing: October 2010

10 9 8 7 6 5 4 3 2 1

Printed in the United States of America

For Steven C., my once and, I hope, future friend.

ACKNOWLEDGMENTS

I'd like to thank my agent Janet Benrey, of Benrey Literary Agency, for her friendship and support. I'd also like to thank my editors at Kensington, Michaela Hamilton and Richard Ember, who I'm sure breathed a sigh of relief when I finally finished.

I'd also like to thank Peoria County sheriff Michael McCoy, Tazewell County sheriff Robert Huston, Lieutenant Mark Greskoviak, of the Peoria County Sheriff's Office, members of the task force that investigated the murders and ultimately apprehended Larry Bright, Peoria County state's attorney Kevin Lyons, and Seth Uphoff and Paulette Fair, of the state's attorney's office.

I would also like to thank the nice lady at the Creve Coeur, Illinois, Police Department who helped this frazzled writer track down some information at the eleventh hour, and the nice gentleman at the Tazewell County Coroner's Office who helped me verify that information.

To my friends, who have had to put up with one canceled social engagement after another—sorry.

And finally a shout-out to Marc J. Schiller, who is doing his best to make me understand the importance of a good outline. I'm trying.

We serial killers are your sons, we are your husbands, we are everywhere. And there will be more of your children dead tomorrow.

—Ted Bundy, serial killer

PROLOGUE

Peoria, Illinois, was incorporated as a village on March 11, 1835. When it was incorporated on April 21, 1845, as a city, it ended the village president form of government and began the mayoral system. Peoria's first mayor was William Hale.

Peoria (named after the Peoria Indian tribe) is the largest city on the Illinois River, and the county seat of Peoria County, Illinois. As of 2007, it had a population of approximately 144,000. It sits midway between Chicago and St. Louis.

In 1830, John Hamlin constructed the flour mill on Kickapoo Creek—and so began the city's first industry. In 1837, E. F. Nowland started another big industry, the pork industry. Over the years a number of industries have cropped up in Peoria, including carriage factories, pottery makers, breweries, wholesale warehousing, casting foundries, glucose factories, ice harvesting, farm machinery manufacturing, and furniture making.

Peoria won the All-America City Award three times, in 1953, 1966, and 1989. In 2007, *Forbes* ranked Peoria number forty-seven out of the largest 150 metropolitan areas in its annual "Best Places for Business and Careers." *Forbes* evaluated the city on the cost of doing business, cost of living, entertainment opportunities, and income growth. In 2009, Peoria was ranked sixteenth best city with a population of a hundred thousand to two hundred thousand in the "U.S. Next Cities List," compiled by Next Generation Consulting.

And who hasn't heard the famous question: Will it play in Peoria? The phrase originated during the days of vaudeville in the early 1920s and 1930s. At that time Peoria was one of the most important places in the country for vaudeville acts to perform. Because Peoria was considered the "typical" American town, new live acts and shows were booked into theaters in Peoria to test the reactions of audiences. If an act did well in Peoria, vaudeville companies knew that it would work throughout the nation.

Today Peoria is still used as a test market by advertisers trying to determine how popular products and ideas will fare around the country.

Peoria also has everything its residents could want: affordable housing, great schools and colleges, excellent medical facilities, shopping, arts and entertainment, and many recreational areas. But despite its growth, Peoria still exudes Midwestern friendliness and warmth.

But there's a seedy side to Peoria—a side inhabited by prostitutes and drug addicts and those who prey on them. A side of the city where a thirtysomething mama's boy could go seemingly unnoticed on a fifteen-month killing spree.

1

He didn't want to do it again.

He knew it was wrong, but it wasn't his fault. It was those damn voices echoing in his head. He tried to fight them, but he was powerless.

"Kill," they said.

And he obeyed.

Under cover of darkness on that warm September evening in 2004, he cruised the backstreets of Peoria in his Chevy Blazer, looking for his next victim. "Hunting," he called it. And then he found her. His prey. She was standing in the parking lot of the furniture store, next to Woody's Bar, like she often did. He pulled up to her and she jumped in. She had no idea it was her night to die.

"You wanna party?" he asked, showing her an eight ball.

"Yeah, but can you take me to get more crack for my friend first?" she asked.

So he drove her to a little house next to a yellow building on the south side of town. He dropped her off, circled the block, and waited for her to come out. Then he took her back to Woody's so she could deliver the drugs.

When she finished her business, she got back in the car and he drove her to his place on Starr Court. They went inside, where they drank whiskey and smoked crack until they were wasted. Then they got naked and had sex. He wore a condom, like he always did, but it broke.

"You can't let her go. You can't let her go. You gotta do it. You gotta do it."

The voices again.

He put his hand on her throat and squeezed the life out of her. He had to get rid of the body, but he couldn't do the fire thing because his mom was home and his grandma was coming the next day. He tried to pick her up, but her body was slick from the lotion she had been wearing, and he couldn't get a grip. So he pulled a bootlace out of one of his work boots and tied it around her neck. Then grabbing onto the lace, he pulled and dragged her off the bed, out of the house, and into the Blazer.

He drove to a place in rural Hopedale that he called "Pitzer's Cabin," although he never remembered ever seeing an actual cabin there. He took the interstate until he spotted a cruiser a couple cars ahead of him; then he turned off, onto Route 98, and drove the back roads the rest of the way. He drove down a dirt road and over a levee. He parked the Blazer on top of the levee, then dragged her body a ways and discarded it by a tree.

He got back in his car and drove home, tossing her clothes and shoes out the window on the way. As he was driving, he realized he didn't have his false teeth. Worried he had lost them when he dumped her body, he turned his car around and headed back to the levee. When he got there, he pulled over and used his headlights to look around. Unable to locate them, he left. When he got home, he breathed a sigh of relief. He had found his teeth.

It was a beautiful early-fall evening. Perfect for camping. Michael McDonough and Casey Kauffman wanted to take advantage of the weather, so they packed up Kauffman's truck and headed to their favorite spot, near the Mackinaw River on King Road. When they arrived at about 9:15 P.M., they noticed a blue Dodge Neon and a gray Ford Ranger parked near the exact place they had planned to camp. They realized that the owners of the two vehicles were having sex, so Kauffman drove a little farther and parked his truck along the trail.

He and McDonough unpacked the truck and set up camp. They spent forty-five minutes trying to light a fire, but the wood they brought with them didn't want to burn. So McDonough set out with his flashlight to gather up some small sticks and branches, while Kauffman set up the tent. The other two vehicles had since left the area, so McDonough walked over to where they had been parked to find some wood.

What he found, instead, was the nude body of a black woman lying on her back on the ground in the woods, her head facing toward the right. The woman had what looked like some kind of string or necklace around her neck. He yelled for Kauffman, who called 911 as soon as he saw the corpse.

It was just about half past ten at night when Deputy Sergeant Darryl Stoecker and Deputy Sheriff Dan Nieukirk, of the Tazewell County Sheriff's Office (TCSO), were dispatched to King Road to investigate the discovery of the body of a black woman who had been found naked in the woods. A gravel road, King Road ran north about a half mile from Wildlife Drive, coming to a dead end at the Mackinaw River. Detective Hal Harper and Deputy Dave Wilson were also en route to the scene.

Wilson was the first to arrive. He parked his squad car at the crest of the hill at the end of King Road. When he got out of his car, he saw McDonough and Kauffman standing at the base of the hill where the road split into three sections. As Wilson walked down the hill, he noticed one of the men pointing to a wooded area to the east of the roadway. As he moved closer, Wilson saw the body of a black woman lying on her back on the ground. By then, the other investigators also had arrived.

Wilson walked back to the campers and listened as Kauffman explained how he happened to find the woman's body. The detectives asked for the license plate numbers of the vehicles that belonged to the man and woman who had been having sex. Then he telephoned them to determine what, if anything, they had seen. The couple told police all they saw before they left were the two campers and a farmer working in a field.

As they continued to investigate, the deputies stopped a red Ford F10 that was leaving one of the farms. The driver said he and his five-year-old son, as well as his buddy, who had been driving a silver Chevrolet Tornado, had been camping in the area on property owned by a local farmer.

Wilson talked to the men, then turned the scene over to task force members, Detective Cy Taylor, Captain Bobby Henderson, and Detective Hal Harper, who had arrived with a crime scene technician to investigate and process the scene.

The woman's nude body was lying a few feet from a large tree in a grassy area covered with leaves on the right side of the dirt road, just over a steep rise. She was lying on her back with her arms extended up from her body. Her legs were slightly apart and extended, but it didn't appear her body had been posed. There was a black-and-tan–striped shoelace or bootlace around her neck. Police couldn't figure out if there were two laces or one lace that had been wrapped around her neck twice. There were leaves on the left side of her head and maggot eggs on her face, genitals, and the other openings on her body.

Police also found empty shopping bags and facial tissues near the woman's body, which they collected as evidence. About a hundred feet away from her body in the shoulder-length grass next to the road and near a bean field, police found a white tennis shoe with blue striping on it. A short distance away, police discovered the other tennis shoe in a thicket. It appeared that someone had tossed each shoe separately into the brush from the road, because police didn't find any evidence that anyone had trampled on the scrub in the area. Police also observed a glove that had been tied as some sort of marker on the top of a hand-made barbed-wire fence, most likely by a farmer.

The woman's body was photographed and sealed, then recovered by employees of a local funeral parlor under the direction of an assistant coroner. Investigators conducted a thorough search of the area, but their observations were limited because it was dark. Detectives finished up a little after two-thirty in the morning. Henderson and Harper went back to the Peoria Police Department (PPD) to try and identify the body. They looked through mug shots and missing persons reports, but they couldn't figure out who she was.

At just about the same time Harper was on the phone at the Peoria Police Department trying to identify the body, a woman from East St. Louis, Illinois, called the police with information that her sister Benita might have been murdered in Peoria. The woman said someone had telephoned her to give her that information.

The woman said a female called her at home and, trying to disguise her voice, said Benita had been murdered. Then a man, who identified himself as "Detective Mike Williams," also called Benita's sister to say Benita had been murdered and that the family should go to Peoria.

The problem was that police hadn't yet released the information about the body found on King

Road. So they were worried that the person or people making the phone calls had "suspect knowledge" about the crime. However, the female caller and the "detective" said the body had been found in Peoria, not in Tazewell County where it was actually found.

So police went to Benita's home in Peoria to check on her and discovered she was alive and well. She had no idea why someone would think she had been murdered. When her family arrived, they were relieved to find she was safe.

The next day Benita met Harper at the Peoria Police Department. She told him she had been having problems with her friend Sherry, who also lived in Peoria. Benita said Sherry had recently been arrested and charged with smashing out the windows in Benita's car. Benita said she also believed Sherry had broken into her apartment and was probably the person who had made the phone call saying she was dead. Harper, however, didn't quite believe Benita's story. He figured there had to be more to it than what Benita was saying.

The next evening Harper and PPD detective Chris Hauk went to Sherry's house to talk to her. Sherry told them that she and Benita were fighting because Benita had stolen some jewelry from her. But she was adamant that she hadn't made any phone calls to Benita's family in East St. Louis as a prank or for any other reason. And she said she had never smashed the windows in Benita's car. She said Benita was lying to get her in trouble.

After he got back to the station, Harper called Benita and informed her that Sherry denied making the phone calls or doing anything else to her. He told Benita he believed she was lying to him and that she had actually called her family to tell them she was dead. Angry, Benita said she would "take the rap for all of it, if that's what the cops wanted," but she hadn't done anything.

Later that night, Sherry and a man named Conroy showed up at the station to talk to Harper. Sherry said Conroy had helped Benita make the calls to her family and she wanted police to clear her as a suspect. Conroy told Harper he was sorry he ever let Benita talk him into pulling the prank on her family. And he wanted police to know that no one was killed, and he didn't know anything about anyone being killed.

Conroy said Benita asked him to help her get back at her family for pranking her. Benita said someone in her family had called her to tell her a friend was dead, and she wanted to turn the tables on them. So with Benita listening in on an extension, Conroy called her sister and told her that Benita had been found dead and they needed to get to Peoria as quickly as possible.

But when Benita's sister became terrified and panicky, Conroy realized it wasn't funny anymore and immediately hung up the phone. Conroy decided to come forward to the police because the incident seemed to have sidetracked a real homicide investigation. Conroy told Harper he didn't care if he was arrested for the stupid stunt he pulled on Benita's family but he wanted to be cleared as a suspect in the real murder.

Harper called Benita's sister and told her what had happened was just a practical joke gone horribly wrong. However, the timing of the prank was extremely coincidental, to say the least.

At about five in the morning, Detective Eric Goeken and other members of the Tazewell County Sheriff's Office went back to collect evidence from where the body had been found. Goeken and Detective Cy Taylor took the evidence back to the Morton Crime Lab and began the process of trying to identify the victim.

While they were there, crime lab technicians were able to identify the woman by her fingerprints. She was forty-year-old Linda Kay Neal. After learning that Linda had been staying on Cass Street with Chucky Clinton, Goeken and Taylor went to pay him a little visit.

Chucky told police he hadn't seen Linda since Thursday, September 23, when they were both at home. He wanted to know why the police were so interested in Linda, but he wasn't at all prepared for their response. When he found out she was dead, he lost it and started crying and pacing around the house.

"Me and her were boyfriend and girlfriend, but I asked her to move out Thursday because she liked crack more than me," he said. "I thought she went to stay with a friend, Alexander Lee, on George Street."

Chucky told the police that Linda, whose nickname was "Chocolate," often "dope-dated," which meant she traded sex for drugs. When guys picked her up, she'd take them to one of the many hotels in East Peoria, and a lot of the times, she'd be gone all weekend.

"Was she strangulated?" Chucky asked.

"We're not totally sure," Goeken said. "We're still looking into it."

According to Chucky, Linda used to hang out with a bunch of white guys from a local towing company. Every Thursday, she'd buy drugs and take them to her "boys" at the tow lot. She also hung out at Woody's Bar and Roger's Place, bars located near the tow company.

"I tried to convince her not to be dope-dating," Chucky said. "She told me she was raped by a white guy she didn't know, who was driving a smaller dark-colored truck. Linda used to wear wigs to make her hair longer when she went out, and the guy took her wig as a souvenir before he let her go."

Linda saw the guy drive by Chucky's house as she was getting ready to leave on Thursday, and she screamed for Chucky, who was in the back room. But by the time Chucky got there, the guy was gone. Linda waited in the house for a short time, then left, most likely headed to Woody's or the tow company.

The next day one of Linda's regulars, a black guy in his fifties with a twisted face named Doe-Doe, went by Chucky's house looking for her. When Chucky told him Linda was gone, the guy drove away.

Around ten on Saturday night, Chucky walked to Roger's Place to get some cigarettes. He saw a white guy who hadn't been around for a long time sitting at the bar. He was talking to the bar-

tender, who was Roger's sister-in-law. The guy
knew Linda and had been with her before. Chucky
asked the guy, whose name he couldn't remember,
if he'd seen Linda, but he said he hadn't. Chucky
told police Roger's sister-in-law might know the
guy's name.

After talking with Chucky, the detectives went to
Roger's Place to talk to the bartender, who told
them she last saw Linda about eleven on Friday
night. She said Linda only had one beer, then left
by herself.

Linda's stepbrother, Kevin, told police she had
called his house on Saturday, sometime during the
second quarter of the Illinois-Purdue football
game. When Kevin asked where she was, she told
him not to worry about where she was and to let
her talk to their dad, R.C. Kevin didn't think anything of it because Linda had a great relationship
with her father.

"The call lasted maybe three to five minutes,"
Kevin said. "Even though R.C. talks to her, he for-
gets the conversation right away because he has
Alzheimer's."

Kevin suggested police talk to Penny, one of
Linda's friends. Penny said Linda used to call her
every day to tell her how things were going, but
the last time she heard from her was Wednesday.

"She called me and said, 'I got a new man,'"
Penny said. "She told me she was just around the
corner, and that meant somewhere near my
house. She said she couldn't talk long, because she
had to fix her new man breakfast."

Detectives also talked to Linda's friend Sabrina,
who said she remembered that Linda had been

raped recently. She said there was a rumor going around that at some point after she had been raped, Linda spotted the guy in his car, and she and some people she was with beat him with a baseball bat.

"That's really all I know, but I'll try to get more information for you," she said.

The police also talked to several of Linda's other friends, but they really didn't get any information to help them in their investigation.

Harper also went to talk with Alexander Lee, who said he was a close friend of Linda's. In fact, he called Linda "his girl." Lee said Linda had been sexually assaulted by a guy driving a dark red Ford pickup truck, with white wagon wheels. He said he thought her assailant lived on War Memorial Drive in Peoria.

Toward the end of September, Peoria Police Department detectives Sean Meeks and Chris Hauk met with thirty-nine-year-old Tiffany Hughes at Peoria's South Side Mission. They wanted to talk to her about Linda Neal.

Tiffany knew Linda and the other women who had been murdered. And although she wasn't sure if the information she had would help police find the person who was killing her friends, she decided to tell them her story, just in case.

Like the other women, Tiffany sold herself to get money for drugs. She started when she was just a teenager. A hard life, to be sure. So it was no surprise that when a stranger in a beautiful sky-blue Dodge Dakota—not the normal color for a truck—pulled over and asked her if she wanted to get high, she immediately jumped in. The man, who was white, was between thirty and forty years old and had a normal build. He had shoulder-length reddish brown hair, a moustache, and green eyes. His face and arms were covered with sores.

It was sometime in the beginning of September. Tiffany had just left her aunt's house on Aiken Street. The guy caught her by surprise when he asked if she wanted to get high. Usually a john asked for sex in exchange for money, but Tiffany didn't care that this man was different. She just wanted drugs.

The guy told Tiffany he had some crack, but it was back at his house. She went with him without a second thought. It didn't matter that she didn't know the man. It never did. It didn't matter that so many women—women she knew—had turned up missing or dead. All that mattered was getting high.

Tiffany told the man she knew a house in the neighborhood where they could buy some crack. He wasn't interested. Instead, he drove her to his house on Starr Court, just outside of the city. When they arrived, he parked in the front yard. The pair got out of the truck and walked through a large gate attached to a tall wooden fence to get to a small ramshackle house. As they made their way to the man's residence, Tiffany also noticed another larger house and a pond.

Once inside, Tiffany noticed a bed on one side of the shabby one-room apartment. There was a bathroom, but no kitchen. She also saw some drugs and drug paraphernalia in plain sight on a table in front of a couch.

Before she knew what was happening, the man grabbed her from behind and began beating her and squeezing her throat.

"Bitch, you say anything and I'll fucking kill you," the man said as he pushed her down on the bed and started raping her.

Afraid for her life, Tiffany told him that her family would be looking for her if she wasn't around. She told him her aunt had seen her get in his truck and would go to the police. In fact, she said, some of her relatives were in law enforcement. She was terrified and just wanted him to let her go.

When he was finished, he told her he was a cop, so there was no point telling anyone he raped her because no one would believe her. He also said that neither the truck nor the house was his, so she had no way to identify him. Then, without saying another word, the man walked Tiffany to his truck and drove her back to where he had picked her up.

Tiffany saw the stranger again later that month. It was September 24. Tiffany was walking on Laramie Street with several women, including Linda Neal, when she saw the guy driving his pretty blue Dodge Dakota. Tiffany recognized the man immediately. She warned Linda not to get in the guy's truck, because he was crazy, but Linda said she'd be fine. She told Tiffany not to worry about her. Tiffany never knew if Linda went with the guy. She only knew that the next day, a group of campers found Linda's body along a gravel road in a nearby town close to the Mackinaw River.

After hearing about Linda's death, Tiffany decided to tell police about her run-in with the man in the sky-blue truck. She explained that she had been distressed to see the man in the area again after he raped her. Tiffany told police the guy took her to a house at the end of Starr Court. Police had had previous dealings with a suspect who lived in that area on unrelated charges, so they showed Tiffany some photos of white men, including that suspect.

But Tiffany didn't recognize any of the men in the photographs as the person who had picked her up, then raped and beat her. Police knew that the suspect they had in mind drove a sky-blue Dodge Dakota pickup truck, so they asked Tiffany if he was the man she saw driving the truck. But she said she was 100 percent sure that he was not the person driving the truck or the man who had raped and beaten her.

Tiffany told police she would be more than willing to cooperate further, and told them where she would be staying. They gave her a card and told her to call if she had any other information to pass along.

2

March 21, 2001, started out as an ordinary day for Ken Givens, but it ended up being anything but.

It was about two in the afternoon. Givens, who lived in Norwood, was fixing the steps of the First Presbyterian Church of Pottstown, when he noticed a guy taking his dirt bike out of his truck. A short time later, he heard the biker calling out to a friend.

The dirt biker had almost ridden over the body of a woman in a vacant lot near a dry creek bed. He assumed she was sleeping and wanted his friend to help wake her up. But even though they continued to yell at her, she didn't respond. Wondering what was going on, Givens went over and looked at the woman. She was a black female. She was wearing a sweatshirt and pink sweatpants, which had been pulled down. Givens checked for a pulse. There was none.

Investigators soon identified the woman as forty-year-old Wanda Jackson, of Peoria. She had been strangled and left in the field off Illinois Route 8 in Pottstown. A deputy had seen Wanda about eleven-thirty walking near Main Street on Farmington Road. He was responding to a call from someone who reported that a woman was walking in the street. The deputy told her to get off the street. There was little else he could do, because she wasn't engaged in any illegal activity and she wasn't drunk.

Witnesses told detectives with the Peoria County Sheriff's Office (PCSO) that they saw her get into a four-door cream or off-white car at just about that time. The man driving the car was in his late thirties or early forties. His sandy blond hair was tied in a long ponytail. The last time anyone saw the car, which was thought to be a 1990s Buick LeSabre or an Oldsmobile Delta 88, it was headed south on Western Avenue, at Martin Luther King Jr. Drive.

Wanda's body was found approximately two miles north of where another woman's body had been found the previous October. The partially mummified body of thirty-one-year-old Kimberly Avery had been found in a field about two months after she had been murdered. Investigators were unable to figure out how she had died because her body had been so decomposed. Investigators said they didn't have any reason to think the murders of the two women were related.

During their investigation police learned that Wanda had used crack cocaine and had been arrested for prostitution and shoplifting. She lived off and on with either her parents or her oldest daughter. But sometimes the streets were home.

Family members told the local newspaper that she had used crack for years, and she had been in and out of rehab. Wanda had nine children—the youngest was nine, the oldest twenty—two grandchildren, and eighteen brothers and sisters.

Like other women caught up in the vicious cycle of drugs and prostitution, Wanda Jackson wasn't a bad person. She was a good person who had made some bad choices and had done some bad things, but she hadn't deserved to die for her mistakes.

In August, investigators, who were trying to solve Wanda's murder, got some particularly gruesome news. A human skull had been discovered by a man fishing in Kickapoo Creek, near Edwards. The man found the skull in about three feet of water in the creek on August 17. Sometimes, though, the creek could be eight feet deep, and it was possible that the skull had drifted downstream before it was found.

Thinking it might be some kind of artifact, the fisherman took the skull home, but a friend convinced him to turn his find over to the Peoria city police. After the discovery investigators from the Peoria Police Department, the Peoria County Sheriff's Office, and the Peoria County Coroner's Office (PCCO) went to the creek to search for more bones. They did find some, including what looked like a leg bone.

Although officials knew that the bones were human, they didn't know much else. They didn't know how long the bones had been in the creek or if they had belonged to a man or a woman. And they certainly had no idea how the person had died. They just had no way of knowing what they were dealing with, and they also had no way of knowing how much worse things were going to get.

Police set about trying to match the victim's teeth with any missing persons on file in both the city and county police departments. They also asked an anthropologist to inspect the bones, to try and get some answers. About ten days later, the anthropologist determined that the skull belonged to a woman over eighteen. Investigators then set about matching the teeth to the dental X-ray records of seven or eight women who had been reported missing in the area.

Several of the women had already been linked to two other area serial killers. Valerie Sloan, of Peoria, who was twenty, and Stacey Morrison, twenty-five, of Pekin, had been missing since the fall of 1993. Police said they were probably victims of serial killer Joseph Miller. And Peoria native Arlie Ray Davis, who had been convicted of murdering one woman, most likely had something to do with the murder of a Peoria woman and the disappearances of four other Peoria women, who had been reported missing in the mid-1990s. However, he was never charged in those cases.

In July 1994, Miller was found guilty of murdering three Peoria prostitutes, whose bodies were found along roads in western rural Peoria County in the fall of 1993. In 1995, he also pleaded guilty to having murdered eighty-eight-year-old Bernice Fagotte around the same time he murdered the prostitutes. Investigators matched blood in Miller's apartment and Bernice's car to the three slain women. The link was established by analyzing the DNA in the blood. The Miller case was the first time in the history of Peoria County that DNA had been used by prosecutors to obtain a conviction.

Before he killed the four women in Peoria, Miller had served fifteen years in prison for the 1976 and 1977 murders of two Chicago prostitutes. He had been out of prison for only five months before killing the Peoria prostitutes. Miller was sentenced to death for killing the prostitutes. However, he pleaded guilty to killing Fagotte and received a sentence of life in prison without parole. In 2003, just days before he left office, the governor, George Ryan, commuted the death sentences of Miller and 167 inmates on death row in Illinois.

In May 1996, Arlie Ray Davis was convicted of raping and strangling Laurie Gwinn, of Kewanee, and was sentenced to die by lethal injection. But police were convinced he was a monstrous serial killer.

Laurie's nude and decomposed body had been discovered in the Hennepin Canal, near Annawan, about fifty-two miles northeast of Peoria. Before she was murdered, Laurie met Davis and his cousin at a bar in Kewanee. After a night of drinking, Davis told Laurie she was too drunk to drive and offered to give her a lift home. But Davis drove Laurie and his cousin to another relative's home, where he had set up a tent in the yard. When Laurie said she wanted to leave, Davis choked her, dragged her into the tent, coughing and gasping, raped her, then finished her off. The next morning Davis and his cousin, who was also charged in the case, tossed Laurie's body into the Hennepin Canal. Davis's cousin, who testified against him in court, pleaded guilty to the murder and was sentenced to twenty years in prison.

Even though Davis was only convicted of murdering Laurie Gwinn, police figured him for the murder of Ginny Miles, of Peoria. Ginny's nude body was discovered in a shallow grave next to a creek in Menard County in 1994. After Davis died in prison of a heart attack in 2002, authorities said publicly that DNA recovered from Ginny's body matched Davis's DNA, indicating that he had had sex with her before her body was buried. But because there was no other evidence to tie Davis to her murder, prosecutors had been unable to bring him to trial.

In addition to Ginny's murder, Peoria investigators believed Davis was linked to the disappearances of Stephanie Gibson, Loretta Tinkham, Sheryl Murwin, and Cheryl Murray.

About quarter past five in the evening on Sunday, July 27, 2003, a farmer found a partially clothed woman's body in his cornfield along Augustin Road, about four miles northeast of Tremont, Illinois.

The farmer, who owned the land, was checking the field with his children when he found the body of a black female, four rows into the cornfield. She was lying on her back, with her head facing to the west and her feet to the east. She was nude, except for a pair of red panties and a pair of shorts, which had been pulled down around her ankles. The farmer immediately called police, and Detective Sergeant Jeff Lower, of the Tazewell County Sheriff's Office, responded to the call.

Lower figured that as her body was being dragged into the field, her pants probably caught on a cornstalk, which caused them to come down. The woman's body was taken to the morgue by the coroner's office, where her fingerprints were taken. A forensic technician then ran the prints through a database and matched them to thirty-six-year-old Sabrina Payne. They were also able to identify her by the repair plate she had in her right ankle.

During the investigation detectives determined that her boyfriend, Brian Montgomery, had been the last person to see her alive. That was on the Friday before her body was found. No one had seen her after four o'clock on Friday afternoon. Sabrina and Brian had met three years earlier when they both had lived in Chicago. Before she was killed, they had been planning to get married.

Police also learned that Sabrina had a drug habit. In June 2002, she was convicted of unlawful possession of a controlled substance and sentenced to thirty months of probation, fourteen days in jail, and treatment for drug and alcohol abuse.

On the Thursday before her body was found, she was at home with her boyfriend and two other people smoking a whole lot of crack. The other two people supplied most of the drugs. At one point they gave Sabrina some money to go out and score more crack. When the pair left Sabrina's the next morning, her boyfriend was still with her, but he left at about four o'clock that afternoon. Sabrina's neighbor saw her leave her house a little after that.

Police questioned Brian for hours the next day about Sabrina's disappearance. He said the last time he saw her was about one on Friday afternoon. She left the house, saying she would be gone for a few minutes. The next morning, when she hadn't come home, Brian figured she had gone to Chicago to visit her three teenage children, who still lived there. But he really got worried when she wasn't back by Sunday.

On August 28, 2003, Tazewell County coroner Robert Dubois held an inquest into Sabrina's death.

In Illinois, the coroner's verdict has no civil or criminal trial significance. The verdict and inquest proceedings are held to determine the facts of death. However, if a person is implicated as the murderer, the outcome of the coroner's inquest could have an effect on an arrest. But that rarely happened because the state's attorney (SA) usually called a grand jury to indict a suspect.

At the inquest Lower told the jury about how Sabrina's body was found, and Dubois told them about the results of Sabrina's autopsy. He said that the doctor who examined her body didn't find any evidence that she had been murdered. He categorized her death as undetermined, although he thought it could be drug related because she had cocaine, as well as alcohol, in her blood.

However, he couldn't, with absolute certainty, rule out that someone might have killed her without leaving any evidence. That's why he said she probably died from an overdose of cocaine. He just couldn't be sure what killed her, since there was no sign of trauma, disease, or any other congenital anomalies.

Lower also testified that he had no evidence to conclude that Sabrina had been murdered. He said it appeared she had died from a cocaine overdose, and someone dumped her body in the cornfield.

After deliberations the jury decided that the manner of Sabrina Payne's death was "undetermined."

It was about half past seven in the morning on Thursday, February 5, 2004. Neal Barry had just left his house to drive his wife to work, when he noticed something unusual in a ditch—a woman's body. She was lying on top of the snow, not far from his house on North Valley View Road in Edwards. She was wearing jeans and a T-shirt, but no shoes. She had been dumped facedown on the side of the two-lane road, off Kickapoo-Edwards Road. Her feet were sticking out into the road. Barry drove by the body, backed up, then drove home to call police.

During their investigation police determined that the body of the black female could have been there since the previous evening. They canvassed the neighborhood, but no one reported seeing anything unusual. The woman's body was dumped about four miles from where Wanda Jackson had been found three years earlier.

By the next day, police had identified the woman through her fingerprints. Her name was Barbara Williams. She grew up in the Harrison Homes housing development in Peoria, and still lived in the area. Even though police knew who the woman was, they still had no idea how she had died or how she had ended up in the snow. But even so, they were treating her death like a homicide.

Although she hung out with the wrong crowd, and got into drugs, she wasn't really a criminal. She had been arrested in 1999 for battery, but prosecutors never pursued the case.

After Barbara's body was found, members of her family talked to the *Peoria Journal Star* about her. Barbara came from a large family—eleven brothers and sisters. But she also had ten step-brothers and stepsisters. Her sister Shelley told the paper that no one had heard from her for a couple days before her death. Although she lived in the area, she was always moving around. Sometimes Barbara stayed with her mom, which was where her nine-year-old daughter lived. Barbara didn't have a job at the time she died, but she had worked as a housekeeper.

Shelley had recently quit a job in Kansas City, Missouri, to care for their mother after she had triple bypass surgery. She described her sister as someone who was always smiling and always making people laugh.

An autopsy on Barbara's body was inconclusive, and until they had something concrete to go on, investigators with the Peoria County Sheriff's Office weren't about to speculate on how she died. Dr. Violette Hnilica, the forensic pathologist who did the autopsy, found several injuries on Barbara's body that she had received before she died.

Barbara, thirty-six, had a contusion on the right side of her face, a contusion and abrasion on her left shoulder, and an abrasion on her left wrist. The doctor also found some injuries that Barbara had received postmortem, including a dislocated left wrist, abrasions on her left arm, and lacerations and contusions on her left hand. She also had scrapes, most likely drag marks, on her left arm, both heels, as well as drag marks on her clothing.

In her medical opinion, Hnilica said Barbara died of a cocaine overdose, because Barbara had toxic levels of the drug, as well as a small amount of alcohol, in her system. The doctor couldn't find any evidence that Barbara had been smothered or strangled.

If police thought that was the last body that was going to turn up, they were dead wrong.

On Saturday, February 21, just a little more than two weeks after Barbara's body had been found, Michael Hodges was driving an all-terrain vehicle (ATV) along a rural road near Hanna City in Peoria County when he made another grisly discovery—a woman's body partially covered with snow, lying in the tall prairie grass.

The discovery slammed the door shut on Michelle Brown's hope that she would ever see her twenty-nine-year-old sister, Frederickia, again. Since she reported her sister missing to the Peoria police on Christmas Eve, she held on to the hope that her sister would turn up safe. Now there was no more hope.

Police said Frederickia had been found about thirty feet from the roadway. They identified her through her fingerprints. She was thought to be wearing a red coat, a long-sleeved shirt, and blue jeans the last time anyone saw her. Detectives with the Peoria County Sheriff's Office wouldn't say what she was wearing when her body was found.

Lieutenant Mark Greskoviak, a sheriff's detective, said she wasn't walking in the area when she died, but it appeared she had been there for quite some time. Police said Frederickia, a known prostitute, was last seen in the North Valley neighborhood, where she often stayed. Someone saw her get into a yellow car or a red truck driven by a white male around three-thirty in the morning on December 17 or December 18. But Michelle said her sister might have been seen again a couple days before Michelle had reported Frederickia missing.

Frederickia, who shared an apartment with her boyfriend, was also addicted to drugs. She had three children, who were in foster care. Over the years Frederickia had been arrested for prostitution, aggravated battery, robbery, mob action, and commercial burglary.

When her body was found, Greskoviak said it was too early to determine if Frederickia's death was connected to the deaths of Barbara Williams or Wanda Jackson. But a few days later, police said she didn't die of a drug overdose, but they refused to disclose exactly how she had died. Peoria County sheriff Mike McCoy said police were keeping that information from the public in order to determine who was responsible for her death. Ultimately a Peoria County coroner's jury determined that Frederickia's death was a homicide. She had been strangled; then her body was dumped in the snow.

On August 22, one of Laura Lollar's friends told police he was concerned because he hadn't seen her for about three weeks. Typically, he heard from her at least every three or four days. Laura's ex-husband was also worried that she wasn't around. He usually saw her at least once a week, and their three oldest children saw her regularly as well. He looked for her in all the usual places, but he hadn't been able to find her. And no one he talked to seemed to have any idea where she was. Her ex-husband filed a missing persons report on the thirty-three-year-old woman on August 26.

On August 28, Shirley Ann Trapp-Carpenter's boyfriend filed a missing persons report on her with the Peoria Police Department. The man told police he hadn't seen the forty-five-year-old woman for a couple days, and he was worried because it wasn't like her not to contact him.

Shirley's family said the last time they saw her was August 25. They were concerned because she had diabetes and needed medication to control her condition. They had contacted her pharmacy to determine whether she had picked up her medication. She had not.

Twenty-nine-year-old Tamara "Tammy" Walls had been missing for about three weeks. On September

22, 2004, her sister finally reported her missing to the Peoria County Sheriff's Office. Tammy never went that long without checking in with her family, and they were worried.

After the discovery of Linda Neal's body on September 25, Tazewell County sheriff Robert Huston said there were enough similarities between her death and the deaths of the four other women found since 2001 that police were investigating any possible links.

Police described Neal, who had a history of prostitution-related arrests, as having an "alternative lifestyle," much like the previous four women whose deaths they were investigating. All five cases were similar enough that the Peoria Police Department and the sheriff's departments in Peoria and Tazewell Counties decided to form a task force to solve the crimes. But investigators admitted that finding the person or persons responsible for the women's deaths could prove difficult because of the type of lives the victims led, moving around and living with different people.

After Linda Neal's death, the task force began working hard to come up with any connections among the deaths of the five black women. However, the words "serial killer" hadn't been spoken— yet. Maybe that was because serial murder was relatively rare, according to the FBI—although Peoria seemed to have more than its share. In fact, less than 1 percent of all murders in any year are attributed to serial killers. And those serial killers don't always fit into the mold that society seems to have cast for them. So trying to zero in on a serial murderer wouldn't be easy.

Interestingly, the majority of serial killers aren't reclusive, social misfits who live alone. They're not monsters, and they really don't appear strange. Because they often have families and jobs, they're able to hide in plain sight in their communities.

Take Robert Lee Yates, for example. During the 1990s, Yates killed seventeen prostitutes in the Spokane, Washington, area. He was married, had five children, lived in a middle-class neighborhood, and was a decorated U.S. Army National Guard helicopter pilot. During the time period of the murders, Yates routinely sought out the services of prostitutes. Yates buried one of his victims in his yard, beneath his bedroom window. He was eventually arrested and pleaded guilty to thirteen of the murders.

Contrary to popular belief, all serial killers aren't white; rather, they span all racial groups. Charles Ng, a native of Hong Kong, killed numerous victims in Northern California. Derrick Todd Lee, an African-American, killed at least six women in Baton Rouge, Louisiana. Rafael Resendez-Ramirez, a native of Mexico, murdered twenty-four people in Kentucky, Texas, and Illinois, before he turned himself in.

And just because the women killed in Peoria and Tazewell Counties were all prostitutes, it didn't mean their murders were sexual in nature. Serial murderers killed for any number of reasons, including anger, excitement, money, and even because they thought they were ridding society of people whom they considered to be less than desirable.

In the past the definition of "serial killer" was someone who killed three or more victims in separate events, with a cooling-off period in between. But a more recent definition developed by the Behavioral Analysis Unit (BAU) of the FBI described serial murder as *the unlawful killing of two or more victims by the same offender(s), in separate events.*

A mass murderer, on the other hand, is someone who kills several people at one time. Richard Speck, for example, was a mass murderer. In 1966, Speck killed eight student nurses in one night in South Chicago.

And a spree killer is someone who murders his victims in a short period of time. Andrew Cunanan is an example of a spree killer. In 1997, Cunanan shot and killed five men, including renowned clothing designer Gianni Versace, in a cross-country murder spree before he turned the gun on himself. Unlike serial murders, there wasn't a cooling-off period in between Cunanan's kills.

If a serial killer was on the loose in Peoria and Tazewell Counties, forming a task force was exactly the right thing to do, because it was important for all the law enforcement agencies to work together. They reviewed all the incoming information, collated the information, and assigned leads to various members of the task force. Throughout the investigation the task force received over a thousand leads, and assigned a priority—low, moderate, or high—to each one.

They got a number of leads related to the death of Linda Neal. One caller told police that Linda had been arguing with her roommate the week before Linda's body was found. The caller said the roommate's cousin told Linda, "I'm going to kill you."

Linda Neal wasn't the last black woman to turn up missing or dead in Peoria and Tazewell Counties.

Shaconda Thomas's grandmother went to the Peoria Police Department on October 7, 2004, and reported the thirty-two-year-old woman missing. She hadn't seen her granddaughter, who lived with her, since the last week of August.

About eight o'clock in the morning on Friday, October 15, the body of forty-one-year-old Brenda Erving was discovered in a ditch in Elmwood Township. An employee of the New Horizons Dairy in Elmwood who found her shook her toe to see if she was still alive. When she didn't respond, he went back to his truck and called the police.

Brenda was found lying faceup in the mud. She was nude, except for a pair of white socks. In the mud near her body, there were fresh tire marks that went north in a bean field for about half a mile, then turned back onto Taggert Road. But the only footprints in the mud were those of the deliveryman.

Brenda's mother hadn't seen her daughter since Wednesday, when a male friend had picked her up. Although Brenda had been convicted of unlawful possession of a controlled substance, she had never been convicted of prostitution. Brenda Erving had three young daughters.

Dr. Violette Hnilica performed an autopsy on Brenda on Saturday and determined that she had been asphyxiated, but she had also suffered blunt-force trauma to her head. Medical tests showed that she had toxic levels of cocaine in her system.

Although the task force was doing everything it could to find out what had happened to the missing and murdered women, area residents didn't think police were doing enough to investigate the murders of Brenda Erving, Linda Neal, Frederickia Brown, Barbara Williams, Sabrina Payne, and Wanda Jackson, plus the disappearances of Shirley Trapp-Carpenter, Shaconda Thomas, Tamara Walls, and Laura Lollar.

To air their grievances, nearly five hundred residents held a town hall meeting at City of Worship Refuge Center with members of the task force on Monday, October 25. Photos of the dead and missing women adorned two posterlike maps of Peoria and Tazewell Counties at the front of the congregation hall. The pictures of the dead women were placed on the spots on the map where their bodies had been found.

At the meeting Gary Poynter, the interim chief of the Peoria Police Department, told the residents that authorities had added more people to the task force. In total, there were ten detectives just working on the investigation.

Peoria County sheriff Mike McCoy said although

the task force didn't have any solid suspects, the investigators were gathering information. But, still, the people in attendance wanted to know why police waited until five African-American women had been murdered to form a task force.

Police hadn't formed a task force earlier because the deaths of the women weren't all the same. Although there were similarities, there were also a number of differences.

Residents also wanted to know why the task force was made up of only white officers from the Peoria Police Department, the Illinois State Police (ISP), and deputies from the Peoria County and Tazewell County Sheriff's Offices. They believed an African-American officer might be able to get more information from members of the African-American community.

For police, though, race wasn't an issue in the investigation, and investigators were treating the deaths like they treated any other deaths, without regard to the race or lifestyles of the victims.

Although the task force was working with an FBI profiler, an FBI agent wasn't part of the task force because a federal crime hadn't been committed.

About four hundred people attended another community meeting held at the City of Worship Refuge Center a couple weeks later. Residents talked about the possibility that a serial killer was stalking women who were drug abusers and worked as prostitutes to feed their habits. They worried that their daughters, sisters, and mothers weren't safe on the streets of Peoria. And they were still concerned that police, who had added three African-American investigators to the task force, weren't doing enough to find out what had happened to the dead and missing women.

3

Toward the end of October, a corrections officer (CO) from the Tazewell County Jail called Detective Hal Harper to let him know that an inmate had some information about Brenda Erving for the task force.

Her name was Tyresa, and she had known Brenda for about five years. The last time "Ty" saw Brenda was a couple days before Brenda was murdered. Ty told the detective that Brenda used to stay at Brenda's uncle Johnny's house on Madison Park Street in Peoria. According to Ty, Brenda and a guy named Kevin, a known drug user, were partying in his car, an older tan Oldsmobile or Buick, about a month and a half before she was killed.

Ty said Kevin was a white man, thirtysomething, with shorter blondish brown hair. He was about five feet nine inches tall and weighed 170 pounds. He always wore a baseball cap.

"One time me, Brenda, Kevin, and another guy were at her uncle Johnny's house, and me and Kevin were in another room kind of on a drug binge," she said. "Kevin started coming on to me. He was rubbing my neck. He was really aggressive. I pushed his hand away because I was so afraid. But he was so aggressive that he scratched me with his keys. I still have a scar."

Ty also told Harper about another white guy who could have been involved with Brenda's death. The man was about forty-five years old, five feet seven inches tall, 150 pounds. He had shoulder-length black hair and blue eyes. The guy drove an older, bigger pickup truck, with a loud exhaust. He lived in the Brimfield area and was a chicken farmer. He traveled to a number of towns in the area, making deliveries. Ty said the "chicken man," as she called him, wanted to go out with Brenda, even though he was married.

Ty also gave Harper the names of two other men, who might have had something to do with Brenda's death. One of the men was a registered sex offender who drove taxis in Peoria; the other was a guy who routinely let the girls use his house to party.

At the conclusion of the interview, Ty told Harper she wanted to do whatever she could to help police in their investigation.

Rhoshanda Fisher called police at the beginning of November with a story about her friend Teracita, who had been with a white guy who tried to choke her. She thought it might be the same guy who had killed the other black women. Police tracked thirty-one-year-old Teracita down at the Dwight Correctional Center in Dwight, Illinois, where she was being held for failure to appear in court. They met with Teracita on the morning of December 10. She agreed to tell them her story.

It happened in July. For as long as she could remember, Teracita had been selling herself on the street to feed her habit. That night she was walking near a local recreation center. It was around six in the evening. She was looking for drugs, when a white guy in a gray Chevy Blazer pulled up next to her. He was in his late thirties or early forties, tall with a slight beer belly. He had short blondish brown hair and grayish eyes. He hadn't shaved for three or four days.

"I got about an ounce of cocaine," he said. "Do you want to get high?"

That's the only thing Teracita wanted to do, so she got in the guy's truck, which was cluttered with tools. As she got in, she looked out the window and saw a man named Tarzie. She wasn't sure if he saw her.

"Do you work construction?" she asked.

"I work on houses and do brickwork."

Teracita didn't have a good feeling about the guy, but her need to get high ultimately overpowered her sense of fear.

"Can you take me to meet some friends so I can tell then where I'm going to be?" she asked.

The guy refused and, instead, drove her back to his house. It was a brown-colored brick house with an unattached garage at the end of a long driveway. There was a lot of stuff in the driveway and in the garage. There was also a table in the driveway with miscellaneous items on it, and some potted plants on the porch.

"You moving?" Teracita asked.

"Nah, my mom is having a yard sale," he said, adding that the house belonged to his mother.

They walked around to the rear of the house and went into the kitchen through the back door. Teracita noticed a large wooden table and chairs, and a square wooden clock hanging on the wall. As she looked around, she also saw some brand-new Barbie dolls still in their boxes.

"Go on down into the basement," the man said, pointing to the door.

Teracita did as she was told, and a few seconds later, her host joined her. Even though it was dark, Teracita could see a big bed and a long wooden table, with a lava lamp on it, as well as a barbell and a space heater. Clothes, used condoms, vibrators, dildos, as well as pornographic books and magazines, littered the carpeted floor. There was also some aluminum foil on a plate under the bed, with what Teracita thought was crystal meth.

A couple seconds later, the man came downstairs, grabbed Teracita from behind, and put a knife to her throat.

"You're under arrest," he said.

"What are you talking about?"

"You're under arrest for prostitution. Get the fuck out of your clothes," he said. "I'm going to kill you, like I killed the rest of the girls."

Frightened, Teracita started taking off her clothes.

"Do what I say, and I'll think about letting you live and see your son."

Teracita had just given birth and she was still wearing a tampon. She pulled the tampon out and threw it on the floor. The man kicked it, and it went under the bed. He then pushed Teracita down on the bed, put on a condom, and raped her anally and vaginally for the next six or seven hours. He placed Ben Wa balls—three small marble-size metal balls used for sexual stimulation—in Teracita's vagina and anus. And he pulled her hair back and stuffed socks in her mouth, to keep her from screaming. Unable to ejaculate, the man became increasingly frustrated. He removed his condom, but he still couldn't have an orgasm.

Finally he told Teracita to put her clothes back on.

"You won't get into another car, will you?" he asked. "I should take your ass down to the station and let them book you on prostitution."

The guy walked her to his truck and drove her back where he had picked her up. As soon as she got out of the truck, Teracita took off running.

A couple weeks later, Teracita saw her attacker again. He was driving the same truck. He looked in her direction, but he apparently didn't recognize her. Angry, Teracita picked up a bottle and threw it at the truck. The guy just kept on driving.

Teracita gave police the names of three other women who had survived similar incidents, one of whom was in the same prison.

A couple weeks later, police went back to the correctional facility to talk to Teracita again. They were trying to locate Jeannette, the woman Teracita had told them was in the facility with her. The detectives pulled out a photo of a woman named Jeannette Smith, who was in the Dwight Correctional Center, but Teracita said she wasn't the right Jeannette. The Jeannette she knew was real short and had dark skin. Her nickname was "Nett," and she lived near Starr Court.

According to Teracita, Jeannette had been picked up in Peoria by a man in a newer model blue or turquoise truck. Despite Teracita's information, detectives were never able to find Jeannette.

Police then showed Teracita two photo lineups. The first lineup contained a picture of a man named Larry Bright, with long hair, and the second lineup included a photo of Larry, but with shorter hair.

The second Teracita saw Larry's face, she pointed at the photo and said, "This is the guy. That's him. I will never forget his face. That's him. That's him. But when he raped me, his hair wasn't that long."

When Teracita looked at the photo of Larry with shorter hair, she again recognized him. "That's him," she said. "That's the guy who raped me. That's the guy I threw the bottle at. I'm positive it's the same guy. His hair was longer in front like the other picture, but it was shorter on the sides. Not as short as this."

The detectives asked Teracita if she had seen any Peoria newspapers while she was in jail, or if she had talked to her family about the deaths of the black women in Peoria. She said she hadn't read any newspapers or talked to her family about the other women. In fact, she said she hadn't even told her mother that she had been raped.

But she did tell her friend Tarzie.

Just after Christmas, Tarzie contacted the police to tell them what he knew about the night Teracita was assaulted. He said that sometime in the summer, he was near his house on West Kettelle Street, and he saw Teracita walking down the street. He also saw a gray or black Blazer in the area, but he didn't see Teracita get in the truck. When he looked up, he saw the Blazer driving away, and Teracita was no-where around. The next time he saw Teracita, she told him she had been raped by the guy in the Blazer. She told Tarzie she thought she knew the guy, and that's why she got in his truck.

"She was crying and acting like something very bad happened," Tarzie told police. "I don't know anything else about what happened, because that's all she told me."

Around the same time they talked to Teracita, members of the task force got a tip that a thirty-five-year-old prostitute named Vickie Bomar had recently been picked up by a man who took her to his house and raped her. Vickie didn't report it to the police because the man had threatened to kill her, and she was afraid.

On November 9, Sergeant Scott Cook, of the Peoria Police Department, went to talk to Vickie at the South Side Mission. Vickie agreed to talk to him.

It was sometime in the middle of July. She was walking near the Harrison Homes, a public hous-ing development built in 1942. She was trying to score some crack cocaine. As she was walking, a white man in a truck pulled up to her and said he was looking to party. He said he had $200 in cash and an eight ball of coke. As soon as Vickie heard those magic words, she hopped into his truck and they drove to his house.

It was a small house with a porch, almost like a summer cottage, that sat behind a larger house. The property was partially concealed by a tall wooden privacy fence. The man opened the gate and the pair walked into the one-room house. There was a bed off to the right, and a couch, coffee table, and some other furniture on the left. There was no kitchen. The door to the bathroom was closed.

Vickie pulled her crack pipe out of her purse. She was looking forward to getting high. Suddenly the guy started talking.

"You have the right to remain silent. Anything you say can and will be used against you," he said.

Vickie figured him for a cop, since he was reading her rights to her.

"You know, I'm going to give you a break tonight," he said. "I'm off duty and I don't feel like going to the office and doing paperwork."

Vickie headed for the door, but the guy pulled a knife on her.

"I won't hurt you, if you do what I tell you," he said. "Take off your clothes."

"But you're a police officer," Vickie said, trying to understand what was happening. Scared out of her mind, and afraid she was going to die, Vickie took off her clothes.

"Now get into the bed. I'm going to fuck you."

Vickie did as she was told. The man started kissing her and sucking on her. He attempted to rape her. He thought he was penetrating her, but he wasn't. After about twenty minutes, the man told her to turn over, because he wanted to screw her in her ass. Vickie knew her life was on the line, but there was no way she was going to let this guy rape her. She had a plan.

"I have to use the bathroom really bad," she said. "Please just let me go. I have to go bad. Please."

Finally, after seven or eight minutes of pleading, he let her go.

Once inside, Vickie locked the door. The bathroom looked like it was being remodeled. She sat down on the floor, with her back against the door, and her feet against the sink. She picked up a board from the floor and put it behind her head, just in case he tried to force his way in.

The guy was getting impatient.

"Come out of there *now*," he screamed.

"No, I'm not coming out."

The man started kicking the door, trying to get it open. After a few minutes, he gave up.

"Come out, and I'll take you home," he said.

Knowing she had no choice but to believe him, Vickie got up and slowly opened the door. She walked out of the bathroom, holding the board for protection. She was shocked to find that the guy was already dressed. She was even more shocked when he let her put her clothes back on. She was in such a hurry to get the hell out of there that she forgot to put her bra on. While Vickie was getting dressed, the guy was going through her purse, probably looking for drugs or money.

Finally the guy led her out to his truck. When he opened the driver's-side door to get in, Vickie took off. He yelled at her to stop, but she kept running. Just then, one of the guy's neighbors, Joyce, pulled into her driveway and got out of her car. The guy jumped in his car and raced away.

Vickie ran over to the woman. She said she had been raped and needed help. Joyce offered to call the police, but Vickie, who had an outstanding warrant for her arrest, said no. She told Joyce the guy was a cop, so what good would it do to call them, anyway? Joyce told her he wasn't a cop, then offered to drive Vickie home.

After giving her statement to Cook, Vickie told him she wanted to get into some kind of drug rehabilitation program. So he made some calls and brought her to Chestnut Health Systems in Bloomington.

The next day Cook and Captain Bobby Henderson went back to the facility to show Vickie a photo lineup of six men, one of whom was Larry Bright.

"That's him. That's him. That's him right there!" Vickie screamed, pointing to Larry's picture.

The police decided they needed to record Vickie's statement, so they brought her to the Bloomington police station, reinterviewed her, then took her back to the health-care facility.

On November 11, police arrested Larry Bright for unlawfully restraining Vickie Bomar and brought him back to the Peoria County Sheriff's Office for questioning.

Deputy Dave Wilson spoke with Larry Bright in the detectives' bureau about the incident. After Wilson read Larry his Miranda warnings, Larry said he understood his rights and agreed to talk to

Wilson and PCSO detective Cy Taylor, who was also in the room. The interview covered a wide range of subjects, including Larry's dating habits, his drug and alcohol use, and even the kind of cigarettes he smoked.

During the interview Larry told police that he had lived at his current address for a little over a year, and he had lived on West McClure Avenue before that. Larry had also live in Canton and Yates City at different times in his life. He had been born in California and had moved to Morton, Illinois, when he was a young boy. He lived in Morton until he finished eighth grade. Then his family moved to Tremont, where he attended high school, although he dropped out during his senior year. His brother, Jerry, still lived in Morton, and his mother lived in the house in front of his house on West Starr Court in Peoria.

Wilson asked if he had ever lived in Racine. Larry admitted he had, but he said he had almost forgotten about it. Larry told police he had lived in Racine for about four months. While there, he stayed with his half sister, Monica, and worked for a company named Holton Brothers.

When asked if he had ever been with a black prostitute, Larry said he had not. In fact, he said, the first time he had been with a prostitute was three months earlier, when he had picked up a white girl named Latisha and took her to his house, where they had sex. Larry said he picked up Latisha at Woody's Bar in his blue Dodge Dakota truck. Larry told police his mother owned a Dodge Durango, but he never drove it. She used to own a gray Chevy Blazer, but she sold it a couple weeks earlier. Larry insisted he had never picked up a black prostitute, and he had never had any problems with prostitutes.

Wilson asked Larry if he knew any of the black girls who had been murdered or had gone missing recently. Larry looked at the police photographs of the girls and said the only one who looked familiar was Tamara Walls. He added that he might have seen her before, but he had never dated her. Larry said the only black girl that he ever dated was a girl named Ernestine. He had met her at a bar about nine or ten months earlier and had partied with her. Although he had sex with her, he never brought her to his house, because his mother wouldn't have approved of him having any kind of a relationship with a black woman.

Larry also talked about his drug use. He said he occasionally used marijuana and had last used crack cocaine about a year earlier. About four or five years earlier, he had gone through a rehab program for an addiction to crack.

Wilson and Taylor also learned that Larry liked to fish, and that he had caught a forty-five-pound flathead catfish in the Mackinaw River, near a broken bridge. He liked to fish for bass so much that he used to be a member of a local fishing club.

Wilson asked Larry if he would be willing to provide DNA to help them with the investigation, and if he'd allow them to search his house. Larry said he'd have to talk with his attorney first.

After Larry was taken to his cell, Taylor stayed in the interview room while lab officers collected the cigarette butts from Larry's cigarettes, as well as the new plastic cup that Larry had used, so they could be submitted for DNA testing.

The same day thirty-eight-year-old Peter Morton called the Tazewell County Sheriff's Office and spoke to Detective Cy Taylor. Police had been trying to track Morton down for about a week. They had received a tip on the Crime Stoppers line from a woman who believed Morton was responsible for the murdered and missing women in Tazewell and Peoria Counties.

The caller said Morton lived with his mother. She also said Morton often traveled to Peoria to pick up drugs, as well as prostitutes, and then he brought them back to his house. The caller said he once told her that he hit a black man in Wisconsin with his car, then left the scene.

"His family has real issues," she said. "I think Pete could be doing these things to these women."

Sometime after getting the call, Taylor went out to Morton's home and spoke with his mother. She said Peter wasn't living with her at that time, but she'd give him the message.

As the saying goes, Peter Morton's rap sheet was as long as his arm. A look at his criminal history painted a picture of a man who had been in and out of prison for much of his life on charges ranging from driving under the influence (DUI) to driving on a revoked or suspended license, from criminal destruction of property to aggravated battery on a police officer and a firefighter, and domestic battery.

After speaking to Taylor on the phone, Morton

agreed to meet him at the Field Shopping Center in Morton. The two talked in Taylor's squad car.

"I'm involved with the investigation of six dead and four missing black women," Taylor said, adding that he knew Morton was addicted to drugs.

"Yeah, I'm addicted to crack, and I used to get it on the south side of Peoria, but I've been clean for a couple weeks, and I've been going to church in Morton. But why are you talking to me?" Morton asked. "I'm not a killer."

"Your name came up in our investigation as someone who frequented prostitutes and sometimes brought them home."

"Sure, I traded drugs for sex, but I never brought a prostitute home. I partied with some girls at my house, but we didn't have sex, and I don't think they were prostitutes," he said. "And I have a girlfriend now. It's been a couple of years since I visited prostitutes. I only know them by Serena and Dannette. I don't even know if those were their real names."

Morton told Taylor he went to prison in January 2000 for driving on a revoked or suspended license and also for aggravated battery to a cabdriver. He was released in January 2001, but was hauled back to prison in November 2003 for violating his probation. He was released on parole in February 2004. Morton said the Department of Corrections (DOC) took his DNA, but he would provide it again, if necessary.

When Taylor asked Morton about the alleged hit-and-run accident in Wisconsin, he said he had never lived in that state. He said he had lived in San Antonio, Texas, for a short time, about four years earlier, and had lived in Illinois a year and a half to two years earlier when he was working for a siding company. For most of the past summer, he and his girlfriend had lived at the campgrounds at Yogi Bear's Jellystone Park in Goodfield, Illinois.

Taylor showed Morton pictures that had been published of the dead and missing black women, along with a recent newspaper article. When he came to Sabrina Payne's photo, Morton asked Taylor if she was the woman who had been found about a mile from his house.

"Yes," Taylor said.

"I don't remember meeting any of these girls," Morton said. "And I wouldn't do anything in my own backyard."

A couple months later, Taylor went to talk to Morton again, because he had received information that Morton and Larry Bright had been friends when they were younger.

"I heard you used to run around with Larry Bright. Do you know him?" Taylor asked after a brief greeting.

"Yeah, I do. We were close friends when we went to high school, until Larry went to prison. I saw his picture in the paper. Boy, it sure don't look good," Morton said, shaking his head.

"What do you mean?"

"For Larry, because of where some of the bodies were found," Morton said. "Larry knows those places. I hope he didn't do it, but it don't look good."

Morton agreed to take Taylor and Henderson, who had arrived a short time after Taylor, to some of the places where he and Larry used to hang out when they were teenagers. First he directed them to a pond on property belonging to Sal Nelson. The pond was east of Ritthaler Road, halfway between Allentown and Augustin Roads. The two boys used to take their girlfriends parking there. Sabrina Payne's body was found not even a couple miles away.

When they got to the area, Morton pointed out Mud Creek. Morton and Bright used to camp and fish under Mud Creek Bridge, which was about one hundred yards from where Sabrina's body was found.

Morton next took police across Augustin Road to a dirt lane, which he and Larry used to drive on when they were kids. The dirt lane ran north from Augustin Road to Allentown, just west of Mud Creek Bridge. Morton said he thought Nelson owned that property, too. He said Larry was also familiar with that area.

Morton then directed police to Broken Bridge, at the end of Herberger Road in Mackinaw. He said he and Larry used to jump from the bridge into the river. Just north of Broken Bridge was an old railroad right-of-way and an old gravel pit, where they used to ride four-wheelers.

At the end of Levee Road, a dead-end street, was another old bridge that had been a party spot when Morton and Bright were teenagers. Traffic to the bridge had been cut off for some time. Linda Neal's body was found within a mile of the bridge.

Morton and Bright also used to party at a place near the old bridge called Pitzer's Cabin. It was the place where he and Larry used to cross the Mackinaw River in their four-wheel–drive vehicles and party. Morton did his best to direct police to the area. After a couple wrong turns, Morton remembered where it was—near the levee on King Road, another dead end. Linda's body was found on the north side of the levee on King Road.

Bright and Morton also partied at the east end of the levee on the north side of the Mackinaw River on Benson Road, as well as at the bridge over the river. The area was near Larry's old house on Robin Hood Lane.

The next day Wilson brought Larry back to the detectives' bureau to speak with him again about the investigation. Larry said he understood his Miranda rights as Wilson recited them, and he agreed to talk to him without an attorney. Captain Bobby Henderson, of the Tazewell County Sheriff's Office, was also present throughout the interview.

Wilson told Larry he didn't think he was telling the truth when he said he had never been with Vickie Bomar. His less-than-truthful denials, coupled with Vickie's description of him, his truck, and his house, added credence to her story. And Wilson said he had a hard time believing that Larry had never been with a black female other than Ernestine.

"I think Ms. Bomar was at your house at some point," Wilson said.

Finally Larry gave in.

"Sometime in the middle of July, I did pick up a black prostitute, and it could have been her," he said.

It was about ten at night. He was driving around the south end of Peoria, an area known for prostitution, in his blue Dodge Dakota when the woman flagged him down. After determining that he wasn't a cop, she got into the truck and asked if he wanted to get high. He gave her fifty bucks to buy some crack cocaine, and she directed him to a house where she could get it.

But when she returned, Larry thought she had ripped him off, because she only had crack worth about $30 on her. Nevertheless, Larry took the woman back to his house, where they smoked the crack.

Larry had the woman perform oral sex on him, and when she was done, she wanted him to pay her $20 more for the sex. Larry told the woman he had already paid her by buying her the crack cocaine and kicked her out of his house. But before she left, she told him to pay her or he'd regret it.

Larry denied having any physical contact with the woman after she performed oral sex on him. And he said he never threatened her or displayed any weapons. When the woman walked out of his house, he followed her and asked her if she needed a ride somewhere. She told him no. Larry watched as she walked over to talk to one of his neighbors.

He told the detectives that the woman didn't leave any clothing at his house. And he said he never told her he was a police officer, and he didn't own a badge of any kind.

"You guys are welcome to look around my house, if you want to," he said.

Wilson asked Larry if he had ever had any problems with any other black prostitutes he had picked up. He said that sometime back in April he had picked up another black prostitute in the south end of Peoria. The girl flagged him down and she was acting crazy. She got into his truck, and as he was driving back to his place, she continued to act nuts. All she wanted to do was get more dope. Larry stopped the truck somewhere on West Starr Court and told her to get out. She was so angry that she kicked the side of his door, putting a small dent in it.

"Do you remember how many black prostitutes you've been with?" Wilson asked.

"Over the last ten years, I guess I've been with about ten."

Then Wilson showed Larry a number of photos of black women and asked him if he recognized any of them. Larry said he he might have been with one of the women, whose name was Julia. Larry explained he often took the women to the Townhouse Motel, and sometimes he took them back to his place. When asked if he knew Tonya Russell, he said no.

As the interview progressed, Wilson asked Larry if he had ever been married. He said he was divorced, and his ex-wife, Cathy Bishop, lived in Galesburg. Larry's best friend, Dan Hosmer, also live in Galesburg. Then, maybe to show police he had nothing against black people, Larry said he had a friend named Harry Cannon, who was a black man. (Cannon was Larry's crack supplier.) He said he last saw Harry a month earlier.

As he did the previous day, Wilson asked Larry,

when had he lived in Racine. He said he had lived there for three or four months in the spring of 1999. Between 1999 and 2002, he went back occasionally to see his sister, Monica.

At the end of the interview, Wilson asked Larry if he would still be willing to let police look through his house and his truck. He agreed, so police drove him to his mother's job to get the keys to his house from her. Then they took him to his house, where he signed a consent form to allow the search.

As the crime lab officers arrived to take photos of Larry's house and collect possible evidence, Wilson went to look into Larry's truck, but it was locked. Larry said his mother had the keys, but he gave Wilson permission to unlock it with a slim jim so the lab officers could process it.

After the search Wilson brought Larry to the courthouse for his first court appearance on the charge of aggravated unlawful restraint. Larry was released on $10,000 bond.

The next day PCSO deputy Doug O'Neill was notified by PCSO detective Dave Hoyle that investigators were searching Larry's house on West Starr Court; they needed him to respond to process the scene.

When O'Neill arrived, the investigators told him that Larry had been arrested on a warrant for unlawful restraint. They also told him that Larry's victim said she had been sexually assaulted.

As O'Neill walked around Larry's apartment, Detective Cy Taylor pointed out some interesting items like a large flesh-colored dildo wrapped in a blue towel by the bed, a black bra in a laundry basket, and three shoes without shoelaces. O'Neill noticed tan or brown stains on the white sheet on the box spring, which was under the mattress. There was also a hitter pipe and a green leafy substance on the coffee table. In one corner of the room, O'Neill saw a copy of the *Peoria Journal Star* newpaper dated February 7, 2004. In the local section, there was an article about the death of Barbara Williams. O'Neill photographed the newspaper and the rest of the house before he went outside.

As O'Neill took pictures of the outside and inside of Larry's truck, Detective Pat Kennedy, who was looking through it, found an advertisement for Camel cigarettes in the side panel of the passenger-side door. O'Neill also took swabbings from the steering wheel, gas pedal, driver's-side door handle, brake pedal, and from the passenger-side door.

O'Neill collected two black floor mats, hairs and fibers from those floor mats, a dirty white towel, with pink flowers, that had red bloodlike stains on it, four pairs of gloves and four single gloves, as well as garbage and some personal items. He took those items and other items from Larry's house back to the lab for processing.

At the lab Deputy Scott Gamboe examined the items that had been taken from Larry's apartment before placing them into evidence. He noted that the laces were missing from two Brahma hiking boots. He also observed brownish stains on the fitted sheet and on the inside of a hooded gray sweatshirt. Also inside the sweatshirt were two strands of Chore Boy, a coarse scrubbing pad, often used to smoke crack cocaine.

Gamboe also saw a whitish stain and a darker stain on a green towel, and dark stains on two white bath towels and a red towel that had come from Larry's apartment. When he examined a pair of leather work gloves, which had Velcro closures, he saw a grayish mass of what appeared to be fibers or hair. He also found what looked to be hairs stuck to the dildo.

4

Typically, serial killers prey on prostitutes and women addicted to drugs because they're vulnerable and available. No one takes a second look or gives a second thought to a man in a car picking up a woman in an area where all too many women walk the streets plying their trade.

And usually when a prostitute turns up missing, no one files a missing persons report. Think about it. Another prostitute won't report it, because she probably figures the police won't even listen to her. And the families of the women often don't know their relatives are missing, because they don't hear from them on a regular basis.

Even the women who escape the clutches of their would-be murderers don't go to the police. For one thing, they don't think the police will believe them or even care about what happened to them. For another, as in the case of Vickie Bomar, the women often have warrants out for their arrests and are afraid to go to the police because they don't want to go to jail.

And sometimes serial killers prey on prostitutes because they think they're doing police a favor by getting rid of women they consider worthless, although that didn't seem to be the case with Larry.

But the reality is, none of these women deserve to die—no matter how they might live their lives. Despite the perceptions and misconceptions about the women who use drugs and turn to prostitution to feed their habits, the truth is they are daughters, and sisters, and mothers, and aunts, and cousins.

None of the Peoria serial killer's victims intended to live their lives high on crack and having sex with who-knows-how-many strangers. They had had jobs and families. They went to church and school. Sure, they had a couple drinks now and then and probably smoked some weed, but that was it—in the beginning. But as time progressed, they suffered tragedies; they got mixed up with the wrong people. They turned to harder drugs, such as crack cocaine or heroin, to dull the pain. They sold their bodies, shoplifted, mugged, and even stole from family members to get the drugs they needed to survive. And the years of addiction took their toll.

They were raped, beaten up, and made to feel worthless. They wanted to find peace, but all they found were places to get high and escape from the world. They lived wherever they could—in shelters, on the streets, with friends, with family. They tried to get off the streets, but they got caught up in the never-ending cycle of using, getting clean, taking up old habits, using again, getting locked up, getting clean. . . .

That's what happened to Brenda Erving.

* * *

By all accounts, Brenda Erving was a good person, a beautiful person. She loved her family, and her family loved her. She was a happy little girl who liked to go out and play and have fun. She went to Manual High School in Peoria, where she excelled in her classes. Brenda was funny—the type of person who enjoyed making people laugh.

But she had a hard life.

When Brenda was young, Cynthia, her baby sister, suffered from cancer. Cynthia passed away when she was just seven years old. Her death affected the entire family, but Brenda took it particulary hard.

"When Brenda was a kid, she was a lot of fun. She was very sweet," said Laverne Young, Brenda's aunt. Laverne's brother William Young Jr. married Brenda's mother when Brenda was just two years old.

"I stayed at their house a lot when Brenda's baby sister came out of the hospital," Laverne said. "Sometimes my brother would get a code blue to go to the hospital because they thought Cynthia was going to die. They thought she was going to die six times before she passed. And when they would go to the hospital, I'd go to the house and stay with Brenda and the other kids. And sometimes she'd stay overnight with me."

Brenda's life just seemed to be mired in tragedy. Her mom, Lee, who passed away a few years after Brenda died, was a diabetic and an amputee. It had hurt Brenda to watch her mother suffer the way she did.

Then, when Brenda was thirty-five, her sister Antoinette passed away. One minute Antoinette was joking and talking with her husband, and the next minute she asked him to take her to the hospital because something was happening with her chest. She died almost as soon as she got there.

"I talked to her after her sister passed," her aunt Laverne said. "I asked her if there was anything I could do. She told me I could do anything because she just didn't know what to do."

By then, Brenda had already started hanging out with the wrong people and doing drugs, but her sister's death really pushed her deeper into life on the street.

"Brenda was doing good," said her stepdad, William Young Jr. "She had three daughters and she was raising them. She was doing good. Then she got in with the wrong crowd."

When Brenda's body was found, her family was devastated.

"It shocked me. I felt bad. I didn't know what to think. My son called me. I was driving. I answered the cell phone. I went home, and the detectives came by the house to tell me what happened," William said.

Laverne, who said she didn't even know Brenda had been missing, called her brother one night just to talk. William told Laverne he and his girlfriend, now his wife, were just about to leave to go over to Brenda's mom's house.

"I said, 'Is Lee worse?'" Laverne said. "He said, 'It's not her. It's Brenda. She's not with us anymore. And that's the way I heard about it. It was terrible. I was abolutely shocked. It was like everything had been taken away from me. I was devastated for him, her, and her mother. And I started thinking back to when she was a little girl and wishing I had been able to be in her life more, and maybe things might have been different. I still think about her and miss her a lot. But it bothers me now when I think of Brenda. I have to put it out of my mind."

Laverne said she didn't even know Brenda was involved with drugs.

"After Brenda died, my brother told me she was into drugs, and he was upset about it," she said. "I told him to try and understand, because she wouldn't have chosen that way if she knew another way. She was trying to deal with what she went through in her life. I told him I still loved her."

Like Brenda, Linda Neal faced a number of tragedies in her life. That doesn't excuse the life she ultimately lived, it's just a fact.

Linda grew up in Joliet, Illinois. She had two sisters and two brothers. She was the youngest girl—a tomboy. But when the kids were in grade school, her parents split, and her dad moved to Peoria. Her mom did everything in her power to raise her five young children the best way she could. The kids often spent summers with their dad in Peoria, a city Linda seemed to take to more than the rest of her siblings.

And it seemed to be working for Linda. She went to Joliet Central High School, where she excelled in sports. An athletic teen, she ran track and was on the gymnastics team. She was also a cheerleader. A great cook, Linda went to Joliet Junior College for a time and initially majored in culinary arts, but she later decided to take up stenography, instead. She dreamed of being a court reporter one day.

In 1982, her mom passed away, at forty. Her mother was the same age Linda was when she was murdered. She had suffered for years from a rare skin disease. At the end she lapsed into a coma and died in a Chicago hospital. All the kids were close to their mom, and it tore them all up.

For a while the family lived with their grandmother in Joliet. Linda eventually moved to Peoria with her boyfriend. They got a house, where he still lives. Things seemed to be going well, at first. She worked in a number of area restaurants. Then tragedy struck again when her twenty-three-year-old brother died. He suffered an epileptic seizure and died in his sleep.

Linda started hanging out with the wrong people, drinking and using drugs. She got into cocaine and started smoking crack. She and her boyfriend started fighting—he was clean and couldn't stand the idea that Linda was using. They split up and Linda hooked up with a number of older men—men on Social Security. It was an easy way to support her habit.

Younger brother Mark, who lives in Missouri, was the first to admit that his big sister was no angel. But she was his hero. He was closer to Linda than he was to any of his siblings.

"We just had so much in common," said Mark, who was four years younger than Linda. "We were so much alike. Instead of a brother following a brother, I followed her. If it came down to going somewhere, I always wanted to be behind her. I learned a lot from her. She wasn't an angel, but she was kindhearted. If you knew her, you couldn't do nothing but love her. She was affectionate toward people, but if you got on her bad side, she was like a rattlesnake. She'd get you."

Mark learned a lot from Linda—more than he learned from any of his other siblings.

"Once I did something wrong to a friend, and [Linda] made me apologize, and I wasn't used to apologizing to people," he said. "And I remember crying, because I had to apologize. She taught me right from wrong in a lot of things. She'd say, 'You don't do this, you don't do that.' If you hurt someone's feelings, she made you apologize."

Linda also taught Mark about life on the street.

"We used to fight together," he said. "I've seen her fight people four foot tall and six foot four. She held her own. She didn't care how big or how small you were. If you got in her face, she was going to get you. She was going to fight you. I've seen her fight two or three girls at one time and whup all of them. That's another thing she taught me—not to be afraid to stand up for myself. She said, 'Don't go running and crying, you fight.'"

Mark admitted things started to go downhill for his sister, once she moved to Peoria for good.

"Every time I'd be around her, there would be a fight with this girl or that girl," Mark said. "People were jealous of her because she held her own. She didn't take nothing from nobody. And a lot of people just didn't like her."

Then there were the drugs. In the beginning

Linda didn't want anything to do with drugs, but things changed.

"She was running with some of the wrong people," Mark said. "I had some other cousins who were into drugs. It's crazy, because she was always against it. I know she smoked marijuana, and drinking alcohol here and there at parties, but that was the extent of it. As far as crack cocaine— no way."

Mark said he was totally shocked when he found out his sister was doing drugs. It didn't make any sense, because she always told her family members who were using that it was wrong and they were going to kill themselves.

"She was so against it for so long," he said. "When I found out the first time she was doing it, I couldn't believe it. I thought no way, not my sister. She couldn't stand the sight of people who did drugs. I couldn't tell you what made her do [it]. I talked to her about why she did it. I wanted to know why she turned to drugs when she used to try and get family members off drugs. But an addict always makes excuses. She'd just say, 'Oh, I only do it recreationally.'"

Beverly Broadway, Linda's sister, who lives in the south suburbs of Chicago, remembered her sister as the life of the party, and as someone who looked out for her family.

"She was hilarious," Beverly said. "We'd sit up and laugh all night, crack jokes with each other, talk about the past. Even when we had picnics or barbeques, she was always the life of the party. She was fun to hang with. But she wouldn't let anyone mess with her family. When we went to a party, she'd say,

'If anyone's messing with you, you let me know.'
She'd have my back. She looked out for me."

But Beverly knew Linda had her problems
with drugs.

"I went through a lot with Linda with that," she
said. "When I was going through my divorce in the
summer of 1998, I asked her to come here and
stay with me. I knew she had a problem. Her addiction was pretty strong. But I thought if I got her
away from there, we could work on some things.
But bringing her into my house was kind of a mis-
take, because some things would come up missing.
And it became more of a problem than a help to
me. She stayed a month with me—then I had to
send her back because she stole my cell phone and
she pawned my car."

Turns out Linda had given her dealer her sister's car for the day in exchange for drugs.

"Sometimes you can give the drug dealer your
vehicle for an entire day, and they can do whatever
they want with it, maybe do drug buys or whatever.
And I ended up seeing my car on the street, and
me and my girlfriend pursued my own car on the
street with this guy driving my car," Beverly said.
"So it started becoming more of a hassle for her to
be staying with me than a help. So I sent her back
to Peoria. We still remained friends, and I understood what she was going through."

But through it all, Linda still tried to do the best
she could for herself and her family.

"She still tried to keep herself up, and I know
she tried to take care of my dad while she was
down in Peoria," Beverly said. "She'd always check
in on him or go to see him. But everybody knew

about her drug habit, and it got to the point [that] when she needed things, they'd rather buy those things for her than give her the money."

Beverly recalled a scary incident that happened to Linda before she met up with Larry Bright.

"There was this one tavern she would always frequent, and that's where she'd hang out and run across people with drugs. Sometimes Linda would hook up some of the guys that were there with people who sold drugs, and she would get something out of it, like smoking the drugs with them," Beverly said. "One time she was in a car with a Caucasian male who choked her and pushed her out of the truck while it was moving, and she was afraid. She talked to the police about it (the description of the guy didn't match Larry) and they wanted her to stay in a shelter for her safety. So she went. What happened to her kind of upset me, so I talked to her and asked her to come up my way. I told her I knew about a facility that was real nice that I could put her in, to help get her off drugs. I knew she did get into selling her body for drugs. I think she was probably arrested once or twice for prostitution. I didn't like her living that life, and that's why I tried to get her to come here."

Linda agreed, and her plan on the weekend she was murdered was to wash her clothes and have her dad put her on the train to Chicago. Larry Bright, though, had other plans, and that's when she came up missing.

"She hadn't called me about coming to Chicago, so I started calling down there asking, 'Where's Linda? Hasn't anybody seen her?'" Beverly said. "They said she left the shelter. So I figured she must have gone out to get that last high before she got on the train to come see me. It made me mad to think that. Then when I heard that they found her body, it was devastating. It just broke my heart."

Beverly later explained how she first heard her sister had been murdered.

"Initially my stepmother called me and said they found Linda, and I said, 'What do you mean "they found Linda"?' That's when she told me she was dead, and they found her in Tazewell County," she said. "From there, I heard it on the news, and they had no clue about who did it, and then they tried to connect all these other prostitutes' deaths. Linda was a fighter. She didn't take anything from people, male or female. She was known to carry her weight. I was kind of surprised when the police said, according to Larry Bright, she didn't fight back. I was thinking she had to be really stoned or high and couldn't fight back."

Beverly cried for weeks after Linda died.

"It was tough. I didn't believe it. I didn't want to believe it," she said. "It was like I was so close to getting her out of there. That's the only thing I kept thinking of—I almost had her, if she had just washed her clothes and come up here. But she just had to go out that night and get that last high in. That's what killed me—knowing I almost had her. It was devastating. Larry Bright must have felt like these women were expendable. They were nothing on the street. They wouldn't be missed, that their families didn't care. Little did Larry Bright know. There was a family who loved Linda and would know if she was missing."

Mark, too, was devastated when he learned about his sister's death.

"My stepbrother called me when she first came up missing," Mark said. "She wasn't known not to keep in touch with her family, even when she had been on a binge for two or three days. We'd lose contact with her then, but after she came down from that little binge, she would call and let us know she was safe. Then he called and said, 'They found Linda.' And I was like, 'Oh, okay, where's she at?' Then he told me she was dead, and I don't remember any more than that. I fell into my closet doors and I passed out. A few minutes later when I came to, I could hear him yelling in the phone. And my girl came running into the room, asking what was wrong. I picked up the phone and I just asked to talk to my dad, because I knew it had to be killing him to lose a daughter. That's all I remember about it."

Mark said he still thought about Linda all the time.

"I still deal with her death every day now," he said. "I look at her pictures and remember all the good and the bad, and I still love her. I don't condone what she was doing, but I still loved her—no matter what problems she had. Months before she was killed, me and my girlfriend were trying to get her to come up with us to get her away from all the drugs. I'll never get over it. I still have dreams about her all the time, and we're still running around as kids or going to parties, like she was still here. Linda wasn't the angel of angels, but she had a good heart. She was generous and kind and had a loving heart."

5

About the middle of November, TCSO detective Hal Harper drove out to Kickapoo Creek Road in rural Peoria. He wanted to talk to Lacy Davis about the S10 Chevy Blazer that her husband, Sam, had recently purchased.

Lacy told Harper that her husband was just driving around "curiosity shopping," with his friend Richard Harrison, when they noticed the Blazer parked in front of a house. The way it was parked made it look like it was used very little, if at all. Sam and Richard decided to knock on the door and ask the person who owned the Blazer if it was for sale.

The owner, Larry Bright, was interested, but he said the sale would have to be approved by his mother, Shirley. Bright exchanged telephone numbers with Sam. Larry later called Sam to say his mother had approved the sale. The two men agreed on a price of $500 and set up a time to meet to complete the transaction. Sam picked up the Blazer, on either November 2 or 3. He had to use a trailer to transport the vehicle because it wasn't running. After he got it home, Sam replaced the master cylinder and it worked just fine.

In response to his questions, Lacy also told the detective that she was a friend of John Long's and Fred Holley, his nephew. Long had stayed in a camper in the Davises' backyard for about a year. After Lacy and Sam sold Long the camper, he moved it to the junkyard behind a nearby meat packing plant, where he was living at that time.

Lacy said she had known Long all her life and he visited her at least every other day. She only knew Fred Holley because of Long, but she didn't trust him. Holley used to visit her almost every other day as well, but he hadn't been around since August.

"He's weird," she told Harper. "I wouldn't get in a car with that guy."

According to Lacy, Long and one of his buddies, a Hispanic guy, who went by the name "Amigo," liked to pick up black prostitutes. Amigo lived in Chicago with his wife, but he often made the trip to Peoria to get together with Long and have some wild, drunken parties with black prostitutes. Lacy said about a month and a half earlier they paid her to drive them to and from Woody's Bar on Adams Street.

Lacy said Long sold rabbits, chickens, and goats to Amigo, who killed them, covered them up, and drove them back to Chicago in his white or cream-colored Blazer. Stacy said Amigo was about five feet seven inches tall and about 160 pounds. He had fairly short black hair and was usually clean-shaven. He typically wore jeans, a T-shirt, and a flannel jacket. He had a thick accent and sported an earring.

According to Lacy, Long never drove anywhere, and always had to have someone drive him wherever he had to go, including to auctions and barn sales. Lacy said Long, who used to live on Pleasant Hill Road, across from the South Side Mission, had recently been in the S10 Blazer that Sam had bought from Larry Bright. After speaking with Harper, Lacy gave the Peoria County crime scene technicians permission to search that Blazer.

Around the same time, PCSO detective Dave Wilson went to talk to Harry Cannon, who had known Larry for about five years. Cannon was Larry's crack connection. Larry typically called him at least once a week, usually Mondays, and Cannon hooked him up with crack cocaine worth about $100. Sometimes Cannon met Larry to make the exchange. Sometimes, though, he delivered the dope to Larry's house, although he had never been invited inside.

"I used to see him around with black women," Cannon told Wilson. "I saw him with Ernestine a lot before she died. I heard from her family that she died of AIDS. I think she might have given Larry the disease, but I'm not sure."

"Did Larry prefer black girls or white girls?" Wilson asked.

"He always said he preferred black women over white women," Cannon said. "Larry was always a little strange. He always used to talk about being in the military, and how he saw action in the Gulf War."

"Did he ever pass himself off as being a police officer or doing some kind of police work?" Wilson asked.

"Not that I heard," Cannon said. "But it wouldn't surprise me that he'd do something like that."

Wilson asked Cannon if he had ever seen Bright drive the Blazer that he sold to Sam. Cannon said he didn't think so, because it was never running.

"I thought about buying that Blazer from him once, but I never did," he added.

The detectives also wanted to know what Larry's ex-wife, Cathy Bishop, could tell them, so two FBI agents went to her mother's house in Knoxville, Illinois, to meet with her.

Cathy explained that she had been introduced to Larry by his sister, Monica, who was one of her good friends. Cathy and Monica had lived in the same trailer park. It was sometime in February 1993. At that time Cathy had a two-year-old daughter, Suzanna, by a man named Jake Brown. Some six months after Cathy and Larry had started dating, her daughter was dead.

It was around one or two o'clock in the morning on August 6, 1993. Cathy, who had put Suzanna to bed, was sound asleep in the trailer she shared with Larry in the Rolling Meadows Mobile Home Park in Abingdon. Cathy had turned in early because she was ill, and she had left Larry in charge of the baby. Suddenly Larry woke her up, saying they had to bring Suzanna to the hospital immediately.

When she asked why, Larry mumbled something about hearing the baby "gurgling," and brought Suzanna's limp body to her. Cathy started cardiopulmonary resuscitation (CPR), then called 911, but she knew it was already too late. Her daughter was gone.

When paramedics arrived, Cathy told Larry she was going to ride to the hospital in the ambulance with Suzanna. Larry said that was fine, and that he would call a friend to drive him to the hospital to meet Cathy and the baby. But almost as soon as he arrived, Larry told Cathy he had to leave.

Hospital personnel thought Suzanna had died from shaken baby syndrome (SBS), but an autopsy failed to confirm that theory. However, the medical examiner (ME) found that the baby had a heart condition, which could have caused her death. There were also no signs of bruising or abuse on Suzanna's body.

Abingdon police who investigated the case wanted Larry to take a polygraph about what had happened, but he refused. The investigating officer wrote in his report: *During the interview with Bright on 8-9-93 this R. O. detected no physical or verbal signs of deception and still have no reason to believe that Bright's version of the death to not be an accurate account.*

So the police then got a warrant and searched the trailer in Abingdon. They said it was a mess. There were ants and dog feces everywhere. Larry, who was read his Miranda rights, told police he had never mistreated Suzanna in any way, and he loved her as if she were his own child. Police ultimately deemed the case against Bright "unfounded."

On August 21, 1993, Larry and Cathy married, and less than a month later, on September 16, Cathy was granted an order of protection against her husband.

"He beat the crap out of me, that's why I left him," Cathy told the FBI agents. "He also raped me, but I didn't press charges against him because I just wanted to get away."

Cathy said things turned from bad to worse in December of that year when she tried to do a favor for Suzanna's father, Jake Brown. Although Brown had moved to Florida, he spent the Christmas after Suzanna died visiting family in Illinois. While he was there, he wanted to get a copy of his daughter's autopsy report. Jake and Cathy tried to get a copy made on Christmas Day, but they didn't have any luck—everything was closed.

Larry called Cathy's mother on Christmas trying to track Cathy down. She told him that Cathy and Jake were out trying to copy the baby's autopsy report. Larry was so furious that he beat Cathy when she returned to their trailer in Abingdon. A few days later, Larry arrived at the Country Kitchen restaurant, where Cathy worked, with a peace offering—a beautiful bouquet of flowers. Cathy threw them away in front of him.

Cathy left Larry, but she soon started seeing him again. She continued to do so for some time. They didn't live together, though, because Larry had moved back to Peoria by then. He drove back and forth to Abingdon to see her. It was during that time that Cathy said Larry raped her.

Finally, on March 2, 1994, Cathy, just nineteen, filed for divorce, claiming "extreme and repeated mental cruelty." Larry contested the divorce, because he believed in his heart that he and Cathy would get back together. That divorce action was dismissed on February 29, 1996, but Cathy refiled her petition for divorce in May 1997. Their divorce was granted June 9, 1997.

In March or April 1994, before the first time she filed for divorce, Cathy went to visit Jake in Florida. One thing led to another, and before she knew it, she was pregnant. And she was still married to Larry. The baby, Andrew, was born on January 3, 1995. Cathy had a paternity test done to make sure that Larry wasn't Andrew's father. Despite those tests, Larry was convinced Andrew was his son, because the baby looked like him. Trying to be fair, Cathy sometimes let Larry visit Andrew. Cathy became pregnant again, by another man, in 1998 and had a daughter.

While Cathy and Larry were together, he was very aggressive when it came to sex.

"Did he have a high desire for sex?" one of the agents asked Cathy.

"Oh, yeah. He'd have sex all day and every night if possible," she said. "He used to go to adult stores to buy stuff. He liked dildos up his ass. Sometimes he lay on his side and put the dildo up his own ass. He always asked me for anal sex, but I always said no. He never forced me."

"Did he ever pay for sex?" the agent asked.

"Not that I know of."

"Do you think Larry was prejudiced?"

"I don't think so. He even dated a black girl

once, but he stopped dating her when he thought he could get back with me," Cathy said. "Larry used to tell me that when it came to sex, he didn't care if the girl was black, white, or Chinese, because they were all the same color on the inside."

About three weeks later, a couple members of the task force went back to Cathy's house to question her about Larry again.

Cathy told the detectives that she and Larry hit it off immediately and they started living together in the trailer park not long after they met. She said Larry was very close to his mother and he'd drive to Peoria to see her almost every day.

"You know, I think Larry's mother used to be a prostitute," she said. "She had a few wigs that she used to wear in her younger days. Larry's father used to call her a 'fucking whore,' and said she did what she had to do to get by."

Despite Cathy's statements to police that Shirley had been a prostitute, police were never able to substantiate that claim, although they continued to question others about it.

The detectives asked Cathy to tell them more about what had happened on the night her daughter had died.

"I wasn't feeling good, so I took some cold medicine and went to bed. I took Suzanna with me, but she was restless," she explained. "So I asked Larry if he could take her so I could rest. A few hours later, Larry woke me up and told me something was wrong with the baby, and that we needed to call an ambulance."

She said while they were waiting for the paramedics, the couple tried to do CPR on Suzanna, but it didn't work. Cathy rode in the ambulance with Suzanna to the hospital, and Larry called a friend for a ride. Once he arrived at the hospital, Larry started acting funny. Before long, he left, although Cathy didn't remember if he left with his friend or by himself.

"Later that day, Larry asked me to marry him," Cathy said. "At Suzanna's funeral my friend, Tracy, saw Larry kneel by Suzanna's casket and say, 'I'm sorry, Suzanna. I'm sorry what happened to you.'"

"Do you think Larry had anything to do with Suzanna's death?" PPD detective Chris Hauk asked.

"I don't really think so, but sometimes I wonder," she said.

"Was Larry ever violent with you?" Hauk asked.

"Yeah, Larry used to beat me, and, once, he raped me."

"Can you tell me about the rape?"

"Well, me and Larry had just split up, and we tried to work things out a lot," she said. "I was at Larry's mother's old house on McClure, and Larry wanted to have sex, and I said no. So he held me down and he forced himself on me. That's when I left Larry for the last time and filed for divorce."

"Do you think he's capable of killing anyone?" the detective asked.

"I don't think so, but he's really gotten into crack cocaine, and that makes people do crazy things," she said. "I haven't had any contact with Larry in years, but maybe I'll go visit him in jail."

6

As the investigation continued, officials of Peoria and Tazewell Counties offered a $20,000 reward for information leading to the arrest and conviction of the person or persons responsible for the deaths of six of Peoria's African-American women.

At about 11:00 A.M. on December 2, 2004, Assistant State's Attorney (ASA) Stephen Pattelli stood before the Peoria County grand jury to seek an indictment against Larry Dean Bright for "aggravated unlawful restraint" for holding Vickie Bomar against her will sometime in July 2004.

"Going on the record, this is the people of the *State of Illinois* versus *Larry Bright,*" Pattelli said. "The proposed bill of indictment in two counts states in Count One that on or about July 15, 2004, through July 30, 2004, in said Peoria County, state of Illinois, Larry Bright committed the offense of aggravated unlawful restraint, in that he knowingly and without legal authority detained Vickie Bomar at West Starr Street, Peoria, Illinois, without her consent, while armed with a dangerous or deadly weapon, being a knife in violation of [Illinois state laws].

"Count Two states that on or about July 15, 2004, through July 30, 2004, in said Peoria County, state of Illinois, Larry Bright committed the offense of unlawful restraint in that he knowingly and without legal authority detained Vickie Bomar at West Starr Street, Peoria, Illinois, without her consent in violation of [Illinois state laws]."

The first witness called by Pattelli was Scott Cook, a sergeant with the Peoria Police Department.

"In your capacity [as a police sergeant], have you and other members of local law enforcement been investigating a series of women who have disappeared, and some of them being found dead, in the Peoria County and Tazewell County area that caused you to investigate an incident that came to your attention where a Vickie Bomar was detained by an individual determined to be a Larry Bright that led to his arrest and prosecution for unlawful restraint?"

"That's correct."

"Could you relate for the grand jury the circumstances of that situation?"

"During the course of my employment being assigned to the detective bureau in the Peoria Police Department, I've also been assigned collateral duty as a member of a task force. As you stated, in doing so, I've worked with Captain Bobby Henderson, who is a police officer in Tazewell County, Illinois. Captain Henderson and I, on November eighth, were working together as partners. Captain Henderson had information from an informant that Vickie Bomar may have information pertinent to our task force investigation.

"Upon locating Ms. Bomar, we spoke with her and asked her if she did, in fact, have information regarding our investigation. We spoke with her at length. She indicated to us that there was a male subject, whom she did not know, that had approached her, telling her that he was in possession of a quantity of crack cocaine, as well as cash, and wanted to party. At that point she went with the subject in order to partake in his offer and wound up at his residence."

"Would that be consistent, in your opinion, to the scenarios that may have occurred to other women that had disappeared?" Pattelli asked.

"Yes."

"In essence, did Ms. Bomar come forward with this originally or pursuant to the publicity by the task force of investigating similar incidents, or did some other person inform the task force that this may have happened to Ms. Bomar?"

"Through the course of the task force investigation, we've been approached by people saying, 'Well, I don't know personally what happened, but an individual has said that they were involved with someone who did commit a certain offense.' That was the case here. We had an informant who called Captain Henderson and said Vickie Bomar may have been involved with someone who unlawfully restrained her, did some things that may be consistent with some violent crimes going on against area prostitutes."

"So that would be one of the type of leads that

you would certainly follow up on in regard to that bigger picture, correct?"

"Absolutely."

"And in following up on that, then I take it that you—the task force was able to converse with her and verify that apparently sometime basically around July, as best you could determine, that this had occurred?"

"Correct. She indicated that it was mid-July. She couldn't be exact on a date, but she indicated somewhere around the middle of the month," Cook answered.

"Was she sufficiently able to describe where this occurred or who the person was to lead you to Larry Bright?"

"Yes. She actually went with Captain Henderson and directed us, as to her recollection, to the area in which Mr. Bright lives. Upon driving in the area, she pointed out locations and had previously described the location as being a garage [that] was converted into a living quarters behind the larger house. It was contained within a privacy fence. Once we were in the area of Mr. Bright's residence, we did see that this was consistent with what Ms. Bomar told us."

"Did she indicate basically what had occurred that had caused the alarm to the police department?"

"Yes. She indicated that she had gone with Mr. Bright, had gone to his residence. Her belief was at that point they were going to smoke crack cocaine. She had a crack pipe with her. At that point she indicated Mr. Bright began by saying, 'You have the right to remain silent, anything you say can and will be used against you,' which is the beginning of the Miranda statements, [which] police officers normally advise suspects of during the course of questioning. Ms. Bomar said she believed at that point Mr. Bright was a police officer, and she was very frightened that she was about to be taken to jail. Ms. Bomar said that Bright told her he was going to give her a break, as he did not want to go into the office to do paperwork, so he was not going to arrest her.

"She began to get her things together, wanted to leave, at which point he produced a knife. Ultimately, Bomar said, Mr. Bright told her to take her clothes off. He attempted to have sexual intercourse with her, both vaginally and anally. She did not wish to have anal intercourse with Mr. Bright. Told him numerous times that she needed to use the restroom. Ultimately he let her go use the restroom, at which point she barricaded herself inside. She stated that Mr. Bright attempted to get into the bathroom by banging on the door. She had her feet propped against the sink and was holding her back against the door. Ultimately Bright made the statement that he—that she needed to come out of the bathroom. He would go ahead and take her home.

"Ms. Bomar advised us that at the time this happened, she went, put her clothing on—however, leaving part of her underwear at the residence. Mr. Bright went out to his vehicle. As he prepared to get into his vehicle, she took off, running. She said that she saw a neighbor, who had just come to her residence, and she ran toward this neighbor of Mr. Bright's and advised her that she had been, in her words, 'raped.' At this point the neighbor wanted to call the police, but Ms. Bomar was reluctant because she believed that this Mr. Bright was the police, and accepted a ride home from the neighbor. In following up on the investigation, we spoke with the [neighbor], and she did confirm that sometime in July she had spoken with Vickie Bomar, who related basically what I just stated," Cook testified.

"Now, was it determined that Mr. Bright lived in the same neighborhood as Ms. Bomar, the victim here, or did they live in a different area?"

"They live in the south end of Peoria. Ms. Bomar does not have a permanent address at this time, but it is the same general area."

"It would not be inaccurate to say that Ms. Bomar has, at least, had a dependency or used controlled substances in the past?" Pattelli questioned.

"Yes. At the time that we spoke with her, she was interested in, and was taken by us to, a treatment center for dependency."

"Is it possible that she also engaged in the prostitution business?"

"Yes, sir."

"Okay. So she would be a person that might have fit the profile of the victims that had been turning up in Peoria County and Tazewell County?"

"That's correct," Cook stated.

"In essence, it appears that she's saying that she was approached and consensually went with the person that she did not know, correct?"

"Correct."

"And then after she went to this person's residence that the person became overly aggressive toward her?"

"Right," Cook responded.

"Now, we're not exactly sure if she [was kept there] after sex acts, or because she didn't perform more sex acts?"

"Correct."

"But she did indicate she was threatened with a knife? He tried to keep her there further by the use of this dangerous or deadly weapon?"

"That's correct."

"This would have been at West Starr Street?" Pattelli asked.

"Yes, sir. That's correct."

"Now, pursuant to her giving a statement to the police department, was a warrant issued, and, in verifying the information she had given by talking to other people, was a warrant issued for Larry Bright?"

"Yes. After the initial conversation with Ms. Bomar, we did compile a photo lineup and present that to her for identification purposes, and she identified Mr. Bright following this, as well as the confirmation by Mrs. Whitby, the neighbor, that Ms. Bomar had been, in fact, in that area in July, stating basically the same facts that she had told us. We presented the information, and an arrest warrant was issued."

"Did that identify the defendant as being a Larry D. Bright, a white male, born July 8, 1966?"

"Yes, it did."

"In fact, was the warrant served, and was he detained by the members of the task force?"

"Yes, sir. He was," Cook replied.

"Was it determined that he, in fact, was living on the property apparently owned by his mother? She lived in a house in the front, and he did live in a converted garage in the rear of the property?"

"That's correct."

"So what the victim had said was consistent, as far as what the premises looked like, correct?" Pattelli questioned.

"The victim was very specific with her description, as far as the outside of the residence. She was also very specific with the description of the inside of the residence, that being going onto a porch, having a—use her words here—having an 'efficiency-type room.' That being the bedroom, the living-room furniture, television, and whatnot was all centrally located in one room, and then a separate bathroom being closed off."

"Okay. Now, Mr. Bright did not make any admissions, correct?"

"No, he did not."

"The property under his control was searched, and no obvious physical evidence belonging to this victim was located there, correct?" Pattelli asked.

"Not that we're aware of at this point."

"There were DNA samples taken from him that are presently being compared to this crime, as well as possibly other crimes? He consented to samples, I believe?"

"I'm not sure on that issue."

"Okay," the attorney stated.

"That was not part of my portion of the investigation."

"Okay. Now, the victim herself, I take it, has her own legal problems, correct?" Pattelli queried.

"Yes."

"And she apparently didn't come forward originally, maybe because she didn't understand the significance, as well as she was wanted, apparently, by law enforcement for some warrants?

"It was her belief at that time she had an outstanding failure-to-appear warrant. So she was not willing, did not come forward, conceivably for a number of [reasons], correct?"

"Correct. When she approached [the neighbor], she indicated that she just wanted a ride home. She did not want to call the police, because she was fearful of going to jail herself," Cook replied.

"Now, that would not be inconsistent with the type of victims that have been determined to be the victims of some of these recent crimes that the task force is investigating, correct?"

"I think it would be very consistent with the type of victims that we're dealing with," Cook stated.

"Okay. Does anybody have any further questions of this witness before we bring in the victim?" Pattelli asked.

"Didn't you also say that he had her believing he was a police officer, and that was one of the reasons she was concerned about calling you people, because she thought he was a police officer?" a juror asked.

"Correct. He began reading what is very commonly known as the Miranda warning, telling her she had the right to remain silent, thereby leading her to believe he was a police officer or someway affiliated with law enforcement," Cook said.

"But he is not and never has been?" the juror asked.

"Not to our knowledge."

"Did he show a gun or badge or anything?" the juror asked.

"Not that she has indicated in the incident, which she reported to us. No, sir," Cook said.

"What is her age and his age?" a juror asked.

"Ms. Bomar was born in 1969. That would make her thirty-five. Mr. Bright was born in 1966, so that would make him thirty-eight years old," Cook responded.

"Anybody else?" Pattelli asked. "If not, we'll have you step down."

Pattelli next called Vickie Bomar to the stand.

"Could you please state your name and age for the grand jury?"

"My name is Vickie Bomar. I'm thirty-five years old."

"Vickie, where do you stay at?"

"Well, right now I reside at the South Side Mission on Laramie."

"And recently did it come to your knowledge, the police department's attention, that you may have had contact with a white male that you did not know that led to you being detained for a short period of time on Starr Street?"

"No, sir. Not on Starr Street. On Grinnell Street."

"Okay. Could you tell us about that, what you know?"

"Well, I met him one night when I was walking with a friend of mine, Clarence. We were walking back to his residence, hoping to—hoping to score drugs. I ran into this guy in a, like, greenish blue— I guess I'd say Honda Chevy. He approached me. He asked me, would I ride with him for exchange of drugs? He told me he had two hundred bucks. He asked me to ride with him, to get in the car and ride with him to exchange sex for drugs, and he said he had two hundred and an eight ball of crack cocaine. I agreed to get in with him. We left from Grinnell Street and rode to a residence of his, over in the county area."

"Okay. And did you go into a residence or a garage or something?"

"I guess it used to be a garage, but it was, like, transformed, you know, like a little summer cottage outside of a residence," Vickie replied.

"Okay. And did you do drugs with him or engage in a sex act with him?"

"Not willingly. No drugs was ever brung up. No money was ever brung up."

"Did he threaten you or display a knife to you at some point?"

"Yes, he did. He told me he was a police officer. He said he was giving me a break that night. He started to read me my rights, and he told me that he was too tired to go back to the station and do a report and whatever, and at that time I thought I was going to be free to go. That's when he came at me with a switchblade."

"Did that put you in fear that he might try to harm you?"

"Yes."

"Did that—did you then seclude yourself or

hide in some part of that garage in the bathroom or something?"

"No. Not at that time yet. That's when he told me I had to get undressed and give him a favor for him letting me leave, by him being the police," Vickie answered.

"Did you perform a sex act?"

"No. Actually, he did. He made me get undressed. He made me get on his bed as he got on top of me. He performed sexual activities on me."

"Did he detain you there longer than you wanted to be there?"

"Yes. Way longer."

"Okay. Now, how did you get away?"

"Well, first I started by telling him I had to urinate."

"Okay."

"After I complained that I had to urinate, for maybe seven or eight minutes, he finally got off me and let me use the restroom. When I went in the restroom, I boarded myself in with the door and the sink, and I put the board over my head, you know, thinking, because he might kick the door in or try to come back in. So after I was in there, like, maybe three or four minutes, he realized I wasn't going to come out. He started kicking the door in. He accepted I wasn't going to come out. He started to scream and hollering to me to get dressed, and he would take me back to where I came from. I still had the—I didn't put the board down. I kept the board over my body because I didn't know if he was going to use the knife or not."

"What did you do then?"

"When I came out of the bathroom, he was getting dressed. He started throwing me my stuff, telling me to get dressed. I got dressed really quick. As we left out, he ran and got into his truck, but I just ran across the field because I wasn't getting back into that truck," Vickie testified.

"So you did not go with him and let him take you home?"

"Huh-uh."

"Did you make contact with somebody you knew then?"

"This lady. I didn't know her, but there was this lady right outside of his [yard] there. She was pulling up in a white car. This older white lady. I started telling her this man had raped me. He said he was the police. She told me to get in and call the police. Then she took me to my designated area."

"Now, let me ask you a couple other questions. As I reiterated to you or indicated to you out in the hallway, we are not interested in prosecuting you for any illegal activity. Just the truth of what occurred here. You did not come forward with this immediately to the authorities, correct?" the assistant state's attorney asked.

"Huh-uh," Vickie answered affirmatively.

"Is there any reason why you—particular reason why you didn't tell the police about this incident?"

"At that time I had a warrant for my arrest."

"So if you would have told the police, they would have arrested you on the warrant?"

"For failure to appear."

"Did you become aware of the police's investigation in other circumstances occurring in the county involving individuals that had some drug problems that were found that were missing, or found dead?" the ASA queried.

"I'm not understanding the question."

"Let me rephrase that. Did you come forward eventually, or did somebody tell the police?"

"I never came forward until Clarence informed the police of the incident."

"Then the police contacted you about this incident?"

"Yes. Henderson and Cook."

"I take it you told them what happened here?"

"Right."

"And you also gave a taped statement, I believe?"

"Yeah. And I picked him out of a lineup also."

"Does anybody have any further questions of this witness before we leave you to deliberate on this case?" Pattelli asked. "Okay. If not, we appreciate you coming down."

With that, the hearing was concluded, and the grand jurors began their deliberations. They returned with an indictment against Larry Bright for aggravated unlawful restraint.

The next day about thirty family members of the dead and missing women marched through downtown Peoria to the Peoria County Courthouse, hoping to make people more aware of who the victims were, not just the lives they led.

Tamika Donelson, Wanda Jackson's daughter, told the *Peoria Journal Star* that she wanted people to know that her mother was a loving and caring person. She said Wanda, the mother of nine children and several grandchildren, was a "happy spirit" and spent a lot of time with her children. Tamika said all the victims were good people, who were loved by their families.

While the families waited for answers, members of the task force worked long and hard to find out what had happened to their daughters, sisters, mothers, and girlfriends. They knew that the more time passed, the more likely they were to find the four missing women dead—although no one really believed they were still alive.

And the detectives weren't even sure if one person was reponsible for the murders. For one thing, the kills seemed disorganized. The bodies of the victims were found in various positions. Some were lying on their backs, while others were found facedown. Some were fully or partially dressed, others naked. Their bodies were dumped in different places—by the side of the road or in more hidden areas. Maybe the killer or killers didn't even live in Peoria. Police in other states, as well as in Canada, were also investigating the deaths of prostitutes.

Authorities hoped the march would keep attention focused on the investigation. Police also planned to hold a news conference every two weeks to update the public. And detectives had already investigated more than five hundred tips that had come in to the task force. One woman even called the task force to say her husband might be the murderer, because he was addicted to crack and liked to engage the services of black prostitutes.

Police were also interviewing the five hundred

reported sexual offenders in the area, and were tracking down reported and unreported rape cases in the counties, particularly rapes of prostitutes.

On December 10, PCSO detectives Dave Hoyle and Dave Wilson went to Larry's house to speak with him. They knocked on the door, but there was no answer. As they were leaving, Larry pulled up to the house, got out of his truck, and approached them.

Wilson told Larry they were there to check up on him and make sure he hadn't had any problems because of the recent article in the *Peoria Journal Star.* Larry said there hadn't been any trouble, but he had no idea what article Wilson was talking about. The detective explained that the newspaper had run a story about a woman named Tiffany Hughes, who claimed she had had a run-in with a guy who tried to strangle her. Wilson said the description Tiffany provided to the reporter about the house where she almost lost her life matched his house. In fact, Wilson told Larry that several people had called the task force and said that the house described in the story *was* Larry's house.

Larry again said he had not had any problems. Then he said he didn't know if he should be talking with them, because his attorney had advised against talking to them, particularly about Vickie Bomar.

"I'm not going to talk to you about the Vickie Bomar case," Wilson said. "But I mght need to talk to you about these other deceased and missing women so I can either eliminate you as a suspect or prove you were involved."

"I'll do whatever I can to cooperate," Larry said. "You know, I wish you'd find out who's killing these girls so you can eliminate me as a suspect."

Investigators were soon notified by the Illinois State Police Crime Lab that the DNA extracted from the two cigarette butts Larry had discarded during his interview with detectives in November matched the DNA that had been found on Linda Neal.

Armed with that information, police were able to obtain search warrants to collect Larry's DNA officially, as well as to search his house, his vehicle, his mom's house, and her vehicle. So they went to pick him up at his grandmother's house, where they knew he had gone. Police had his truck towed back to the station; then they drove Larry to his house so he could unlock the door for the other investigators.

On the way to his house, Larry asked why police had search warrants for his mom's house and car. They explained it was because he had had access to them. When they arrived at Larry's place, the crime scene unit (CSU) was already waiting. Larry unlocked both his house and his mom's house.

Once inside, Deputy Scott Gamboe searched and photographed Shirley's house. In the spare bedroom, next to the master bedroom, he took a picture of a bagless vacuum cleaner. Then he removed and collected the two filters and all the accumulated debris. He photographed and collected a "spoon" ring from the top of the armoire in the same room. One of the victims reportedly had been wearing the same type of ring.

In the top left drawer of the dresser, he discovered a size-38DD Warner's bra, the only item of clothing in the drawer. Thinking that a bit unusual, he photographed and collected it to take back to the lab. He also recovered a computer tower and power cord from the same room.

As Gamboe searched Shirley's house, Detective Doug O'Neill conducted a search of Larry's house and photographed the scene. He collected a number of items, including suspected drug paraphernalia, a mattress pad with stains on it, a couple shirts with stains on them, a sweatshirt with hair and fibers on it, a couple pairs of men's underwear with stains on them, and a flesh-colored dildo wrapped in a blue towel.

Deputy Martin "Marty" Klatt, of the Peoria County Sheriff's Office, also went to the Bright residence to help in the search. He had been asked to remove two Eureka upright vacuum cleaners from the hallway in Shirley's house and take them back to the lab to process them for evidence.

After he took the vacuum cleaners out of the house, Klatt searched the garage attached to Larry's house for anything that Larry could have used for digging, burning, or cutting. He collected a variety of hand tools, garden tools, shovels, rakes, cutting utensils, knives, shearing tools, axes, saws, and chain saws.

One of the most interesting things Klatt collected was a shovel that Larry would eventually tell investigators he used while he burned the remains of his victims. The deputy also found seven Fire Start sticks, which could be used to start a bonfire or campfire.

During his search Klatt found a wadded-up piece of fabric that had been thrown into the rafters above the garage. He retrieved the material and realized it was a dark blue woman's dress. After photographing the dress, Klatt inspected it and found several long fibers, or hairs, attached to it. However, there were no legible manufacturer's tags on the dress. He collected the hair and fibers to take back to the lab.

The dress was thirty-eight inches around at its widest point, fourteen inches wide at the shoulders, and thirty and a half inches long. According to a seamstress who later examined it, the dress was between a size 10 and a size 12. There was a small button at the collar and a small slit on the bottom right. There were sweat stains on the collar and under the arms.

Klatt and the other crime scene investigators (CSIs) looked around to see if there was blood. They had been told that one of the victims had struggled with Larry, then escaped out of his house by breaking a window. During their investigation law enforcement had found a broken window on the south wall of the patio area. They also discovered three small brownish red spots on or near the window. Klatt swabbed the blood so it could be examined later.

The CSIs also found a brownish red spot on the bathroom floor near the closet. Klatt photographed that spot and swabbed it. The investigators also removed tile and carpeting in and near the bathroom, as well as the threshold, searching for more blood.

Then they tested two spots on Larry's mattress and determined they were spots of blood. Klatt took pictures of the spots, and the investigators took the mattress as evidence. They also took a picture of a dark stain on the side of the couch and then swabbed it.

Investigators were also joined in their search by a trooper with the Illinois State Police and his K-9, Goldberg, a cadaver-sniffing dog. The trooper took Goldberg through the house, but he didn't detect anything. While the dog was going through the bathroom, he bit his tongue and was bleeding all over the floor. The trooper collected a sample of the blood for O'Neill to take back to the lab.

Gamboe also searched the garage attached to Larry's house. He discovered a used roll of duct tape on a shelf in the front of the garage. After O'Neill photographed it, Gamboe collected it as possible evidence. Toward the back of the garage, he noticed a plastic bin. Inside the bin he found a makeup kit containing what appeared to be part of a radio antenna, with some kind of residue on one end. Because sections of antennas can be used to smoke dope, Gamboe tested it for cocaine, but the test came back negative. He took the antenna back to the lab for further testing.

When Gamboe arrived at the lab, he vacuumed Larry's Dodge Dakota, and Shirley's Dodge Durango, which had been towed to the jail. He took swabbings of certain sections of both vehicles and also collected some fibers from the seat and carpet of Larry's Dakota. He logged everything into evidence.

After they left Larry's house and were driving on their way to the jail, Detective Hoyle told Larry they were going to be collecting his DNA.

"Why do you need my DNA?"

"We already collected it once, when you left your cigarettes butts in the inteview room, the first time we interviewed you," Hoyle said. "And that DNA matched the DNA that was found inside one of the murdered women."

"And there's only one way that it could get there," said Detective Chris Hauk.

"Yeah, but I didn't kill her," Larry said. "All I did was get her some crack and drop her off at the bar."

Larry paused for a minute, then said, "I can tell you everything and clear my name, but I'm not giving you any names."

Hoyle told Larry that they couldn't question him about anything because of an order his attorney had filed.

"Can I use your cell phone to call him?" Larry asked.

Larry talked to his attorney, Joseph Borsberry, for a few minutes, then told police he could cooperate with all the warrants, but he wasn't going to give them DNA.

"We have a warrant, and we'll take your DNA if

it means we have to use ten cops to hold you down," Hoyle said.

Larry talked to Borsberry again, then told Hoyle the lawyer wanted to talk to him. Hoyle took the phone and explained that police had a warrant for Larry's DNA and they'd take it by force, if necessary. Borsberry acquiesced but asked if he could be present when the DNA sample was taken. Hoyle told Borsberry he'd have to clear that with Lieutenant Greskoviak. Several minutes later, Greskoviak called Hoyle and gave the okay.

When they got to the jail, they waited for Borsberry to arrive; then they took Larry to the medical facility, where Marty Klatt, who had returned from the Brights' property, collected Larry's saliva, as well as twenty-five pubic hairs and fifty hairs from his head. When they were finished, Larry's attorney told police that his client was exercising his right to remain silent. He then drove Larry home.

Wilson and Hoyle went to West Starr Court the next day to arrest Larry for possession of cocaine and marijuana. They arrested him as he was coming out of his house to greet his mother, who had just arrived home from work. Larry asked why he was being arrested, and Hoyle explained that police had found something during the search of his house in November.

Larry had been eating a cheeseburger at the time and asked if he could finish it before he was handcuffed. He was allowed to do so; then he was handcuffed and placed in the back of an unmarked squad car. Once in the car, Larry asked what had been found and what he was being charged with.

Hoyle told him he was being charged with marijuana and cocaine possession and probably violating his bond. Larry asked what that meant, and Hoyle explained that the state's attorney would probably revoke his bond and he'd go back to jail on the original charge in the Vickie Bomar case.

The detective said he would have to ask someone at the state's attorney's office to find out for sure. Larry was concerned, because his mother had posted the bond money and wanted to know what he should do. Hoyle said he couldn't talk to him about the investigation because his lawyer had filed papers stipulating that they not talk to him.

"It's just us in the car, let's talk," Larry said. "I'll tell you what you want to know."

"Larry, you can say what you want, but we can't ask you any questions," Hoyle said.

"Okay, I picked up the girl that was found by Hopedale. She ripped me off," Larry said. "She was with another girl and we got some crack. Then I took them back to the bar and dropped them off. I went to get some more crack and went by the bar again. I saw her getting into a tan van. How's that?"

The detectives had a number of questions they wanted to ask Larry, but they couldn't do so until they checked with their boss to determine if they were able to speak with him again. Hoyle told Larry he'd probably need to talk to his attorney as well.

"Ask me what you want."

"We can't, Larry, until we get permission from someone else first," Hoyle said.

"Can we try to call my attorney?"

At that point they had arrived at the jail. Before they went in, Hoyle let Larry use his cell phone to call his attorney. Unable to get through, Larry called his mom and asked her to have Borsberry call the detectives. Hoyle and Wilson then took Larry to the detectives' interview room, where he waited until they tried again to locate his lawyer. They also called the state's attorney to apprise him of the situation.

A short time later, Shirley Bright called and said she had been unable to find Larry's attorney, but she had left several messages asking him to call one of the detectives. Hoyle told Larry that they hadn't been able to reach his attorney, but they'd talk to him without his attorney *if* they could videotape the interview. Larry agreed. Hoyle said that TCSO detective Hal Harper would also be present for the interview. He also said he would explain the entire procedure before they got started; then he asked Larry if he needed anything.

"Can I take a shit first?" Larry asked.

Hoyle let Larry use the restroom. After he was brought back into the room, Hoyle began going over the standard forms for video consent and explaining them to Larry, who had started chain-smoking cigarettes. About halfway through the consent forms, Larry said he needed to go to the bathroom again.

As soon as he was done, Hoyle picked up where he had left off explaining the forms; then he asked

Larry if he was ready to begin the interview. He was in the middle of smoking a cigarette, so Hoyle told him to finish the smoke and then they'd get started. As he smoked the cigarette, Larry started sweating and breathing heavily.

"Are you ready?" Hoyle asked when Larry had put out the cigarette.

"No, I can't do this," he said. "I think I want to wait until I have my lawyer with me."

Hoyle said that was fine and left the room. Larry was then taken to be processed into the jail. When Hoyle went back to the detectives' area, he received a call from Larry's attorney. Hoyle went over the situation with him, then scheduled an appointment for Borsberry to meet with Larry.

Borsberry arrived at the jail at about eleven o'clock the next morning to talk with his client. Following that meeting, the attorney told the detectives that Larry didn't want to talk—unless he was offered a deal. Hoyle said that he would have to make that request to the state's attorney. Borsberry said he would contact the state's attorney and be in touch.

Although the warrants to search the Brights' homes and vehicles were sealed, the press soon got wind that the police were searching property in Peoria County. They asked Sheriff Mike McCoy to comment on the investigation.

McCoy, however, declined to comment, saying the investigation was going to be conducted in a private and confidential manner. He was worried that it wouldn't be fair to leak Larry's name to the press, in case he had nothing to do with the dead and missing women. He also refused to give out any information about any evidence that investigators might have uncovered.

As far as McCoy was concerned, he'd only release information to the press if someone had been arrested, but the case was far from solved. Just because multiple search warrants had been served didn't mean there had been a break in the investigation. And McCoy wanted people to continue to call in with tips and other information that could help find whoever was responsible for the dead and missing women.

When Larry was arrested on the drug charge, word began circulating that he had also been arrested in November for holding a Peoria woman in his house against her will. Police, however, still officially refused to confirm whether Larry was a suspect in the task force investigation.

During his bond hearing on the drug charges, Larry appeared in Peoria County Circuit Court over the jail's closed-circuit television (CCTV). At that hearing, his bond on the drug case was set at $100,000. The next day Larry was back in court on the matter of his bond on the unlawful restraint case.

During that hearing SA Kevin Lyons told the judge that Larry had been charged with unlawful possession of a controlled substance while out on bond for the unlawful restraint charge. Lyons asked for an increase in Larry's bond. Larry's attorney tried to persuade the judge that his client wasn't a flight risk, and he didn't have a lot of money.

But Borsberry's plea fell on deaf ears as the judge granted Lyons's request and set Larry's bond at $350,000—$250,000 for the unlawful restraint charge and $100,000 for the drug charge. That meant Larry needed to post an additional $25,000 to get out of jail.

Although Lyons didn't mention the investigation into the deaths and disappearances of the local women at the hearing, media reports pointed to the fact that it was highly unusual for Lyons to appear personally at a bond hearing on somewhat minor felony charges. It was also unusual, but not unheard of, for a high bond to be set in an unlawful possession of a controlled substance case, which is punishable by either probation or up to three years in prison.

Although the authorities didn't want to talk, one of Larry's neighbors told the *Peoria Journal Star* that police had been to Larry's house several times in the week before the hearing. She said the neighbors had no idea what was going on, but they were certainly curious.

7

As the investigation progressed, TCSO captain Bobby Henderson and Special Agent Joe Spidle with the Illinois State Police went to Galesburg, Illinois, to talk to Larry's friend Dan Hosmer. Hosmer and his girlfriend, Chris, were in the process of moving when police arrived.

Hosmer told the investigators that he and Larry had been friends for several years. They first met in 1998 through one of Larry's relatives. Hosmer said Larry had been to visit him twice in the previous week, and Larry was supposed to finish helping him move on December 11, but he never showed up.

"Did he tell you anything about being arrested?"

"Yeah, he told me he had gone to a local liquor store, and while he was there, some black woman ran from the area. He said the cops investigated the incident and were looking for a white male suspect who drove a truck like his. The cops thought he had killed some crack whores, but they compared his DNA and cleared him, so they let him out of jail. He told me the cops searched his house and the garage where he stayed."

During the interview the detectives asked Hosmer if he and Larry had ever lived in Racine, Wisconsin. Hosmer said he had lived there from 1996 until 2001, and then moved back to the Galesburg area on February 15, 2001. He wasn't sure when Larry moved back to Illinois.

Hosmer said the two men had lived together for a while in Racine, but he eventually kicked Larry out sometime in 1999 because he got tired of Larry smoking so much crack cocaine. Larry rented his own place after he moved out.

While they were in Racine, Hosmer and Larry also hung out with George Jamison, Hosmer's brother-in-law, who, like Larry, smoked way too much crack.

"I remember coming home one day and found George and a black crack whore there," Hosmer said. "They were both high and I made them leave."

Hosmer said he didn't really remember any-thing about the woman—except that she was short and had small breasts.

"Did Larry and George both use prostitutes?" Spidle asked.

"Yeah, they both used black and white prosti-tutes and smoked a lot of crack with them. I know they even traded crack for sex," he said.

"Was Larry or George ever involved in any type of altercation with any prostitutes in Racine?"

"I don't remember any, but I know George sometimes beats women up. He went to prison for it once," Hosmer said. "George gets violent when he's smoking crack or drinking. Once he beat up his boss's son and got fired."

"Is there anything else you can tell us about Larry?"

"I know he was married to some woman, and her baby died. And everyone thought Larry killed the baby," Hosmer said. "He also had a girlfriend whose name was Mary Stone. She lived in Canton, Illinois, at one time. Larry just recently told me he still loved her."

"Do you think Larry could ever murder any black prostitutes?"

"I don't think he would, and if it turned out he did, I'd be very surprised. I think he could kill someone in a fight, but I don't think he could kill a woman."

Spidle, accompanied by Sergeant Scott Cook, also went to Brimfield, Illinois, to talk to George Jamison. The police were interested in Jamison because the bodies of three of the dead women— Barbara Williams, Frederickia Brown, and Brenda Erving—had been dumped within ten miles of his house.

The interview took place in Spidle's squad car in front of Jamison's house. The detectives began by getting a little background information on Jamison. George worked at a recycling plant in Bartonville, Illinois. He said he hadn't owned a car for about ten years. Although he grew up in Yates City, Illinois, Jamison had lived in several Illinois cities, including Elmwood, Farmington, and Galesburg. He had also lived in Texas and Wisconsin for a short time.

Jamison initially said he had never used the services of prostitutes, even when he was young. He said he never even went out to any bars, preferring to drink at home. Jamison said he had lived and worked in Racine from about 1996 until 2001 or 2002.

"Are you sure you never used prostitutes?" Spidle asked.

"I never used them," he said.

"Well, we have information that you might have used the services of black prostitutes while you were living in Racine."

"Yeah, okay, I used them in Racine. I was also smoking a lot of crack while I was there, and sometimes I traded crack for sex, and sometimes I paid for it."

"Do you ever hang out with Larry Bright?" Spidle asked.

"I haven't seen Larry since the summer when I ran into him one time," Jamison said, adding that he had met Larry years earlier.

"Did Larry ever live in Racine?"

"He might have visited Racine one time?"

"Are you sure?"

"Maybe he lived there while I was living there," Jamison answered.

"Did you ever smoke crack together?"

"Yeah."

"Has he been in touch with you?"

"I don't have his telephone number and he doesn't have mine," Jamison said. "And he's not allowed at my house."

"Why not?"

"I know Larry still smokes crack, and I don't want anything to do with that anymore."

Jamison also told the detectives that although he hadn't read any newspaper articles about the missing and dead Peoria women, he had watched television news broadcasts about them. But he didn't know any of the women.

On December 13, police applied for warrants to search the Bright residences—Larry's and Shirley's—as well as the surrounding area to uncover evidence that could help them in their case against Larry. They were looking for any jewelry, clothing, shoes, boots, as well as bootlaces, and hairpieces worn by the murdered women. They were also looking for anything including blood and body parts that could tie Larry to the murders.

In the application for the warrants, police took great pains to present the judge with a succinct summary of the very complex case. And they began at the beginning.

On March 2001, the Peoria County Sheriff's Office responded to a call about a dead black woman who was found on West Southport Road in Pottstown, Illinois. That woman, later identified as Wanda Jackson, a known prostitute and cocaine user, was found lying in the grass next to a parking lot. She had been strangled to death, and traces of cocaine had been found in her system. Detectives also determined she might have been missing a pair of earrings.

Then, on July 27, 2003, the Tazewell County Sheriff's Office investigated the death of a black woman near Mud Creek in Tremont Township. The victim, Sabrina Payne, was discovered lying four rows inside a cornfield, nude except for her panties and shorts, which were around her ankles. Her shorts and panties had been pulled down around her ankles. She wasn't wearing any shoes or socks, and detectives didn't find them near her body. Also a prostitute and cocaine user, Sabrina died of an overdose of alcohol or cocaine.

The next victim was another black woman, Barbara Williams. Barbara was found on February 5, 2004, lying facedown in the snow. She was dressed only in a pair of jeans and a T-shirt. Barbara's lifeless body was found by police on North Valley View Road in Edwards, Illinois, by officers from the Peoria County Sheriff's Office. Like Wanda and Sabrina, Barbara also sold herself to feed her habit. Barbara died from a cocaine overdose, but she also had bruises on her body. And the medical examiner also found ethanol in her system. Barbara's shoes, socks, coat, bra, and panties were missing.

On February 21, 2004, PCSO detectives responded to a call in the area of Eden Road in rural Hanna City, Illinois, and discovered a dead black woman about thirty feet from the roadway. The naked body of Frederickia Brown was lying facedown in the snow. A prostitute and cocaine user, Frederickia was strangled to death. She also had cocaine in her system. Investigators couldn't find any of her clothing or jewelry.

Another area prostitute and drug user, Frederickia

had been reported missing on December 16, 2003. Shortly after that, Michael Hodges called the task force with information he thought might be pertinent to their investigation of her murder. Hodges said sometime in December 2003, he saw a smaller blue truck, with its lights on, in the area where her body was found. According to Hodges, there was a white male standing at the back of the truck, closing the tailgate. Larry Bright owned a blue 1999 Dodge Dakota pickup truck at that time.

Shirley Trapp-Carpenter, another black woman, a known prostitute and cocaine user, was reported missing, on August 28, 2004, to the Peoria Police Department. The last time her boyfriend saw her was August 26. Shirley's body was never found.

On September 22, 2004, Tamara "Tammy" Walls was reported missing to the Peoria Police Department. Tammy, a black prostitute and drug user, hadn't been seen for three weeks, and her family was worried. Tammy's body was never found.

Three days after Tammy was reported missing, members of the Tazewell County Sheriff's Office responded to King Road, near the Mackinaw River. There, detectives found the body of Linda Neal, naked and lying on her back. There was a shoelace or bootlace tied around her neck, and the medical examiner determined she had been strangled. Larry Bright's DNA matched DNA found in Linda's vagina. And a bootlace in Larry's apartment was similar to the one that was used to strangle Linda.

Shaconda Thomas, another black woman, was reported missing to the Peoria Police Department on October 7, 2004. The last time anyone had seen Shaconda was the last week in August. Her body was never found.

On October 15, 2004, detectives from the Peoria County Sheriff's Office went to Taggert Road, where they found another dead black woman. Brenda Erving, a prostitute and drug user, like the other women were, was found lying on her back off the side of the road at an entrance to a farmer's field. She was naked except for a pair of socks. Erving was missing an earring. Her family members said she always wore a lot of bangle bracelets and a number of rings, some of which were fashioned from spoons. When investigators found her, she wasn't wearing any rings or bracelets.

Brenda died from suffocation, but she also had blunt-force injuries to her head, as well as cocaine toxicity. The medical examiner also found ethanol in her system. During an interview with investigators, Larry said he was once a member of a fishing club, which was about a mile from where Brenda's body had been dumped.

Laura Lollar, a black prostitute and drug user, was reported missing to police on August 26, 2004. Her family told police they had not seen or heard from her in three weeks. Laura's body was never found.

In the application for the search warrant, police told the judge that since they had first interviewed Larry on October 26, 2004, they hadn't received any additional reports of missing women. Police also detailed their interviews with the women who alleged they had been picked up and sexually assaulted by Larry Bright.

* * *

Later, on the afternoon of December 13, Captain Bobby Henderson called Shirley Bright and asked her to meet him at the Peoria County Sheriff's Office. Shirley said she got off work at half past four and it would take her about fifteen minutes to get there.

A short time later, Shirley called Henderson back and asked where he was. Henderson said that he was at the Peoria County Sheriff's Office, and that's where he wanted to meet her.

"Is this about all the people at my house?" Shirley asked, explaining that she had received a telephone call from a neighbor saying the police were at her home.

"Yes, it is," Henderson said. Earlier on that day, the task force had obtained warrants to search Shirley's house and her car, as well as Larry's house and vehicle. In addition, police also had a warrant to obtain DNA from Larry.

When Shirley arrived at the sheriff's office, Henderson took her to one of the interview rooms, where he and Detective Cy Taylor interviewed her. They told her about the search warrants, and they also told her that Larry's DNA had been found in the vaginal tract of one of the dead women.

"Larry couldn't kill anyone," Shirley said, sobbing.

"Did Larry ever tell you why he was arrested in relation to the assault on Vickie Bomar?" Henderson asked.

"He didn't really talk about it all that much,"

she said. "He did tell me he was worried that he would get beat up while he was in custody if people thought he was a suspect in killing these women. He told me he was with one of the girls, but he said he didn't kill her or anyone."

When police asked Shirley if Larry ever used her car, she said he couldn't, because he wasn't covered under her insurance. It seemed Larry had had an accident when he was driving a car she used to own, and her insurance made her sign an agreement that she wouldn't allow him to drive her car again.

Shirley described Larry as a "loner," who really didn't have any friends.

"Do you know a Dan Hosmer or a George Jamison?" Henderson asked.

"No, I've never heard of them."

Shirley was surprised to learn that Larry had lived with Hosmer for a time in Racine, Wisconsin, and that Jamison was around at the same time.

"The three of them used to smoke a lot of crack cocaine, and they used to pick up black prostitutes," Henderson said.

"I know he used to do crack, because he told me, but that was a long time ago," Shirley said. "But I didn't know he used to pick up prostitutes."

During the interview Shirley said Larry had a half sister, Monica, who lived in Galesburg. Larry and Monica had the same father but different mothers. Shirley didn't know Monica's address, but she did know her telephone number.

Shirley told police she and Larry moved to their current home on West Starr Court in August 2003.

Before that, they had lived for about fifteen years on West McClure Avenue in Peoria.

At about quarter past five, Lieutenant Mark Greskoviak entered the interview room to talk to Shirley about the search warrants. The detectives also asked Shirley if she would be willing to give them samples of her DNA. She said she wanted to talk to her attorney, Joseph Borsberry, before complying with that request. Borsberry was in the building and met with Shirley at quarter to six. After speaking with him, Shirley agreed to give her DNA and signed the consent form.

Police turned her DNA over to the Peoria County crime scene technician, who, in turn, sent it off to the ISP Crime Lab.

About a week later, Henderson received some information from PCSO detective Dave Hoyle about a crawl space under Shirley Bright's house. Apparently, that crawl space hadn't ever been searched.

So Henderson, two other members of the task force, as well as Peoria County crime scene technician Marty Klatt, went out to visit Shirley. When they arrived, Henderson explained to Shirley about the mix-up and asked her if police could search it. She agreed.

While the others looked around, Henderson talked to Shirley and asked her a few more questions about her son. Shirley explained that she only had been in that crawl space once since they moved to the house in August 2003. And that just happened to be the previous weekend, with her boyfriend, Cameron Morris. They were checking the water pipes to make sure they wouldn't freeze because of the upcoming cold weather. However, she said, Larry had been in the crawl space numerous times. He even told her that the previous owners had left a lot of junk there.

"What jobs has Larry had?" Henderson asked after Shirley finished talking about the crawl space.

"Well, he does a lot of odd jobs for people," she said. "I guess you could say he's a handyman. He has a hard time getting a job because he has asthma and a bad back."

"When did he last have a job?"

"About two years ago, Larry worked for the Kroger's store on Harmon Highway. But he only worked there for a short time, but I'm not sure how long," she said. "At one time he worked for Heinz Masonry in Kickapoo. They're closed now. He hurt his back while he worked there and got a settlement of about twenty-eight thousand for the injury. That was in 1998. He used the money to buy the car he has now, a blue Dodge Dakota. He tried to get SSI, but he was turned down."

Shirley also told Henderson that Larry sometimes worked with her boyfriend's son-in-law, Dick Wolf, tearing down old barns.

As they talked, Shirley said she had had another baby, a full-term baby, who died at birth. She also lost a set of twins. Then she had Larry. Soon after Larry was born, she and Larry's dad, Gary, divorced. When he was fifteen years old Larry lived with Gary for about eight months. Shirley said Larry's father died of cancer in 1998.

* * *

Investigators wanted to get as much information about their prime suspect as possible, so they also continued to question people who knew Larry.

PCSO detective Dave Wilson interviewed Neal Lablond, whose family used to own the Brights' house on West Starr Court. Lablond said he and his mother lived in the main house and used the rear building as a guesthouse. Lablond said he knew Larry, but he hadn't talked to him for a year or two.

"Is there a basement in either house?" Wilson asked.

Lablond said, although there wasn't a basement in either the main house or the guesthouse, there was a crawl space, under the main house, that had been built by the people who owned the house before the Lablonds. Apparently, they had been planning to put in a full basement but never finished. The main area under the house was just large enough for a person to stand up in, and the rest of it was just four feet deep. Access to the crawl space was through a trapdoor in the closet that was near the front of the house, as well as under the dryer, near the garage area. Police had already searched the crawl space.

A few days before Christmas, Detectives Meeks and Taylor met with a thirty-nine-year-old woman named Genene, who left a message on the task force tip line about a white man who had pulled a knife on her when she got into his vehicle.

Genene's sister, Mary, had called police a few days earlier after reading about one of the women who had been attacked by a local man. Police met with Mary and asked her to have Genene call them. Genene called police after she saw a picture of Larry Bright in the *Peoria Journal Star.* At that time she said, "The man in the paper is the same one that pulled the knife on me." The newspaper had run a story about Bright after he was arrested for violating his bond on unlawful restraint because he possessed cocaine. That story was juxtaposed with a story about the dead and missing women in Peoria and Tazewell Counties.

When police met with Genene at her mother's house, she told them she wasn't a prostitute, but she was a crack user and she worked the street for crack.

About a year earlier, Genene said, she was approached by Larry around nine o'clock in the evening. It was a cool night, and Genene was wearing a jacket. She was walking near Widenham and Steubenville Streets in Peoria when a guy in a raggedy two-door red Chevy Blazer, with plastic on one of the windows, drove by her several times. Finally the guy pulled up to her, so she was next to the driver's-side window. He asked her if he could get a "sixteenth."

Genene told him she could get it for him, then walked around to the passenger side and got in the truck. Larry told her he didn't have any money on him, but he had some at his house. When they arrived at his home, Genene noticed a tall tan or white wooden fence around the property. As Larry parked the truck, he told Genene his parents, who were out of town, lived in the front house, and he lived in the house in back.

While they were still in the truck, Larry pulled out a hunting knife with an eight-inch curved blade and put it up to her throat. Scared to death, Genene peed on herself. She reached for the handle and tried to open the door, but it wouldn't budge. Larry pulled the truck up next to the fence and parked. He got out, then reached in, grabbed her by the hair, and pulled her out through the driver's door.

He opened the gate and dragged her through the yard to the smaller house. Trying to take in her surroundings, Genene noticed a small pond. When they got to the house, Larry opened the outside door, then opened a second door and pushed her inside the house. There was a bed on the right, and a couch on the left. On the long coffee table in front of the couch were four crack pipes and a Brillo pad, but no crack. Genene also saw a television and a brown entertainment center. She knew she had to get out of the house, but she couldn't find a way out.

Holding the knife to her throat, Larry moved her to the couch, forced her to sit down, then sat down beside her.

"Suck my dick, bitch," he ordered, forcing her head down onto his crotch. "I'm gonna kill you, bitch."

Just then, they heard a noise. It sounded like someone else was in the house. As Larry turned his head, Genene slapped his arm and hand, knocking the knife onto the floor and under the bed. Genene fought for her life, grabbing and punching her attacker, until she got away. She reached for the knife, then put it to Larry's throat and demanded he take her back to Peoria.

"Please don't kill me," Larry said. "I didn't mean no harm."

The pair walked back out to the truck. Genene crawled in through the driver's-side door, pulling Larry behind her. Genene kept the knife on him until he stopped at Western Avenue and Butler Street. She told him she was going to call the police, and he told her to do it. Genene rolled down the window on the passenger side, opened the door from the outside, and climbed out of the truck. As she turned to run away, she threw the knife at him.

Genene told police that the guy was white, unshaven, short, stocky, and very strong. And he was high on crack.

"That's him in the Saturday paper," Genene said, pointing to his picture in the *Peoria Journal Star.* "I'll never forget that face."

Genene told police she could probably show them where Larry had taken her. While she went inside to get her coat, Taylor talked to her sister, Mary, about the incident. Mary said she thought Genene had been attacked a little less than six months earlier. She said Genene didn't remember when things happened because of the crack.

Genene came out of the house, got in the police car, and told Taylor to head toward West Peoria. She told them she remembered passing by a hill and a cemetery. She directed police to West Starr Court, and after looking at various houses in the area, she led them right to the back of Larry's house. Genene said she wanted to get out of the car to take a closer look. When she returned, she told police the house behind the tall fence was the closest to what she remembered.

"It was dark and I was cracked up when he took me to his house, so I can't be sure," she said. "But this place really gives me the creeps. Is this the place where the guy in the paper lives?"

Meeks and Taylor said they couldn't give her that information. They asked Genene if she'd be willing to give them a videotaped statement that day, but she said she didn't have time to make herself presentable. She agreed to do it on December 21.

During that interview Genene said she was having trouble pinpointing the exact time of her assault. Initially she thought it had happened about a year earlier, but then she remembered it happened around the time an elderly man was murdered at Hurlburt House, a senior housing development in Peoria. Genene told police around that time she had spoken to two other black women who said they had also been attacked, possibly by the same guy. Unfortunately, Genene could only remember the first name of one of the women. She said it was Shatone, who might live on Millman Street.

Police determined the elderly man had been murdered on July 31, 2004. Genene was very surprised that it had happened in July. She said she was always confused because of the crack. She then asked if she could postpone the interview until she could think about it a little more. Police agreed and drove her home. Genene said she'd call them when she was ready.

After the holidays Captain Bobby Henderson and Detective Cy Taylor went to interview Shirley at home. The first thing they did when they got there was to show her a printout of the movies that had been rented on her account at Family Video, on West Harmon Highway, from March 5, 2004, through July 8, 2004. Shirley said they looked like movies she and her boyfriend had rented, but she said Larry might have rented some as well.

Henderson then asked about movies that had been rented from September 26, 2004, through December 10, 2004. They were all porn movies. Shirley said she never rented those movies, and Larry was the only other person authorized to use her account.

Police then questioned her about the times when neither of them rented any movies, including March 10, 2004, through April 2, 2004; May 3, 2004, through July 2, 2004; July 9, 2004, through September 25, 2004. They wanted to know if she or Larry had taken a vacation or gone out of town. Shirley explained that sometimes she just didn't rent movies from Family Video. When she stayed at her boyfriend's house, he often rented movies from a video store in Germantown. But neither she nor Larry ever rented movies from any other store.

Henderson told Shirley that police were investigating the case of a black female who claimed that Larry picked her up around the first week of

July 2003, took her back to his house, and then sexually assaulted her. Shirley wanted to know the woman's name. She said a long time ago when she and Larry lived on West McClure Avenue, a black lady named Ernestine called the house looking for him. Ernestine died in October 16, 2004, when she was just forty-five. Henderson wasn't talking about Ernestine; he was referring to Teracita, but he couldn't tell Shirley.

He did tell Shirley that Gina Carter had given them permission to search the Brights' former house on West McClure, and after doing so, they realized the layout of the house matched the description given by the woman who said Larry assaulted her.

"The girl said when Larry pulled into the driveway she saw several items in the driveway, and in the garage and she asked Larry if he was moving," Henderson said. "Was that around the time you and Larry were getting ready to move?"

"That was about the time I was planning to have a yard sale," she said.

"I know when you bought the house, you paid seventy-five thousand for it and you put down forty-five thousand," Henderson said. "Where did you get that money?"

"I had some money saved up and I cashed in a 401K."

Henderson told Shirley that the police had subpoenaed her telephone records and asked if she'd sit down with him and go over them. She agreed.

While they were talking, Shirley asked Henderson if the lady who gave Vickie Bomar a ride after she claimed Larry assaulted her was the lady who lived behind her, named Joyce. After Henderson said it was, Shirley said she had had a problem with Joyce the past summer, implying that Joyce was probably lying to get back at her.

"Last July, Joyce's son-in-law was living in a tree stand that borders my property. He was urinating and crapping behind the garage that Larry stays in, so I complained to the sheriff's office, the township, and the health department," Shirley said.

Before Henderson left, Shirley said that Larry wanted to be moved to the general population at the Tazewell County Jail. Henderson said Larry had to put that request in writing and give it to one of the corrections officers.

When Henderson and Taylor went back to talk to Shirley a few days later, they asked for permission for police to search the burn pile in her yard, as well as the garden area next to the garage. After she signed the consent form, Henderson called Peoria County crime scene technician Doug O'Neill, who started sifting through the burn pile as soon as he arrived at the Brights' place.

As O'Neill worked, Henderson asked Shirley a few questions about Larry.

"Why does Larry have false teeth?"

"Larry had bad teeth," she said. "When he was a child, he was on a lot of different medications."

"Do you and Larry have any storage rental?"

"No, we don't, and we never have."

"Do you and Larry have any video-recording equipment?"

"No, we never have."

"When was the pond in the backyard built?"

"Larry and I started digging the pond in 2003 around July, just before we moved in. It took us approximately one month to finish."

"Through our investigation we learned that Larry used to have a girlfriend named Marie Waters. Are you aware of that?"

"Yes, that was a long time ago. Marie had a daughter named Candy," Shirley said. "Larry and Marie lived together for a time, above a bar in Canton, Illinois, but I don't remember exactly when."

"Marie said Larry used to abuse her, and he beat her a few times," Henderson said.

Police had learned that Larry once punched Marie in the face in front of some friends and split her lip open. Blood poured out, soaking her clothes, but Larry wouldn't let anyone take her to the emergency room. Finally Marie left Larry and stayed at the Elks, while her six-year-old daughter stayed with one of Marie's friends.

"Did you know that? Were you ever there when Marie and Larry were fighting?"

Shirley answered no to both questions.

"Marie said she and Larry were arguing one day when she was pregnant, and Larry kicked her in the stomach and caused her to lose the baby. Did you ever hear about that?"

"No. I didn't think Larry could have children," she said.

"Why did Larry attempt suicide in 2001?"

Shirley acted as if she had no idea what Henderson was talking about, so he showed her the police report indicating that Larry had attempted suicide when they lived on West McClure Avenue. According to the report, Larry's half sister called paramedics because he had taken twenty-five Vicodin. At the time Larry told police he had a crack addiction that he couldn't break, and he just didn't want to live anymore. Paramedics transported him to Methodist Hospital for treatment.

"Oh, I remember now," Shirley said after reading the report. "Larry was using a lot of drugs. He was trying to quit, but he couldn't. I think that's why he tried to kill himself."

"Did you know that Ernestine, the black woman Larry used to have a relationship with, allegedly died from AIDS last October?" Henderson asked. "Do you know if Larry has AIDS, or if he's ever been tested for AIDS?"

"All I know is that Larry used to give blood at a place on the corner of Nebraska Street and Sheridan Street in Peoria. I don't remember the name. It was 'bio' something or other. Anyway, Larry stopped giving blood. He told me he stopped because they wanted him to read something and sign it. Larry doesn't read very well, and he was embarrassed, so he just quit going back. But just the other night, he told me he stopped giving blood because he has AIDS."

Detective Dave Wilson went out to the Brights' place again to speak with Shirley and to get her consent for his department to search the grounds around her house. Shirley had given the Tazewell County Sheriff's Office permission to search the premises the previous day. Shirley agreed to cooperate in any way she could, but she told Wilson she didn't think police would find anything.

While he was there, Wilson talked to Shirley about her son.

"Do you think Larry could be involved in the deaths of the black women from Peoria?" he asked, getting right to the point.

"I hope he didn't," she said.

Shirley explained that there were some things about Larry she didn't know about before the investigation into the murders of the black women. She said she never even knew that he spent a lot of time with black women. She did know, however, that Larry smoked marijuana, even though she did not approve of that habit. According to Larry, it was helping his asthma. Shirley said her husband used to smoke marijuana, and that's why she left him.

"You know, I recently got a phone call from a man who sounded like a black man," Shirley told Wilson. "He said his name was Jason. My caller ID said he was calling from a Bloomington phone number. I'm going to give the phone number to Captain Henderson the next time I talk to him."

Shirley signed the consent form, then said she had to go to work, but she didn't mind if the police conducted the search while she was gone.

The next time Wilson and Henderson went talk to Shirley, they met her at her mother's house in Bellevue, just west of Peoria.

"Does anyone besides Larry burn anything on your property?" Henderson asked.

"No, just me and Larry," she said. "Larry does most of the burning. He burns all the time. Last summer me and Larry cut up a lot of the hedges on our property and we burned them."

Shirley said she asked Larry many times if he had killed any of the women, but he said he had not.

"When I bailed him out of jail on that [unlawful restraining] charge, I asked him out by the tree in front of the house if he killed these girls," she said. "He told me he didn't. I told him if he did kill them, then he needed to write a letter confessing it and then commit suicide so he could save our family from all the attention. But he kept telling me he didn't do it."

Henderson wanted to know exactly where in their yard Larry did the burning.

"Did he ever burn on the west side of his garage?" he asked.

"Yes, he did."

"Do you remember ever walking back to that area while Larry was burning and the odor was terrible?" Henderson asked. "If you did, did you ask Larry what he was burning?"

"Now that you mention it, I do remember that. Larry said he was burning plastic."

"Do you ever recall him driving the Blazer?" Henderson asked.

"Well, one time Larry's Dodge Dakota was broke down for about a year. I think it was in late 2002 and into 2003. I think it was fixed in November 2003," she said. "During the time the Dakota was broke down, Larry did drive the Chevy Blazer. I don't think he drove it after the Dodge was fixed, because he said the brakes were bad. But I don't really know if that's true or not. I've had a hard time believing half of what he said for the past year or so, because I caught him in a couple of lies."

Henderson wanted to know how the Blazer's back passenger-side window had been broken. Shirley said Larry was mowing the yard and the lawn mower hit a rock, throwing it against the window, breaking it.

"I saw it happen," she said.

"When did Larry go to Racine, Wisconsin, and when did he come back?" Henderson asked. Larry had been dating a woman in Racine, who was found murdered on February 24, 2000.

"I'm not exactly sure, but I think he left to go to Racine in December 1999. I think he came back to Peoria sometime in February 2000," she said.

8

Although she was eighty-six years old, Larry's grandmother, Mary Simmons, was still very active and very competent. So competent, in fact, that she held down two jobs: on Tuesdays and Fridays, she cleaned houses; the other days she worked at a local home-building company.

On a cold December afternoon, members of the task force paid Mary a visit at her home in Bellevue to talk to her about Larry. According to Mary, Larry was about seven years old when Shirley moved the family from California to the city of Tremont in the Peoria area, where Larry attended high school. They later moved to the house on McClure, and finally to the house on Starr Court. Mary knew that several years earlier Larry had lived in another state, but she couldn't remember where.

Since the beginning of December, until Larry was arrested, he and Mary's son, his uncle Denis, who lived in East Peoria, had been doing some remodeling work on the kitchen in the basement of her house. Larry and Denis hadn't really seen each other much until they started working on Mary's house. Mary said after Larry was arrested, Denis packed up and went to a log cabin he owned in the southern part of the state.

"Larry's a good handyman," she told police. "He does odd jobs and works generally in that fashion. He's kind of a loner. He loves to dig ponds. He never had what I would call a real job. I pay him for things he does around the house, and I'm always loaning him money for gas. But he never pays me back."

The detectives also questioned Mary about the cars that Larry drove.

"He don't drive my car, and I don't think Shirley lets him drive hers, either," she said, adding that Shirley owned a Dodge Durango. "I guess Larry caused Shirley some grief in the past over a car accident. But I think he uses the Chevy Blazer that used to belong to my daughter, who died from colon cancer in 1993. You know, there was a motor home that Shirley kept at her house on McClure. It was kind of a running joke that the motor home was never used for camping. Now, I think it's over at Shirley's boyfriend's house in Metamora."

Even though Mary was having a hard time dealing with Larry's possible involvement in the murders of the black women, she understood that he wasn't a model citizen. And she knew drugs had grabbed hold of him real good and weren't letting go.

"He was married for a while to a girl who got him in all this trouble with drugs. She led him down this path of drug use. I don't remember her name, but I know they lived in Galesburg. She got pregnant, and Larry thought the child was his, but Shirley paid for a DNA test and they found out the baby was not his. The baby died eventually," Mary said. "I never saw him do drugs, but I was aware of it because Shirley tried to get him into rehab twice."

After talking with Mary, the detectives also met with Larry's brother, Jerry, and his wife at their home in Morton to see if they knew anything about Larry's possible involvement with the dead women.

"I haven't had anything to do with Larry in years. When we were younger, he used to pound the shit out of me on a regular basis. I can't even remember the last time I talked to him," Jerry said. "Larry is notorious for ripping off friends and family members because of his drug addiction. He's been sponging off Mom all of his life, and I can't convince her to break off ties with him. More than likely, she'd cover for anything that he might have done."

Jerry told police he didn't know any of Larry's current or former friends or where they used to party. And he had no idea whether Larry had ever dated black women or picked up prostitutes, but he said it wouldn't surprise him.

"I doubt Larry would even keep a friend for very long," he said. "Larry's not welcome at my house, so he wouldn't think of coming here if he was in trouble."

When police asked the couple if Larry had

ever lived out of state, Jerry's wife said she remembered that he had lived in Racine, Wisconsin, for a short time.

The day after they talked to Jerry and his wife, task force members paid a visit to Larry's uncle, Denis Simmons, at his home in Goreville. Denis owned seventy-five acres of land there, which he had bought in 1995. It took him five years to build his house. He moved into the house in 2000 and spent most of his time there. He also had another home on Eastwood Road in East Peoria, where he lived until he retired and moved to Goreville.

Larry had only been to Denis's East Peoria house once, in 1990 or 1991, to pick up a washing machine and clothes dryer. Larry brought his girl-friend, but Denis didn't remember her name. A couple times Larry took care of Denis's dog, Sassy, when Denis was out of town, but Denis always dropped Sassy off at Larry's place. Larry didn't have a key to Denis's house in East Peoria, and he had never been to the house in Goreville.

Denis confirmed his mother's story that he and Larry had been doing some remodeling work at her house.

"He helped me for about a week before he was arrested," Denis said. "All we really talked [about] while we were working was the remodeling job. He didn't mention anything about his personal life. He did talk about applying for a job, but I don't re-member where. He said a guy he knew told him he better get his application in fast, if he wanted any chance of getting the job. I didn't know anything about this investigation until you guys went to my mom's house to talk to her."

Denis said Larry was an introvert who didn't have any friends while growing up. According to Denis, Shirley and Larry's father, Gary, separated when Larry was a child.

"I think he lived with Gary in Elmwood, Illinois, for a time when he was a kid and went to school there," Denis said. "Gary died when Larry was twenty."

Denis said Larry didn't usually interact with family members, either.

"We used to attend family events at their house when they lived on McClure Avenue, but Larry always stayed in the basement," Denis said. "Larry and his brother, Jerry, didn't even get along. Jerry felt that Larry was too dependent on their mother for money and a place to live."

What Larry did for work to get cash other than odd jobs wasn't all that clear to Denis.

"I think he used to work at Kroger, on North Sterling Avenue in Peoria, for a little while, and then he worked for a brick contractor. But he hurt his back and got a settlement that he used to buy a pickup truck," Denis said. "I think he also worked for Dick Wolf, Shirley's boyfriend's son-in-law, for a time dismantling old barns and reselling the wood."

As police were working the case, a woman called police around the middle of December with information she thought might be related to the recent disappearances and murders of the women in the

Peoria area. She decided to contact police after reading Tiffany's story in the *Peoria Journal Star* on December 5. The woman said sometime toward the end of summer, someone had picked up and raped her thirty-five-year-old daughter, Renee. Members of the task force went to meet the woman and her daughter on December 16.

Renee told police she was walking alone in the area of Butler and Shelley Streets around midnight or one in the morning. It was a cool night, and she was glad she had worn her dark blue hooded sweatshirt. Suddenly a white man in a gray-and-black Chevy Blazer pulled up next to her. He had short dirty blond hair and green eyes. He said he had an eight ball, but it was back at his house. Always looking to party, Renee got in the truck.

The guy drove to his house, somewhere near Starr Court and Moffatt Street. He parked his car and the two entered the yard through the gate of a tall wooden fence. Once in the yard, she noticed a main house, a smaller house, and a pond. The guy said his mother lived in the other house. He also told her the pond was real deep. When they got to the house, he opened a sliding glass door, then unlocked a wooden door.

It was just one room, with no kitchen. The bed was on the right and the bathroom was straight ahead. There was a couch and chair on the left. There was a crack pipe and a steel wool Brillo pad on the coffee table in front of the couch, but no drugs. There was also a knife with a four-inch blade on the table.

Renee sat on the couch, and took off her

sweatshirt and her belt. Before she knew what was happening, the guy grabbed the knife, held it to her throat, and pushed her back onto the couch. He yelled at her and told her to give him oral sex. Scared to death, Renee urinated on herself and the couch.

"You don't have to do this," she said.

For some unstated reason, the man let her up. When he did, Renee climbed on top of the coffee table and started screaming at him. But by that time, he had calmed down.

"Have you ever done this before?" she asked. "Are you the serial killer?"

The guy didn't answer her. He just told her he'd take her back where he had picked her up. Glad to be alive, and happy to get away, Renee forgot to take her sweatshirt and belt with her.

Renee told the investigators that she had heard the same thing had happened to two other women she knew. With her mother driving, Renee directed police to where the guy took her. It was Larry Bright's house. The two women then went to the Peoria Police Department with the officers so Renee's statement could be recorded.

Toward the end of December, Henderson and Taylor met with Gina Carter at her home on West McClure Avenue in Peoria, the house that Shirley and Larry had lived in before they moved to West Starr Court. Carter lived in the house with her son and her boyfriend, Eric, who was then in the Peoria County Jail on drug charges.

Before purchasing the house in April 2004,

Carter said, she had never met either Shirley or Larry, but they both seemed like nice people. When the Brights lived in the house, Shirley lived upstairs and Larry lived in the basement. Carter said, since she bought the house, Larry had stopped by twice, the last time on June 3, 2004. He wanted to see how things were going.

After Carter gave police permission to search the house, Henderson went into the kitchen from the back. Once he stepped inside, he noticed a door that led down to the basement. He walked down a few steps and came to a landing. He walked down a few more steps to the basement.

Henderson walked down a short hallway and saw a room on the left that contained a toilet and sink, as well as a washer and dryer. On the right was another small room. The hallway opened up into a large room, with a drop ceiling, where Larry used to keep his bed. At the end of that room was a small storage area.

Henderson lifted up one of the ceiling tiles and noticed two towels. He called up to Gina and asked if she had ever put anything in the drop ceiling. She said she hadn't done anything to the basement since she moved to the house. Henderson called CSI Martin Klatt, who was also at the house, to come down to the basement to photograph and collect possible evidence.

As Henderson and Klatt continued searching, they found more towels, as well as packages that contained numerous sexual toys, including vibrators, an ejaculating butt plug, and pleasure balls. Police also found two different-size ropes in the ceiling, a receipt with Larry Bright's name on it, and a liquor bottle. Gina also pointed out a bed sham set, which, she said, the Brights left when they moved out.

Gina said none of the items belonged to her or her boyfriend. She never even knew they were up there. The next day, then, Henderson and Taylor met with Eric in the jail. Like Gina, he said he had no idea where the items in the ceiling came from.

The investigators confiscated the evidence and took it back to the police station. Klatt went back to the house the next day and, with Gina's permission, used an alternate-light source to check for stains, which he found on the basement carpet. Klatt took swabs of the stains so they could be analyzed.

After the holidays Detective Dave Hoyle spoke to a guy named Chip Dawson to see what he knew about Larry. Chip started the conversation by saying he had nothing good to say about Larry. In fact, he said Larry was an asshole who had stolen Chip's dead father's tools.

Chip said his father dated Larry's mother from 1987 to 1988, and the families lived together in a house on Route 117, just east of Rapatee, Illinois. When they were teenagers, Chip and Larry attended several parties together, north of 117, off Route 78.

"Can you describe any of these areas in detail?" Hoyle asked.

"Well, we went north on Route 78 and turned

right, heading toward the Inman Dairy Farm," he said. "There was a lake on that road that we swam in and partied at. The kids called it 'the zone.'"

Hoyle realized that the area Chip described was the spot where Brenda Erving's body had been found.

Members of the task force also wanted to try and get some additional insight into Larry from his half sister, Monica, who was about thirteen years younger. So in the second week of January, Special Agent Joe Spidle, of the Illinois State Police, who had already interviewed Monica in the middle of December, drove the nearly fifty miles back up to Galesburg to talk with her again.

Spidle asked Monica about someone named Marie, a white woman from Canton with whom Larry had lived at one point in his life.

"I remember I was about fourteen, and Larry and Marie picked me up in Galesburg at least twice," she said. "I think one time they took me to Lake Story in Galesburg, and another time they took me to lunch in Peoria."

"Has Larry ever talked about Marie recently?" Spidle asked.

"Larry told me he was seeing Marie after she was married to a rich, older man in Canton," she said. "I think he said Marie visited him when he lived on McClure Avenue."

"Did Larry ever abuse Marie?" he asked.

"Not that I knew."

"Did you ever see Larry with any type of knife?"

"I never saw any, but he might have carried one

that I didn't know about," Monica said. "My ex-stepfather, Dan Hosmer, used to collect knives, and he started getting rid of them last year."

Spidle asked Monica what she thought about Larry's relationship with his mother. As far as she knew, Shirley would do anything for Larry.

"I never saw Shirley have any problems with anyone," she said.

Shifting his line of questioning, Spidle tried to get information from Monica that could help them obtain physical evidence to tie Larry to the murder of Linda Neal.

"Do you ever remember Larry leaving a pair of boots at your house, or maybe giving or receiving shoes or boots from your fiancé?"

"I really don't remember anything about shoes or boots, but there was one time when Larry came over to my house without shoelaces in his shoes," she said.

When Spidle heard that, he pressed Monica for more information. He was very interested in the part about the shoelaces, because there was a shoelace wrapped around Linda's neck.

"What else do you remember about that?" he asked.

"Well, Larry came over sometime in the warm weather last year and he didn't have socks on or shoelaces," she said. "I asked him if he wanted me to give him some shoelaces, because everyone knew that I keep a large glass filled with different shoelaces, but he said no. It was kind of weird that he didn't have any shoelaces in his shoes."

"Do you know what kind of shoes they were? Do you think they could have been tennis shoes?"

"I really don't remember."

"Can you remember exactly when this happened?"

"No, I really can't."

Now it was Monica's turn to ask some questions.

"Do you know the exact dates when all the girls were murdered?" she asked. "I wonder if there were any significant dates in Larry's life that triggered him to do something."

"All the dates when the bodies were discovered have been in the *Journal Star.*"

"Were any of them found in February? Our dad died in the middle of February and was cremated then."

"Well, Barbara Williams was found on February 5, 2004, and Frederickia Brown was found on February 21, 2004," he said.

"I was curious, because Larry talked a lot about our father in 2004," she said.

"I know I asked you this in our first interview, but can you think of any place where Larry might have dumped any other bodies—places where we could search?" Spidle asked.

"My mother and I had been talking about various locations, and we even thought about searching ourselves."

"We'd rather have you just point out locations to us, instead of searching [by] yourself," he said.

"We'll do that so we can help the girls' families get closure."

Spidle said he'd make arrangements for the women to help police locate any additional dumping grounds.

* * *

Spidle next telephoned a woman named Paula to find out what she knew about Larry. Paula and Larry's father had a daughter together. During the conversation Paula asked Spidle if police ever suspected that Shirley had been a prostitute. Spidle asked why she thought that.

"Well, when Gary was married to Shirley, she had a lot of wigs, and Gary told me Shirley kicked him out of the house because he destroyed them all by burning them," she explained. "He never told me specifically that Shirley was a prostitute, but I always suspected it, because she always drove nice cars and seemed to have more money than she made at her job. And when she was raising her two boys after they divorced, Gary never paid her any child support."

Spidle asked Paula if she'd be willing to point out places where Larry used to go when he was younger—places where he could have dumped dead bodies. Paula agreed, but she said she preferred to do it on the weekend because she didn't want to miss work. She also told Spidle that the police should look around West Jersey, Illinois, because that was where Larry's dad was buried.

"I think Gary's second ex-wife owned the cemetery plot where his ashes were buried," she said.

"Do you know anything about her?" Spidle asked.

"I don't think she ever remarried. I think she lives outside of Toulon," she said. "You should search the area around her house, because Larry would be familiar with that area."

"Did you ever notice anything unusual about Larry and Shirley's relationship?" Spidle asked.

"Well, Shirley constantly gave Larry money, and she'd do anything for him," she said.

Paula also said that when Larry was younger, he had asked her for sex. It happened sometime in 1982, when she was living with Gary, and their daughter was a baby. One day when his father wasn't home, Larry went into her bedroom and asked her if she'd have sex with him. Paula said although they never had sex, it made her feel very uncomfortable.

Spidle also drove up to Toulon, Illinois, to meet with Connie, Larry's stepmother. Connie had been married to Larry's father from 1990 until he died in 1998. Connie and Gary met and started dating in 1984; they began living together in Toulon in 1986.

"How did Larry's father die?" Spidle asked.

"He was diagnosed with cancer in 1997. He was sick for almost the entire year, and toward the end, he needed round-the-clock care."

"When was the last time you had contact with Larry?"

"He called me collect from jail about three to six weeks ago to ask me if I had heard anything about why he was arrested," she said. "He told me not to believe anything I heard. He also asked if I'd write to him, because he'd probably be in jail for a long time. The last I heard from him before that was earlier last year when I was in the hospital and Larry and Monica came to visit me."

"What was your relationship with Larry like?"

"He was always polite and helpful," Connie said. "When Gary was sick, Larry would come to Toulon occasionally to take care of him so I could go out."

"What was Gary's relationship with Larry?"

"I think Gary was closer to Larry than all his other children," she said. "When Gary and I were together, Larry visited him the most. He hasn't come to see me regularly since Gary died, but I always try to call him every Christmas."

Connie told Spidle that Larry moved in with them when Gary was sick, but he only stayed a few months. Connie and Gary kicked Larry out after finding a crack pipe in their basement.

"I get the feeling that Larry's had trouble with drugs in the past," she added.

"Did Gary ever tell you why he and Shirley got divorced?" the detective asked.

"Gary never really talked about Shirley or their marriage, but he would never say anything bad about her."

"Did you ever think, or did Gary ever say, Shirley had a lot of extra cash?"

"I always thought that she had more money than she was making at her job," Connie said. "But I think I heard that Shirley's mother was rich, and she frequently gave her money."

Then Spidle asked Connie an odd question that sort of threw her.

"Did you ever hear about Gary hiding bottles of whiskey under rural bridges?"

"Gary drank alcohol when we met, but he quit drinking after we were married," she said. "But I remember that after he died, I found some old whiskey bottles hidden around the house, but I never heard of him hiding anything under rural bridges."

Spidle's colleague State Trooper Don Filkins talked to a couple guys who had owned the motor home that had formerly belonged to Shirley. They were trying to determine if there was anything in the motor home that could tie Larry to any of the dead and missing women.

Troy Gilmore told police he purchased the 1984 Chevrolet motor home from Shirley for $7,200, sometime in the fall of 2003. Gilmore said after he bought it, he and his wife thoroughly scrubbed the ceiling with harsh chemical cleaners. He said they removed all the furniture and shampooed the carpets. They also cleaned all of the walls with Pine-Sol. The couple replaced the wallpaper in the kitchen and the bathroom, as well as the paneling, carpeting, and mattress in the bedroom.

Gilmore told the police he didn't find anything that belonged to either Shirley or Larry Bright in the motor home, nor did he find anything that might have tied Larry to the deaths of any of the women.

But the Gilmores didn't own the motor home any longer. They used the vehicle to take a trip to Kentucky to attend a motorcycle rally in June 2004, then sold it to Doyle Tabor in November. Police talked to Tabor, but he didn't have any information that could help them in their investigation.

* * *

The police also wanted to talk to Dick Wolf, the son-in-law of Cameron Morris, Shirley's boyfriend, to see if he knew anything that could help in their investigation. So a few days before Christmas, Special Agent Filkins met Wolf at the police department in Morton, Illinois, the town where Wolf lived.

Wolf told police he had known Larry for four or five years. One time he had attended an Easter egg hunt for the Bright family children at Larry and Shirley's house on McClure Avenue. He had also attended a July 4 family barbeque at the Bright's Starr Court home, but Larry wasn't there. Wolf said Larry usually kept to himself.

"Do you know any of Larry's friends?" Filkins asked.

"No, I don't," he said. "I don't know very much about his personal life."

"Did Larry ever work for you?"

"Yeah, I own Barns-N-Boards, and Larry worked for me as a laborer. He helped me tear down barns and salvage the wood," Wolf said. "We'd go all over Illinois dismantling barns. We'd take the wood back to Morton, clean it and ship it to customers."

Wolf explained that his company dismantled forty to fifty barns per year, and each job usually lasted seven to ten days.

"We'd usually travel within seventy-five miles of Morton," he said. "Larry would meet me at my house around six in the morning, and we'd be home by six at night. For the past year or two, Larry worked at my shop in Morton pulling nails and trimming boards."

"Where were some of the barns you dismantled located?" Filkins asked.

"About three years ago Larry helped tear down a barn in Diona, and about two years ago, we demolished one near Port Byron," he said. "Another time, in the beginning of 2004, he helped me with a job at a barn near Danvers and Congerville. He also helped me strip a tin ceiling out of a building in Clayton. There were so many, I can't remember them without checking my records."

Wolf agreed to check his records and contact Filkins later to give him the information. The next time they talked, Wolf told Filkins that Larry had worked with him on at least eight jobs. He provided Filkins with more specific information about the locations of those job sites. One of the jobs involved dismantling a barn near Illiopolis from February 19 to February 27, 2004. That barn was three miles west of Illiopolis in Sangamon County. Wolf said the two men rode to the job together.

"Larry also helped me tear down a barn near Granville. That was from the twelfth of February to the thirteenth last year. We might have gone back to finish that job on the seventeenth and eighteenth," Wolf said. "That barn was located south of Granville, off Illinois Route 89 in Putnam County. We rode to and from all the jobs together."

"What were some of the other sites Larry worked at?" Filkins asked.

"Well, he helped with the demolition of a corncrib and barn near Danvers in January 2001," he said. "When I talked to you before, I thought it was in 2004, but my records show that it was 2001. The barn and corncrib were located off the Danvers-Congerville Blacktop in McLean County."

Wolf then told Filkins that in the fall of 2000, Larry had worked with him to demolish a barn east of Port Byron in Rock Island County. Sometime in 2001—Wolf wasn't clear on the exact dates—he and Larry tore down a barn that was located off Route 130, near Diona, either in Coles County or Cumberland County. Around that same time, they demolished a barn situated southwest of Effingham in rural Effingham County.

On November 11 and November 13, 2002, Larry and Wolf removed the tin ceilings in some buildings located in Clayton. Those buildings were situated within the city limits of the town, which was located in Adams County. In February 2004, the two men dismantled a barn northwest of Astoria in Fulton County.

"I'm sure he helped out on other jobs, but I can't remember the dates or locations," Wolf said once more. "But over the past year or two, Larry spent a lot of time working at my shop in Morton. If I remember anything else, I'll let you know."

A month later, Filkins met with Wolf, again, at the old Ace hardware store in Morton. In the lot behind the building, Wolf stored materials that he and his employees had recovered from the barns that they demolished.

"How often do you clean this place up?" Filkins asked.

"Me and my work crew have cleaned it up at

least twice, and we hauled two Dumpsters full of trash since last October," he said.

"Did you or your crew find any clothing, jewelry, or anything unusual on the lot?"

"No, we didn't find anything like that."

"Can we search the property?" Filkins asked.

"I don't own it, you'll have to call the owner for that," Wolf said, giving Filkins the man's name.

Wolf also clarified some of the information he had previously given Filkins.

"That job we did near Illiopolis was in February 2002, not 2004," he said. "Me and Larry tore down three chicken coops. Larry came with me to the site a couple times and went to the site alone on one or two days."

9

Following up on every lead, Sergeant Scott Cook, of the Peoria PD, and Captain Bobby Henderson, of the Tazewell County Sheriff's Office, went to the Peoria County Jail to talk to Tonya Russell. Tonya had written to Cook, saying she wanted to talk to him about her involvement with Larry Bright.

Tonya had already spoken to the police about her meeting with Larry, but at the time she had been on drugs and her memory was a bit fuzzy. In fact, at the time of the first interview, Tonya had been up for three days. She was so out of it, she fell asleep several times. But since being in jail and off drugs, her mind had cleared up and she wanted to do another interview with the police.

Tonya told the police that one day at the end of August, or the beginning of September 2004, she was walking by a shop near the intersection of South Western Avenue and West Millman Street. She was heading toward West Lincoln Avenue when she noticed a two-tone red Blazer—an older model with the back passenger-side window missing—passing right by her. When she got to the intersection of West Lincoln Avenue and South Warren Street, Larry pulled his car over to her and asked if she wanted to play. He said he had some drugs back at his place.

Already high on crack, Tonya was ready and eager to play. She got into Larry's car and he headed toward the south end of town, by the South Side Mission, Peoria's oldest rescue mission. They finally ended up at his house. The pair got out of the Blazer, and Larry unlocked the gate to a fence. When they walked into the backyard, Tonya noticed a little pond. The couple walked up to the porch of the house, and Larry unlocked the door.

Once inside, Tonya saw a bed, a brown couch, and a coffee table covered with drug paraphernalia, including a Tupperware container filled with marijuana and crack pipes. Tonya sat down on the couch and started smoking some dope. Larry went to the back of the house. When he returned, he was carrying a knife.

"Get naked," Larry said, standing in front of the terrified woman.

"Why are you doing this to me?" Tonya asked, crying.

"Just shut up and do what I say."

Afraid for her life, Tonya stood up and took off her clothes. At that point Larry began raping her on the couch. Suddenly he grabbed Tonya, walked her toward his bed, pushed her down on it, and continued raping her. Once they were on the bed, Larry put his hands around Tonya's throat to hold her down.

When he had had enough, Larry got off Tonya, stood in front of her, and ordered her to perform oral sex on him, but she refused. Angry, Larry told her to get dressed. He walked her back out to his car and drove her back to where he had picked her up.

"Did you know where you were then, when this was going on?" Cook asked after Tonya finished her story.

"No, 'cause I've never been on that side of town. But being in the situation I was in, I remembered where he took me, so I paid attention to where we were going," she said.

"But during the incident and immediately after, you did not know where you were," Cook stated.

"Right."

"[You were] a long ways from where you'd been picked up," Cook said.

"Right."

"Now, earlier you mentioned the vehicle that he was driving when he picked you up," Cook said. "I think you said it was a Blazer. Can you kind of describe that for me?"

"It was a two-toned red Blazer. It was an older model. There was a window missing on the passenger side. It was the back window. It had plastic on the window. It was fairly junky in the inside. I think the radio was missing out of it, 'cause there was wires and stuff hanging," Tonya said.

Cook and Henderson then began asking Tonya what happened when Larry was raping her.

"Did he actually choke you, or what was going on when he had his hands around your throat?" Cook asked.

"It was more like he was just holding me there and not choking me. I could breathe while he had his hand around my throat," she said, demonstrating how Larry was holding her throat.

"At no point, did he choke you to where you could not breathe, is that correct?" Henderson asked.

"I was breathing while he was choking me."

"Did he wear a condom?" Henderson asked.

"No."

"Did you make any mention at all, ah, him having any sexually transmitted diseases?" Cook asked.

"No, I didn't."

"Did he ask you if you had any?" Cook asked.

"No."

"So there was no conversation about any STDs or anything like that?"

"[No]."

"Did he do anything else sexually, besides having intercourse with you?" Cook asked.

"He wanted me to perform oral sex on him. He stood in front of me and told me to do it, but I didn't."

"Was this before or after the intercourse?"

"After."

"So, at that time, it's your belief that he did not have an orgasm then?"

"I don't believe he did."

"Did you and he do drugs while you were there, or drink alcohol?" Henderson asked.

"Yeah, I did."

"Was he under the influence of drugs or alcohol?"

"He appeared to be under the influence of drugs, by the way he was acting."

"Had you been smoking any [crack cocaine] prior to him picking you up?" Henderson asked.

"Yes, I had."

"Would you say you were under the influence of crack cocaine at the time?"

"Yes."

Cook then asked Tonya if she wanted to add anything to her statement.

Tonya told Cook and Henderson that she ran into Larry again toward the end of September. This time he was driving a blue truck. Larry pulled over and Tonya got in his truck. She said she recognized him immediately, although he didn't recognize her. Larry asked Tonya if she wanted to party. She said, "No thanks," then got out. She tried to get his license plate number, but he drove off too fast.

Tonya said that around the same time she and a friend were standing at the end of the Proctor Recreation Center baseball field when she saw Larry drive past. Her friend tried to get him to stop, but Tonya told her not to get into the truck with him. But her friend said he was "bait" and that she had dated him before.

While some task force members were conducting interviews to gather as much information as they could on Larry, PCSO detective Doug O'Neill was at the Brights' property looking for any physical evidence, such as women's jewelry and clothing, that could help task force members build a case against Larry. During a search of the burn pile, O'Neill found a gold-colored necklace, with what appeared to be a hair stuck in one of the links. The necklace was in a partially burned cardboard box. After notifying his superiors of his find, he was instructed to stop the search and resume it the next morning, because it was raining and it was also getting dark.

The next day CSI Pat Kennedy, a detective with the Peoria County Sheriff's Office, helped O'Neill and State Trooper Mike Oyer search Larry's yard. When they arrived, the first place Kennedy and the investigators searched was the burn pile on the east side of the property, where they had found two pieces of what appeared to be bone. They also dug in the area around the pond, where the soil was soft. When the CSIs started to dig, Kennedy noticed an odor that was associated with a decomposing body. When O'Neill started digging in the area where the smell was coming from, he found fragments of what looked like bone. But the investigators couldn't tell if the bones were from a human or an animal.

Kennedy took custody of the bones and brought them to a forensic anthropologist to determine their origins. But the anthropoligist couldn't determine if they were human or not.

Ten days later, Kennedy and Lieutenant Mark Greskoviak met with another anthropologist, Alan Harn, at the Dickson Mounds Museum, to see if he could identify the bones.

Harn's preliminary examination indicated that they were most likely human. He said some of the bones had been part of a vertebrae, and he knew they were definitely human bones. Some of the other bones were so small that he couldn't easily identify them, but they also looked to be human. All of the bones had been burned at a high temperature.

Harn said he wanted to take the bones to the Illinois State Museum in Springfield to confirm his findings. The next day, Harn called investigators and said the anthropologist at the state museum had, indeed, confirmed his findings. He said the bones consisted of fragments of vertebrae, ribs, a long bone that was part of the tibia, and a bone splinter that might have been part of the ulna.

However, Harn told police that he really couldn't tell them anything else about the small bones, or if they came from one person or more than one person. But, he said, the pieces of vertebrae appeared to come from the same person, most likely an adult female, based on their size. He also said, based on its size, the rib fragment came from a woman.

As the investigation continued, Detective Cy Taylor got a message to contact a woman named Sarah in Pekin, Illinois. Taylor had previously interviewed Sarah when she was a guest of the Illinois Department of Corrections in Decatur.

Sarah called police because she had heard that a man on Starr Court had been arrested for unlawful restraint, and it reminded her of something that had happened to her at the beginning of 2004. Sarah didn't call police at the time because she didn't think they'd believe she had been assaulted.

Taylor picked Sarah up later that day and brought her back to the Tazewell County Sheriff's Office for a more in-depth interview.

Sarah said it happened one evening in March. It was around six o'clock. She was working the north end of Peoria, near Jefferson and Voris Streets, when a white guy—the same guy she recently saw on the news—pulled over and asked if she was working. He was driving an older full-size tan pickup truck with a topper. The truck was in pretty bad shape; it was rusted and dented.

When Sarah got in the truck, the guy told her he had an eight ball at his house and he wanted to get high. So he drove to the south side of the city, passing Manual High School, and ended up on Starr Court. The man parked in the back of the house. The two got out of the truck and walked into the yard through the gate of a tall wooden fence. Once inside, they turned left, and Sarah saw a pond with a waterfall.

The man led her to the smaller of the two houses on the property. He entered through sliding glass doors. Sarah noticed a five-drawer dresser, a bed, and a TV, as well as a couch and a table in the one-room house. On the table, which was at the end of the couch, was a half-empty bottle of Canadian Superior whiskey and a lamp.

After the man closed the door, he told Sarah to sit down and he would get his crack pipe. He walked over to the dresser, opened the top drawer, and took something out. Sarah suddenly felt something pointed touching the right side of her neck. It was a butcher knife with a silver handle.

"Take your clothes off," he ordered.

Sarah took her clothes off, but for some reason left her socks on.

"Suck my dick," the man said, still holding the knife to her neck.

Sarah did what he told her.

The guy then grabbed Sarah by the hair, and she stopped performing oral sex on him.

"Put the knife down. I'm doing what you want," Sarah stated.

"If you do what I tell you, I won't hurt you," he said.

"Then you don't need the knife."

The man put the knife down on the couch, but Sarah told him it was too close.

"I'm trusting you, now you trust me. We're going to party," she said as she moved the knife onto the table.

The guy picked up the bottle of whiskey and handed it to Sarah.

"What's in this?" she asked.

The guy didn't answer. Instead, he put the bottle to his lips and took a drink. He gave the bottle to Sarah and she took a drink. Then the guy raped her anally and vaginally without a condom. She wasn't sure if he ejaculated. As he was raping her, they drank whiskey and smoked pot. The guy also made a couple phone calls trying to get crack, but he never reached anyone.

Sarah told him she knew where she could get the money for the crack. He handed her his white cordless phone, and she called a guy she knew only as Lenard. She told the guy that Lenard owed her money. Lenard and Sarah had been drinking buddies in the past, although she had told him her name was "Denise." Lenard moved around a lot and sometimes lived on the street, so tracking him down wouldn't be easy.

But it was easier than she thought. He answered his phone right away.

"This is Denise. You got that money you owe me? I got a ride. I'll be there in fifteen minutes," she said, apparently not giving Lenard a chance to speak. Then she hung up.

Sarah and the guy got dressed, finished a joint, and drank more whiskey. Sarah told him they needed to get the money so they could buy some crack. He agreed and they left his house. She directed him to the Southside Manor Apartments. When they arrived, she got out of the truck and told the guy she'd be right back. As she was walking through the first set of doors, she turned around and saw the man pull away.

Sarah walked back to her place on Madison, where she was living with her boyfriend, Tomas. It was around 8:30 P.M. or so. She told Tomas what had happened, but he didn't believe her because she refused to call the police. Sarah figured the police wouldn't believe her, anyway. Not only that, she was afraid she'd be arrested for prostitution.

Sarah told Taylor the guy was about five-ten, with a thick build. She said he had shoulder-length hair that was dirty blond. However, she said, she didn't think she could pick him out of a lineup. After the interview Taylor drove Sarah back to where she was staying.

A few days later, Taylor went to see Tomas, who said he and Sarah were no longer together. Taylor asked Tomas if Sarah had ever told him that she had been assaulted. Tomas said that around March or April 2004, Sarah told him a guy had picked her up and forced her to do things. Tomas explained that he didn't believe Sarah, because she wouldn't call the police.

Trying to learn more about the Brights, around the end of January, Special Agent Don Filkins spoke with some of their neighbors. One of the people they spoke with was Jennifer, who had lived in the neighborhood for eight years, even before the Brights had moved into their house on Starr Court.

Jennifer told police the people who lived in the house before Larry and Shirley had raised peacocks, and they kept the pen in the middle of the backyard. The pen, though, had since been removed. Jennifer said the previous home owners had rarely burned leaves or anything else in the yard.

"I met Larry one time last summer," she said. "Larry's cocker spaniel had chased one of my kids, and Larry went after the dog so he wouldn't bother the kids. He just seemed like an average person."

"Did you ever see the Brights burn anything on their property?" Filkins asked.

"Yeah, I saw a fire on the south side of the Brights' backyard more than a few times," she said. "I saw a fire there, about twice a week, during last summer and fall."

"Did you ever smell anything unusual?"

"No, I never did smell any strange odors," she said.

"Did you ever see anyone else bring brush or other debris to the Bright residence to burn?"

"No, I just assumed they were just burning their own debris."

Jennifer added that in late summer or early fall, she saw Larry digging by a big tree near his garage in the backyard.

"He was using a shovel, and that was the only time I ever saw him dig," she said.

Task force members also received a tip from a man named Ron, who said he had information about Larry's possible involvement in the murders and disappearances of the area women. Ron told the investigators that he had lived near the Tremont house that Larry had lived in when he was younger.

"I used to hang out with Larry. He was kind of a

Brenda Erving. *(Courtesy of the Peoria County Sheriff's Office)*

Linda Neal. *(Courtesy of the Peoria County Sheriff's Office)*

Barbara Williams. *(Courtesy of the Peoria County Sheriff's Office)*

Shaconda Thomas. *(Courtesy of the Peoria County Sheriff's Office)*

Shirley Trapp-Carpenter. *(Courtesy of the Peoria County Sheriff's Office)*

Laura Lollar. *(Courtesy of the Peoria County Sheriff's Office)*

Tamara Walls. *(Courtesy of the Peoria County Sheriff's Office)*

Sabrina Payne. *(Courtesy of the Peoria County Sheriff's Office)*

Larry Bright's booking photos.
(Courtesy of the Peoria County Sheriff's Office)

The bed in Larry Bright's apartment where he raped and murdered his victims. *(Courtesy of the Peoria County Sheriff's Office)*

Larry Bright's apartment. *(Courtesy of the Peoria County Sheriff's Office)*

Burn pile in Larry Bright's yard where he burned his victims.
(Courtesy of the Peoria County Sheriff's Office)

Hole dug in Larry Bright's yard by investigators looking for
evidence. *(Courtesy of the Peoria County Sheriff's Office)*

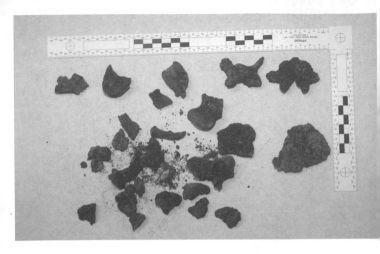

Remains of the women murdered by Larry Bright.
(Courtesy of the Peoria County Sheriff's Office)

Shovels most likely used by Larry Bright to bury the remains of his victims. (Courtesy of the Peoria County Sheriff's Office)

Aerial view of the Brights' property on West Starr Court.
(Courtesy of the Peoria County Sheriff's Office)

The cauldron Larry Bright used to burn his victims.
(Courtesy of the Peoria County Sheriff's Office)

Investigators searching for evidence on Larry Bright's mattress.
(Courtesy of the Peoria County Sheriff's Office)

Members of a local metal detectors club searching for evidence.
(Courtesy of the Peoria County Sheriff's Office)

A victim's ring is discovered. *(Courtesy of the Peoria County Sheriff's Office)*

An underwater search team searching the Mackinaw River for evidence. *(Courtesy of the Peoria County Sheriff's Office)*

House where Larry Bright used to live with his mother on McClure Avenue. *(Courtesy of the Peoria County Sheriff's Office)*

Ceiling in the basement of the McClure Avenue house where evidence was discovered. *(Courtesy of the Peoria County Sheriff's Office)*

Evidence found in the McClure Avenue residence.
(Courtesy of the Peoria County Sheriff's Office)

Investigators searching for evidence in the Brights' backyard.
(Courtesy of the Peoria County Sheriff's Office)

Investigators digging for evidence in the Brights' backyard.
(Courtesy of the Peoria County Sheriff's Office)

Bone dump sites. *(Courtesy of the Peoria County Sheriff's Office)*

Deputy Scott Gamboe, Peoria County Sheriff's Office. *(Courtesy of the Peoria County Sheriff's Office)*

Deputy Patrick Kennedy, Peoria County Sheriff's Office. *(Courtesy of the Peoria County Sheriff's Office)*

Deputy Martin Klatt,
Peoria County
Sheriff's Office.
*(Courtesy of the Peoria
County Sheriff's Office)*

Peoria County Sheriff
Michael McCoy
*(Courtesy of the Peoria
County Sheriff's Office)*

Douglas O'Neill, Peoria County Sheriff's Office.
(Courtesy of the Peoria County Sheriff's Office)

Peoria County State's Attorney Kevin Lyons.
(Courtesy of Kevin Lyons)

Tazewell County Sheriff Robert Huston. *(Courtesy of Robert Huston)*

Task force members. *Back row, left to right:* David Wilson, Peoria County Sheriff's Office (PCSO); Donald Filkins, Illinois State Police (ISP); Cy Taylor, Tazewell County Sheriff's Office (TCSO); Robert Henderson, TCSO; Shawn Meeks, Peoria Police Department (PPD); Chris Hauk, PPD; Joe Spidle, ISP; Scott Cook, PPD; Mike Johnson, Bloomington, Illinois Police Department. *Front row, left to right:* Hal Harper, TCSO; Michael Wiegers, ISP; Kirk Perry, ISP; Mark Greskoviak, PCSO; David Hoyle, PCSO. *(Courtesy of the Peoria County Sheriff's Office)*

river rat who raised himself, because his mother was never home," he said. "And he knows all the area in rural Tremont, Mackinaw, and Hopedale."

Ron told police he believed Larry was responsible for murdering the prostitutes.

"Maybe he's rebelling against his mother for leaving him alone all the time," he said. "I think his mother used to be a prostitute, although I couldn't tell you who used her services. But it was understood that she was working the Grimm's Truck Stop parking lot in Morton. You could talk to this guy Bill Carson. I think he could tell you about Shirley being a prostitute, or he can point you to someone else who knows."

(It's unclear if police ever talked to Carson.)

Larry Bright was also a "person of interest" in the murder of Linda Fields in Racine, Wisconsin. Linda's body was found just after one-thirty in the afternoon on February 24, 2000. Larry dated Linda when he lived in Racine. He moved back to Peoria that same month her body was found.

Thirty-seven-year-old Linda was found strangled to death and her body dumped under a tree near a home on Lake Avenue. She was wearing only her nightgown; her shoes were placed neatly on the ground next to her. A person walking by noticed her and called police.

Linda, a certified nursing assistant, worked in the area's nursing homes. Unlike Larry's victims, Linda had been a professional, a woman who didn't do drugs. Her friends and family—she had two sons and one daughter—said her downfall might have been that she was just too trusting. Her daughter, Laurie, said her mother changed when she met Larry. Laurie was certain that Larry introduced her mother to drugs, and also abused her.

In fact, according to reports, Linda's family urged her to leave Larry, but she didn't listen to them. She lost her home and ended up on the streets, resorting to prostitution to feed her drug addiction. She was never able to recover.

According to Laurie, someone saw Linda go off with a white guy the night she was murdered. That person begged Linda not to go with the guy because he was known to abuse women. The person said he had even choked some people.

Racine police interviewed Larry, but they didn't have any evidence to connect him to Linda's murder. And Larry claimed he didn't kill Linda. But Laurie was convinced Larry murdered her mother and dumped her body like trash on that cold February night.

Linda Fields's murder has never been solved.

And police in Creve Coeur, a little town in Tazewell County, were also wondering if the disappearance of forty-five-year-old Karen Hobdy-Cage, who had been missing for more than fifteen months, was connected to the missing and murdered women in Peoria and Tazewell Counties.

Although the Creve Coeur police weren't sure

foul play was involved—Karen had a history of emotional, mental, and drinking problems that could have caused her to act erratically—they couldn't rule it out, either. So the Creve Coeur police, aided by the Illinois State Police, were trying to figure out if Karen was one of the victims of the serial killer in Peoria, alhough she really didn't fit the profile. But they thought because she suffered from depression and had a drinking problem, she might have fallen into the clutches of a serial killer.

Karen, who grew up in Indiana, married while she was still a teenager and had two kids. But several years later, she suffered a nervous breakdown. Ultimately she and her husband divorced, and he took the children and moved to the West. Karen ended up in Creve Coeur around 1989, when her parents moved there from Colorado. In 1999, she married again, but she was divorced a couple years later.

Karen suffered from osteoporosis and fibromyalgia. She was also bipolar, but when she took her meds, her moods and behavior would even out. The problem was, she'd often stop taking her medication and start to act irrationally. And drinking just made things worse.

When Karen was reported missing, police checked the home of a friend where she had been staying. What they discovered was confounding at best. It appeared that Karen had been cooking a meal, but she left in the middle of it. A heavy smoker, she had also left a package of cigarettes in the kitchen.

Local police searched the area but didn't find anything that explained what had happened to Karen Hobdy-Cage. So they asked the state police for help, but their efforts didn't turn up anything, either.

10

As part of their investigation, members of the task force wanted to know if Larry or Shirley had been in trouble with the law when they lived in Tremont. Officer Taylor contacted Officer Nate Troyer, of the Tremont Police Department (TPD), and asked him to check the department's files for any reports on the pair.

Troyer called Taylor to tell him there were some reports indicating that both of them had been booked at the Tremont Jail: Shirley, for a contempt-of-court warrant in 1976, a probation violation in 1977, and a failure-to-comply warrant in 1982. And Larry had been a suspect in a 1983 burglary, when he was seventeen. He also had been arrested for illegal possession of alcohol in 1987 and for DUI in 1991.

Troyer sent Taylor the incident report for Larry's burglary arrest, which explained what had happened.

* * *

On October 17, 1983, Floyd Carlson called police to tell them that a number of stolen black wallets had been stashed in a blue Vega station wagon parked at a house on East Tazewell Street. Floyd suspected his son, David, who was fifteen, had something to do with the theft.

So Officer Tom Conover went to the house and talked to the owner of the car, one of Larry's relatives. Conover explained the situation to the woman and asked if he could search her car. She agreed and went with him to the vehicle.

Inside, Conover found five black wallets with different logos on them: two had the Jack Daniel's logo, one had the Def Leppard logo, one had the Harley-Davidson logo, and one had the Led Zeppelin logo. He also discovered one heart-shaped watch locket on a gold chain, a square-shaped locket watch, with a gold chain, and one Bible, with a white cover with the name Connie Carlson in it. Conover confiscated the items, gave the woman a receipt for them, then took them back to the station.

About twenty minutes later, the woman called the station and asked Conover to return to her house because she found what she believed was another stolen item inside her house. When Conover arrived, the woman gave him a Starling-brand portable AM/FM radio with headphones. Again after giving her a receipt, he took the radio back to the police station and put it with the other items.

Almost an hour later, Conover found David Carlson walking on South Chestnut Street and stopped him to talk about the robbery. David explained that three other boys, including Larry Bright, had taken the items to sell, and the four of them were planning to share in the profits. David also told him they stole a Mustang-brand graphic stereo equalizer amplifier and some knives, but he didn't know where those items were. David said the robbery wasn't his idea, but he refused to name the mastermind.

David told Conover that he was afraid his father was going to beat him for his part in the theft. The officer advised David against running away from home and suggested he tell his father his side of the story before he found out from someone else. David agreed that was the best way to handle things, and he agreed to go home to talk to his father.

An hour later, Floyd Carlson called Conover and asked him to meet him at his house. When he arrived, Floyd told him that someone had been in his house sometime during the day. Floyd said he knew that David had been in the house at noon, but he didn't know if the items were missing at that point. Conover explained that David was supposed to have talked to Floyd about what had happened. Conover then explained the situation to Floyd and described the items that had been recovered.

Floyd said he'd have to check his supply of wallets to determine how many were missing. He said some of his wife's things were missing, and they seemed to match the items Conover recovered from Larry's relative. As they were talking, David came home and told his dad what was going on.

Later on that evening, nineteen-year-old Frank Brady, who went by the name "Tony," went to the police station to make a statement about the robbery. He said he was scared because he knew Floyd Carlson was out looking for him. After he was read his rights, he confirmed everything David had said—except for one thing. Tony said David Carlson was behind the theft. According to Tony, David got the wallets and the other stuff and gave them to the others to sell. They had originally taken eleven wallets, but the other accomplice, Phillip White, who was the same age as Larry, gave five of them back to David after the robbery had been reported.

Tony put five in the Vega and one in his pocket. He eventually gave that one back to David after they had been found out. Tony said David gave him the two watch lockets for no apparent reason. He said he took the Carlson Bible from another friend's house after David had forgotten it there one day after church. Tony said he didn't know anything about the radio, but he thought Larry had the stereo booster and was planning to hook it up to his pickup truck. Tony thought Larry also had a couple knives that David had given the three of them to sell.

Tony said David went back to school because he was late for his fifth-hour class. Then he, Larry, and Phillip went to Larry's house so Phillip could hook up the stereo booster to Larry's truck. But as he was working, his mother and Larry's mother confronted him and chased him away. Tony said he left with Phillip.

Tony agreed to take a polygraph if David agreed to take one.

Conover interviewed David and Floyd Carlson the next day. David waived his rights and agreed to talk to the officer. Conover first showed Floyd the items he had recovered, and Floyd confirmed they belonged to him and his wife. Conover gave Floyd the Bible because it wasn't needed as evidence.

Then it was David's turn. He told Conover he had come home from school for lunch to take his medicine. On his way back to school, he met up with the other three boys in the area of Tremont Park. They were in Larry's pickup truck. According to David, Larry, Tony, and Phillip convinced him to let them have some of his father's merchandise to sell. In exchange, they would share with him whatever money they got.

When David agreed, Larry drove the truck around to the apartments located behind the Carlson residence. The three boys got out of the truck and went to the back of David's house. David, meanwhile, used his key to open the front door and went inside. He immediately went to the back door to let Larry, Tony, and Phillip in. Larry and Tony went into the garage, while David and Phillip went to find the wallets. The boys also took three folding, lockback-type knives with wooden handles and brass ends.

David wasn't sure if his friends took the radio and stereo booster at that time, because it wasn't the first time something like that had happened. In fact, David had taken merchandise from his house to sell on other occasions. He also had given Tony the two watch lockets a couple weeks earlier, but he said he never got any money from the sale of any of the items.

Floyd Carlson said the total value of the items

was about $164. Floyd also said he was missing a bottle of whiskey.

After leaving the Carlson residence, Conover went to find Phillip White. He picked him up a short time later. The officer told Phillip he was a suspect in the theft, and he read the Miranda warning to him. Phillip waived his rights and agreed to talk with Conover.

Phillip said he met up with Tony and Larry in the alley behind Beechams Grocery Store. Tony and Larry were in Larry's pickup truck. He got in and they rode around for a bit. That's when they spotted David walking through Tremont Park on his way back to school. They stopped and talked to him, but Phillip didn't hear the entire conversation because David was standing next to the driver's-side window.

He said the plan was for them to meet up with David back at his house. When they got there, David let them in the back door, and he and Larry went to the garage, where they got the stereo booster. Phillip knew it was there because he had seen it another time when he was at David's house. Phillip admitted he took five or six wallets, but he said he gave them back after his mother found out what he had done.

After taking the merchandise, the three boys left David and went to Larry's house to install the stereo power booster. Phillip said he didn't see the whiskey and didn't have any of the knives. He did have one of the knives in his coat pocket for a short time but lost it.

Phillip told Conover the theft from the Carlson residence wasn't prearranged. They only decided to do it after talking to David, who said it would be easy to steal the stuff because his father wasn't home.

The next day Larry's mom, Shirley, brought the stereo power booster and one knife to the police station. Five days later, Conover interviewed Larry about the case. Like the others, Larry waived his rights and agreed to talk. Larry confirmed the story that Phillip had already told Conover. He added that they had taken six knives, and he had taken two of them. He gave one to Phillip and he kept the other, but he didn't know what happened to the rest of them. He said his mom removed the stereo power booster from his truck and turned it over to the police. Larry told Conover he had never received any merchandise from Carlson before, although he thought that Tony and David had stolen stuff to sell in the past.

In February 1984, Conover called Floyd Carlson and told him charges were going to be filed against the four suspects. He explained that the state's attorney wouldn't prosecute the case *unless* all the boys were charged. Floyd said he didn't want his son prosecuted, and he understood the case would be dropped. Floyd said he knew that two of the boys were being prosecuted for other crimes, and his case wouldn't make much difference, anyway.

Floyd knew that Larry and Tony had been charged with battery for beating up his son at the beginning of December. David and a friend had just left the high school and were on their way downtown to get something to eat. Just then, Phillip White drove up in his mother's car. He had several friends in the car with him. He pulled over near the east entrance to the high school and called David over to the car. Instead, David and his friend took off and headed downtown.

About an hour later, David and his friend walked to the back of Beechams and met up with some friends. Larry, Phillip, Tony, and a number of other kids were just standing around. Larry called David over to talk to him, saying he wasn't going to hit him. Taking Larry at his word, David walked over to where Larry was standing. Before David knew what was happening, Larry grabbed him by the back of the neck, forced his head down, and kneed him in the head. Then Larry kneed him twice in the gut and punched him in the face a couple times.

As Larry was beating him up, David heard him ask, "Is that enough for four bucks, Tony?" At the time David had no idea what Larry was talking about. All he wanted was to get the hell out of there. As they were leaving, Larry told David if he ever talked to the police, he'd get more of the same. Despite the warning, David and his friend went to the police station to report the incident.

After talking to police, David went back to school. His teacher asked him about the very noticeable bruise under his eye, then sent him to the nurse's office to have it taken care of. She also notified the principal, who talked to David about what had happened. David told the principal that he knew that Larry Bright had been paid by Tony Brady to beat him up. The principal then questioned Larry about the incident, but David believed that Larry had lied about it.

Conover then went to interview John, one of

the other boys who was at Beechams when Larry beat up David. John admitted he was there and said he knew David had been in a fight, but he said he didn't watch it, so he really didn't know what had happened. He said he heard that David took a swing at Larry first, and Larry only hit David in self-defense. According to John, the fight started because David called Larry names.

Conover explained to John that even though he didn't participate in the fight, he was still at fault because he didn't try to stop it. Conover asked John why he didn't run and get the store owner. John said he didn't think of it at the time.

That evening Conover interviewed Phillip White about the incident. White said he was at the grocery store when the fight took place. He said the problem between David and Larry started at noon in the driveway of the high school when students were let out for lunch. Apparently, David and Larry had words, and David gave Larry the bird, then started running home but ended up behind Beechams.

But Phillip said he didn't see the actual fight, because he and a couple other boys were looking at the engine of his car. All he saw was David picking himself up off the ground. Phillip said he didn't know where Tony Brady was at the time, and he didn't hear anything about Tony offering Larry money to beat up David. And he didn't see Tony give Larry any money. When the fight was over, Phillip said, he took Tony back to where he was staying, then drove Larry back to the high school.

Larry ultimately was charged with battery, but

the charge was dismissed as part of a plea agreement. It's unclear what happened to Tony.

It appeared that Larry, who seemed to have a penchant for knives early on, also liked beating people up and threatening them.

Leaving no stone unturned, Detectives Dave Hoyle and Dave Wilson went to talk to Kara, Larry's sister-in-law. They met her at a department store in Morton. While Kara talked to police, her husband, Jerry, sat in a car nearby. Kara said she had known Larry for about twenty-eight years. They met through mutual friends who lived in the Morton area.

The detectives asked her about Larry's ex-wife, Cathy, but she said they had never met. She told police Larry and his brother had a rather rocky relationship. She said Larry used to beat up Jerry when they were kids, and Jerry didn't take kindly to that.

"When you were teenagers, did you ever party at a place called the 'broken bridge'?" Hoyle asked.

"Yeah, I used to party there when I was about twenty, and Larry used to be at the parties."

Kara said she got along fine with Larry's mother, although she felt that Shirley coddled Larry and was overly protective of him.

"Is there anything that indicated that Larry and his mother had a sexual relationship?"

"No, but they had an abnormal relationship."

"Do you know if Larry has ever been with any black women?"

"When Larry used to live on McClure, Jerry

caught him with a black girl one day," she said. "You know, about a month ago, Shirley told me she thought Larry might have AIDS."

A couple days later, Deputy Scott Gamboe went to the Brights' property to search Shirley's house. From her bedroom closet, he confiscated two pairs of hiking boots, a pair of size-8½ Wrangler Heroes, and a pair of size-7½ Route 66s. In the top drawer of the dresser, he found two knives with their sheaths. One of the knives had a curved blade, like the one Genene alleged Larry used to threaten her. On top of the dresser, Gamboe found Larry's wallet containing his Illinois ID card and a receipt for $150.

He found sixteen videotapes in the dresser in another bedroom. In the laundry room, he photographed and recovered three screwdrivers from a toolbox, and in the kitchen, he photographed and confiscated a butcher block, with nine knives and a sharpener—one knife was missing from its slot.

11

Detectives Dave Hoyle and Cy Taylor met at the Tazewell County Jail at a little after seven o'clock in the morning on January 26 to serve a search warrant on Larry for his house and the rest of the property on West Starr Court. The warrant also authorized police to search his mother's house, as well as dig in certain areas, including the crawl space under her house, the yard, and the fishpond, which they were in the process of doing.

One of the corrections officers brought Larry to a common area to meet with the detectives. When they told him they were there to serve the warrant, Larry asked if they could go back to his cell for privacy. Once inside the cell, Larry sat down on his bed, and Hoyle sat down next to him. Taylor remained standing.

When Hoyle told Larry he was going to read the warrant to him, he said he wasn't supposed to talk to them without his lawyer. Hoyle explained they were only there to serve the warrant, not to ask him any questions. He added that he could answer any questions Larry had about the warrant.

Hoyle told Larry that during the earlier search of his yard, police had dug up bones that were later confirmed to be human bones. Based on that information, police obtained the search warrant.

After Hoyle read the warrant, Larry asked where police were going to be searching.

"We're searching and excavating the side yard where the burn piles are located and where the bones were found," Hoyle responded. "We're also searching the crawl space under your mother's house, as well as the area around, in, and under the pond."

Larry hesitated for a few seconds, then said, "There's no need to look in my mom's house or the pond. There isn't anything there."

"We have no choice, because of the bones we found," Hoyle said.

"I'll tell you everything. Leave my mom's house and the pond alone."

"Okay, if we find and identify the remains of any of the missing girls, there won't be any need to dig up the pond or under your mom's house," Hoyle said. "But we can't talk to you without your attorney."

"You can, if I say I want to talk to you, right?"

"Yes, but you'll have to sign a waiver."

"I'll sign it."

"You know, in the past a lot of inmates tell stories because they want to get out of their cells," Hoyle said. "I don't want you playing me for a cigarette."

"I'm not. I want to talk. I'll tell you everything,"

he said. "But there's nothing in my mom's crawl space or in the pond, so don't search there. I don't want to put my mom through any more sorrow. I already put her through enough."

"Those missing girls have mothers, and they loved them very much. And some of them were mothers," Hoyle said. "We need to locate these girls for closure for the families. But if we find them and identify them, I don't see the need to search those areas. But I can't make you any promises."

The detectives then moved Larry into a detectives' conference room so they could videotape the interview. Once in the room, Taylor went to get Larry a soda, while Hoyle reviewed the Miranda forms with him. Larry had to wait to sign the forms until Taylor returned to witness his signature. Larry also had to sign a waiver saying he wanted to talk, despite his attorney's advice. With the paperwork out of the way, Hoyle began the interview.

"What's up?" Hoyle asked.

"I did it," Larry said.

"How many?" Hoyle asked.

"Only eight," Larry said, burying his face in his hands and crying.

"When did it start?"

Larry said it started with the girl—Sabrina Payne—who was found in the cornfield outside of Tremont Township in Tazewell County.

"I killed her at my house and I took her to the cornfield, because I didn't know what to do," he said. "I was on cocaine. Every time I was on cocaine."

He said the second girl, who had been identified

as Barbara Williams, was the one police found by North Valley View Road in Edwards, Illinois. Larry used to date a girl named Tracy, who lived in the same area. Her parents still lived there.

"We were doing drugs and I caught her trying to steal my money, so I hit her in the throat. She started choking, and I lost control," Larry said, explaining how Barbara died. "She died at my house. I don't know why I dumped her body there. I just wanted to get rid of her."

At that point Larry again asked police not to dig up his mother's yard. So Hoyle called the investigators who were searching Larry's property and asked them to hold off digging, because Larry was going to tell them where he had put the women's bodies.

Hoyle then asked Larry to go over the girls he had killed and then talk about their murders in more detail. Hoyle first asked Larry about Frederickia Brown, the woman whose body was found in the snow along the railroad tracks in Hanna City.

"Not me," Larry said.

The next girl Larry said he murdered was one of the missing girls, who were Shirley Trapp-Carpenter, Shaconda Thomas, Tammy Walls, and Laura Lollar.

"Where is she?" Hoyle asked.

"Where you guys dug up. Where the ashes and stuff was at. I burned the bodies. I dug a hole and got the fire going real good. Then I put the bodies in it. Forgive me, Lord," Larry said as he started crying again. "I dumped her along the Kickapoo Creek on Kickapoo Creek

Road," he said. "I can explain where, but it would be better if I showed you."

The detectives listened as Larry told them what he had done with the remains of the missing women.

"After I burned the bodies, I shoveled the ashes out of the hole and put them in buckets. Then I took them to Kickapoo Creek by a big sledding hill near a church," he said. "I parked by the side of the road and carried the buckets of ashes down a trail to the creek and dumped them. Then I threw the buckets away in the same area."

"How did she die?" Hoyle asked, referring to Larry's third victim.

"I strangled her."

"Did all four of the missing girls die that way?"

"I strangled all of them with my hands."

"What about the girl with the shoelace around her neck?" Hoyle asked, meaning Linda Neal.

"I was watching Court TV and I wanted to make it look different."

Larry said he dumped Linda's body by the Mackinaw River near a place where he used to party when he was younger. He dumped the body of Brenda Erving, the last woman he murdered, on Taggert Road in Elmwood. He drove her body there, uncovered, inside his truck. He was trying to find some strip mine lakes in the area where he used to swim when he was a kid, but he panicked before he could find them and just left her on Taggert Road. He said he threw her jewelry out, including several rings, as he was driving on Farmington Road, although later he said he threw it over the fence on the side of his mom's yard.

"How did she get the bruises on her head and face?" Hoyle asked.

"I don't know, but she did struggle with me."

"What did you do with the women's clothes?"

"I burned them in, like, a witch's cauldron–thing in the yard."

"Did you tell anyone else what you did?" Hoyle asked.

"No," Larry said, breaking down again. "The only reason I'm telling you is because I don't want my mom to go through anymore. She doesn't deserve a son like me."

Larry told the detectives the main reason he started looking for black prostitutes was because he thought he got AIDS from a black prostitute named Ernestine. He found out he had the disease when he tried to donate plasma at the plasma center. Hoyle told him he could get help from the medical staff in the jail if he wanted it.

Before Larry started to go into more details about the murdered women, he again told Hoyle he was concerned about his mother's house being dug up. So Hoyle called the investigators at the scene and told them not to resume digging because Larry was telling them where he had dumped the bodies. They agreed to only dig in the area where he had burned the bodies, as long as he was telling them the truth.

Assuring them that he was, Larry started talking about his first victim, Sabrina Payne. Sabrina was hanging out on Lincoln Street in the south end of Peoria, an area known for prostitution, when he picked her up in his Blazer. He took her back to his house on McClure Avenue, where he lived at that time. Larry thought Sabrina, like Barbara Williams, was ripping him off, and he lost control. The next thing he knew, she was dead, so he put her body in the front passenger seat of his Blazer and drove her to the cornfield in Tremont, where he used to grow weed. He dragged her body by the arms out of his Blazer and into the cornfield, where he dumped her. Then he threw her clothes in a nearby creek, went home, and drank a "bunch of whiskey."

"I hear these voices in my head telling me to do things, and I can't stop," he said, crying. "It's the crack. If I stay away from the crack, I'm okay."

"Were the first two accidents?" Hoyle asked.

"Yes, but after the second one, I knew I was going to kill the girls when I picked them up," Larry said. "I was hunting."

Larry said he brought home about twenty other black prostitutes he didn't kill.

"Why didn't you kill the other girls you brought home?" Hoyle asked.

"I don't know," he said. "I really didn't want to do it. I was fighting the voices in my head."

When Hoyle asked Larry if he had murdered Bonnie Fife, a missing white woman from Canton, Illinois, Larry stopped speaking in a soft whimper and his voice became very strong.

"I never did nothing with Bonnie Fife," he said. "I knew Bonnie, but I didn't do anything to her. We were friends."

* * *

Larry next went over the circumstances surrounding the death of Barbara Williams. Larry
picked Barbara up in the south end of Peoria and
took her back to his place. Typically, Larry asked
the women if they wanted to party, and after determining he wasn't a cop, they went with him. However, he said, sometimes he told the women he was
a cop, but he never killed those women.

Barbara and Larry smoked crack and had sex.
Earlier in the interview, Larry said he caught her
trying to steal his money, so he punched her in the
throat, but he had a different story now. It appeared that Larry was confusing the murders of
Sabrina Payne and Barbara Williams.

This time Larry said Barbara had smoked a lot
of crack and was really out of it. She started choking and then passed out. When she started to wake
up again, he strangled her. He figured she would
have died, anyway, even if he hadn't killed her.
Trying to cover up her needle tracks, Larry put
her clothes back on her. Her body sat at his house
until the next day, when he got rid of her.

He had a place in mind to dump her, but it was
too muddy. He was also spooked by a police officer who was driving behind him on Taylor Road
while he had Barbara's body in his Blazer. The officer pulled off into Wildlife Prairie State Park in
Peoria, and Larry drove to nearby Edwards and
dumped Barbara's body, like a piece of garbage,
off North Valley View Road.

"A couple days later, the cops came to my house
looking for someone who used to live there,"
Larry said. "They should have caught me then. It
would have saved lives. After that one I stopped

smoking crack for a few months. Then the first time after I smoked crack again, I killed the next girl. Then even when I wasn't doing crack, the voices in my head kept saying, 'Do it, do it, do it.' I need help. If I've learned anything, it's to stay away from crack."

Larry stopped and started to cry, so Hoyle gave him some time to compose himself. After a few minutes he began describing how he murdered the third woman, who was later identified as Shirley Trapp-Carpenter. Larry picked her up in his Blazer in the north end of Peoria, where the prostitutes hung out, although he wasn't sure of the exact location, and brought her back to his house on West Starr Court. Before picking up each of the women, Larry always got crack from Harry Cannon. If he didn't have the crack, he wouldn't do it.

As Larry was talking, Taylor left the room to get some photographs of the missing and dead women to show Larry. When he returned with the pictures, Larry said he didn't want to look at them yet. So the police agreed to wait.

Larry continued.

Once back at his place, he and Shirley smoked crack and had sex. Sensing something bad was going to happen, the woman started to struggle. During the struggle she made a hole in the wall behind the television. She broke the window in the living room, and she almost got away. But Larry hit her hard in the head, and that, most likely, killed her. But he also strangled her with his hands. He then moved the broken window onto his porch.

After killing Shirley, Larry got the idea from a television show to burn her body. He said he was watching the History Channel and saw something about Hitler's body being burned. So he built a fire and let it burn for hours, until the coals were very hot. Then he carried Shirley's body out to the fire and let it burn for an entire day. Finally he shoveled her ashes into a bucket and took them to Tremont, near where he lived when he was a child.

"Where's the shovel you used?" Hoyle asked.

"It's at my house, but you won't find anything on it, because after I sobered up and realized what I did, I used water and a scrub brush on it," he said. "But I must have missed some bones."

"Was she wearing any jewelry?"

"All the girls had a little jewelry, and I usually threw it out of my car as I drove down the road," he said. "And I threw some from my mom's yard toward the church. I never pawned any of the jewelry, because I was trying to cover my tracks."

Larry picked up his next victim near the Harrison Homes, a housing development on the south side of Peoria. High on crack, Larry was already hearing the voices in his head telling him to kill a girl.

"Is the killing part of the sex act?" Hoyle asked.

"No, it wasn't about the sex," Larry said. "It was revenge for killing me by giving me AIDS."

After Larry picked up the woman, he took her back to his house, where they smoked crack, drank whiskey, and had sex. They were having sex missionary style, and as soon as he ejaculated, he started strangling her. She put up a struggle and scratched his face pretty bad with one nail. When his mother asked him what had happened to his face, he told her a stick scratched him.

"My mom didn't know anything about any of this," he said.

After he killed that girl, he kept her in his bathroom for a day and a half. He had to wait to burn her, he said, because it was raining. He always moved the bodies to the fire late at night when his mother was sleeping or at her boyfriend's house. While he was burning her body, his mother came back home. She asked him what he was burning because it smelled funny.

"A body gives off a terrible odor," he said. "So I told her it was plastic. I want to let you guys know that I never had sex with the girls after they were dead."

When the body was thoroughly burned, Larry carted the ashes and bones away in two buckets, took them to the Kickapoo Creek, across from the old Aspen Ski Hill, and dumped them in the water. That's where he also dumped victim number five. But he said he could only dump victim number six close to the water because the water level was too high.

Later, however, Larry changed his story and said he dumped the sixth woman in a different area, since there were people at the place where he disposed of his fourth and fifth victims.

* * *

After he murdered the fourth girl, his urge got stronger, and he began killing with more frequency. He picked up his next victim outside Woody's Bar in his Blazer. Again he was high on crack. He took the woman back to his place, where they smoked crack, drank whiskey, and had sex. After he ejaculated, he strangled her, just like he strangled his previous victim.

The only difference was, this woman was too wasted to put up a fight. After she was dead, he went outside to start the fire. After it got going real good, he tossed her body into the flames. Then he waited for her ashes to cool off, because one other time he removed a victim's ashes too soon and his bucket melted. He dumped her remains along the Kickapoo Creek, though now he said he didn't remember if he dumped her in the water or just close to it.

"What time of day did you pick her up?" Hoyle asked.

"I picked them all up after dark."

"Was she wearing any jewelry? What did you do with it?"

"This was the only girl I ever kept anything from," he said, not really answering the question. "That blue hitter pipe you found in my truck was hers."

When Hoyle told Larry that police had also found Barbara Williams's obituary in his truck, he was surprised, because he never read or kept any newspaper articles about the murders.

"Did you ever try to get rid of any evidence?" Hoyle asked.

"Once I was sober, I tried to cover it up."

The end came to the sixth victim pretty much the same way it came to numbers four and five. A doped-up Larry picked up the woman, brought her to his house, where they smoked crack, drank whiskey, and had sex, just like every other time. He ejaculated, strangled her, built a fire, and burned her body the same night. Two days later, when the ashes had cooled, he dumped her body along the Kickapoo Creek Road.

Linda Neal was Larry's seventh victim. As Larry began to talk, Hoyle left the room for a few minutes; Taylor continued the interview. Larry said he picked up Linda in the parking lot of Woody's Bar and asked her if she wanted to party. She did, so they went to his house, where they partied and had sex. Then he put his hands around her throat and strangled her. She didn't put up a fight, but he continued choking her until he was certain she was dead. Because his mom was home, he couldn't burn her body and had to dispose of it intact.

"Did you rape her two or three weeks before you killed her?" Taylor asked.

Larry said he did not.

Hoyle returned to the interview room as Larry was describing how he disposed of the women's clothing. He said he burned it in a metal cauldron in his yard and dumped the nude intact bodies. When he burned the other women's bodies, he burned their clothes with them. He told police that there were bones by the shed in his yard, and he used the pond on the west side of his house as a burn pit.

Larry said he used a condom when he had sex with the women—although he didn't know why, since he was already infected. However, the condom he used when he had sex with Linda Neal broke, he said. He also said he killed all the women by strangling them on his bed. It didn't take long, and he could tell when he crushed their windpipes. He said his dad had taught him how to do it when his father came back from Vietnam.

The last woman Larry murdered was Brenda Erving. He wasn't sure where he picked her up, but he remembered picking one girl up in the north end of Peoria, where the prostitutes strolled. When he picked her up, he already had some crack, so they went right back to his house, where they smoked for about an hour, then had sex, including anal sex.

Brenda put up the biggest fight. She scratched him in the chest and stabbed him with a screwdriver. She almost got away, but he was able to grab her and keep her from running out of the house. Although the medical examiner found blunt-force trauma to her head, Larry didn't remember hitting her in the head. After he killed her, he took her out by Elmwood Township in Peoria County and threw her body out on a dirt road. Then he covered up his footprints. After he got rid of her body, he continued driving east until he came to Inmans Dairy Farm. Then he turned around and drove back by the body.

"Did any of the girls try to say anything to you as you were killing them?" Hoyle asked.

"They couldn't say anything. They just gurgled."

Larry finally stopped killing because he stopped using cocaine. He said he was so desperate to stop that he even called in a tip on himself to the Crime Stoppers line from a pay phone after he burned one victim. His message was that police should investigate Larry Bright on West Starr Court. He even tried confessing to his mother over the phone but he didn't have the guts to go through with it.

The interview ended about half past nine after Larry agreed to direct the investigators to the dump sites. The detectives gave Larry a coat, then escorted him handcuffed and shackled to Taylor's squad car. Hoyle rode with Taylor and Larry, while Detective Hal Harper and Special Agent Don Filkins followed in another car.

As the interview with Larry progressed, Illinois State Police CSI Matt Davis went to the Peoria County Sheriff's Office to meet with members of the task force, who explained that while searching Bright's property, they discovered a burn pile, where they suspected he burned his victims. The task force members wanted Davis to reexamine and process the yard.

After leaving the sheriff's office, Davis went to Bright's house, where he met with archaeologist Alan Harn. Harn had also been asked to help in the recovery of additional human remains. Before Davis began processing the scene, PCSO detectives told him that Bright was willing to cooperate with investigators. They asked Davis to hold off examining and processing the scene until investigators brought Bright back to his house.

Several hours later, Lieutenant Mark Greskoviak contacted Davis and told him that Larry pointed out several locations on his property where he buried some of the women's remains. Greskoviak told Davis that Larry allegedly burned several bodies in a pit on the west side of the garage and scattered some remains next to a set of tire tracks that ran along the south side of a storage shed in the backyard of his house.

Larry also said he threw some jewelry belonging to the women in a landscaped area on the west side of the house. Greskoviak asked Davis to search the large fishpond in the backyard and the basement of the larger house for burned body parts. Larry also had allegedly scattered some women's burned remains in wooded areas adjacent to his grandmother's house on South Anna Street in Bellevue, just west of Peoria and adjacent to a house on North Willow Street in Norwood, Illinois. The backyards of both of those houses bordered wooded areas.

For the next three days, the police examined, photographed, and processed the area around Larry's house, his grandmother's house, and the house on North Willow. Investigators going over the scene at Larry's house measured and mapped the inside and outside of Shirley's house and Larry's garage and drew pictures of the crime scene.

Davis and Harn examined the area on the west side of the garage, the area along the wooden privacy fence, as well as the area along a metal Cyclone fence next to the garage. On the other side of the metal fence was a park, as well as a ball field. They also noticed a small fishpond in the area to the west of the garage. It appeared that someone had enlarged a preexisting pit and created the small pond.

That pond consisted of a small depression in the ground that had been covered with a black plastic tarp. It was about one-quarter filled with ice. The two men constructed a series of ten-foot-long by ten-foot-wide grids using string and stakes that covered the area on the west side of the garage.

They then did a walk-over search of each unit in the grid, examining the area and removing the surface debris and rocks. They removed the ice, rocks, and plastic tarp from the small pond and immediately noticed that some of the ground surface around the pool, which consisted of about one inch of topsoil, had been disturbed. Davis and Harn used shovels to clear away the soil disturbances. Harn next dug up the small pond and the area where the soil had been disturbed. Then, using one-quarter-inch and one-eighth-inch screens, crime scene investigators processed the soil removed from the area and looked for evidence. The soil excavated from the base of the fishpond contained dark-colored burned debris and topsoil.

Investigators had previously uncovered human remains in an area just south of the small fishpond. Harn also excavated that area using shovels and trowels and processed the material to search for evidence that would be pertinent to the case. Harn found small pieces of charred wood, other burned debris, and bits of bone in the dark-colored soil. After Harn finished working in the area around the fishpond, the ground surface was slowly scraped away by a backhoe in an effort to locate any other remains. That search, however, was fruitless.

While Harn was doing his work, Davis was examining the large burn pile in the backyard that consisted of miscellaneous burned trash and other debris. Despite his best efforts, Davis didn't find any human remains or any other evidence in the burn pile, or in a woodpile that was near the shed. After the large fishpond was drained and the liner removed, Davis used a shovel to clear away about three inches of topsoil and examined the bottom of it. He didn't find any evidence in the large fishpond, either.

Davis also searched the crawl space/basement under the large house. The basement was a large, open area under the house, and there was a sort of alcove directly under the front porch. The walls of the basement were concrete, but the floors of the open area and the alcove were made of dirt. Davis walked through the entire area but didn't notice anything out of place, including the soil. There was no evidence in the basement.

Davis also examined a set of tire tracks on the grass near a shed in the backyard of the Starr Court property. The tire impressions consisted of two shallow depressions in the ground that extended more than twenty feet out from the landscaped area. Davis took twelve-inch-deep core samples at six-inch intervals along the center of both tire tracks. In one area he dug down about two inches and unearthed small fragments of charred wood and bone. The CSI removed a six-foot swath of soil approximately six inches wide and four inches deep. He collected the soil in five-gallon buckets so he could examine it later at the lab.

As he was examining the tire tracks, Davis noticed some exposed soil in a grassy area. The exposed soil measured about one foot wide by one foot eight inches long. When Davis looked closer, he saw small sections of bone, as well as bits and pieces of plastic and metal. He collected the items in small cardboard boxes, then continued excavating the area until he was sure he had retrieved all the bone and charred material.

Crime scene investigators removed ice, charred wood, and debris from a large metal cauldron next to the large fishpond and put them in a five-gallon bucket, which they brought back to the lab.

Davis and the other crime scene investigators also searched the area around Larry's grandmother's house in Bellevue. First they walked around the wooded area south of Mary Simmons's house, marking all the potential skeletal remains, clothing, and other potential evidence. After completing their search, they realized the evidence was located in three main areas along a line that ran parallel to the tree line and several feet into the woods. The CSI constructed grids, some as large as twenty-five feet by twenty feet, using colored strings and stakes. Then they removed by hand all the surface debris that hadn't been burned, including leaves, vegetation, and trash from the grids. To their trained eyes, it didn't appear that any remains had been buried there.

The investigators placed numbered evidence

markers next to each of forty-nine additional clusters of burned debris containing skeletal remains, clothing, and other evidence. They photographed the evidence and then collected each cluster, along with the frozen topsoil under the cluster. The police then packaged each of the forty-nine clusters in a paper bag and placed them in five-gallon buckets to transport back to the laboratory to be examined.

Davis later determined that the burned debris containing the skeletal remains, clothing, and other evidence had been dumped in the three main clusters at different times. He also concluded that the rain had most likely washed some of the evidence down the sloping ground, thereby forming the other forty-nine clusters. It also appeared that the remains had been burned elsewhere.

Forensic anthropologist Dr. Stephen Nawrocki led the investigators in their search of the house on North Willow Street. When they arrived at the location, they walked around in the woods next to the house and looked for evidence. They noticed several downed trees and branches in the area, and a cluster of burned debris and several fragments of skeletal remains next to the trees.

The investigators removed twigs, leaves, and branches from the area by hand. Then they cleared a twenty-foot by fifteen-foot area around the fallen trees, but they didn't find any more bone fragments. However, they did recover some pieces of bone on top of the fallen logs. In total, police found eight clusters of burned debris that contained pieces of bone and other evidence. They removed approximately four inches of frozen topsoil that contained most of the evidence and placed it in five-gallon buckets to take back to the lab for further examination. Some of the remains were packaged in small cardboard boxes and placed inside paper bags.

The investigators again determined that the remains had not been burned at that site. They also concluded that the person who had dumped the remains there had made no attempt to bury them.

Davis's subsequent analysis of the skeletal remains from the three locations indicated that they were from three people—people whose flesh had been burned off their bodies. But identifying those people wouldn't be easy, if it could be done at all. Their bones had been so fragmented and destroyed by the intense heat it would prove to be impossible to reconstruct their skeletons. It was even hard figuring out the age, height, sex, or ancestry of the victims. All Davis knew for sure was that none of the victims was a child. He also estimated that they were all over the age of eighteen.

He also knew that one of the victims found near the house on North Willow Street had had orthopedic surgery to the mandible.

The interview with Larry continued as they drove to the dump sites. Larry explained that he would purposely pick up girls he didn't know. There were a few occasions that he went out hunting but couldn't find prey. Contradicting his first story, Larry now said Harry Cannon was with him the night he killed Barbara Williams. The three of them

were smoking crack and partying, and both he and
Harry had sex with her. But Harry left before he
killed Barbara. He said Harry had no idea what
happened to her.

During this conversation Larry said the buckets
he used to cart the bones and ashes around were
his mom's white frosting buckets from when she
worked at a Kroger's supermarket.

It was nearly ten-thirty in the morning when
they arrived at the site where Larry dumped the
bones and ashes of one of his victims. The area was
along a levee at the Mackinaw River in rural
Tremont near Robin Hood Lane, where he had
lived when he was a boy. Larry and Hoyle got out
of Taylor's car and got into Deputy O'Neill's sport
utility squad car. O'Neill and Deputy Dave Wilson
had arrived together to videotape the scene.

O'Neill drove down the levee and Wilson oper-
ated the video camera as Larry told his story.

He explained that when he got to the site, he
parked along the side of the road and walked
down into the woods, following a path he had
known about from his childhood. He walked quite
a distance, carrying the buckets, before he started
dumping the remains along the trail. He didn't
dump any in the water. Although he didn't remember which day of the week it was, he did
remember that it was the third girl he killed, and
the first one he burned. The first girl he killed was
the one he dumped by Tremont in the cornfield.
She was later identified as Sabrina Payne. The
second girl he killed was Barbara Williams. Her
body was dumped at the Evans place.

One of the detectives asked what made him quit burning the bodies.

"It was raining the night I killed the last girl," he said. "And I didn't burn the one before that because my grandmother was coming over the next day."

At that point he again explained his process for burning the bodies. He made sure the fire was very hot; then he let them burn all day to ensure that they were thoroughly burned. After they were burned, he was easily able to crush the pieces of the charred bone in his hands.

It was almost eleven when they headed out for dump site number two—a cornfield south of Augustin Road at Mud Creek Bridge in Tremont Township. As they approached Augustin Road, Larry pointed out the turn he took to get to the spot. When they got close to the field where Sabrina was dumped, Larry directed police to the bridge he drove across to get to the cornfield. Then he told them he dumped her a few rows in and pointed to the place where investigators recovered her body. Police then had Larry explain what happened as Wilson videotaped his confession. When he finished, Wilson and O'Neill drove back to videotape the scene.

Next they went to King Road, off Wildlife Road, in rural Hopedale, Tazewell County, where Larry disposed of Linda Neal's body. Larry couldn't determine the exact dump site because the road had been damaged by recent flooding from the Mackinaw River. As they drove down Wildlife Road, Larry showed police where he had thrown Linda's clothes out the window of his Blazer. Again police videotaped Larry's statement. Then after letting Larry urinate on the side of the road, the group left for North Valley View Road in Edwards, the place he dumped Barbara Williams. Larry rode with Taylor and Hoyle to the dump site.

As they drove, Hoyle talked to Larry about a variety of subjects, some unrelated to the investigation. They talked about prayer and how Larry had been spending his time in jail. He said he prayed for the families of the victims every day. And he told Hoyle he felt especially bad about the second to last girl he murdered, because she had cried and told him she had eight kids. It upset him to take a mother away from her kids.

Larry then began to talk about his own family. Crying, Larry told Hoyle he was sorry he had upset his mother so much, because she had always been a good mother to him and his brother. But his dad wasn't worth crap, until he got older and tried to get Larry off crack. Larry said he started doing drugs to fit in with his dad. Larry mentioned the influence he had on his nieces and nephews and said he hoped they learned from his mistakes.

Larry told Hoyle he had been scamming money from his grandmother. He said every time he asked her for money, she always wanted him to show her a receipt. So he bought a receipt book and started making out fake receipts to show her so he could get money for crack. He said police should be able to match a receipt to each day that one of the girls was killed.

Thinking about his mom, Larry again asked that police not tear up the pond he had built for her.

"But if you have to tear it up, at least don't kill the fish," he said, adding that there were thousands of dollars' worth of fish in the pond.

Hoyle told him that police had already contacted the Department of Natural Resources (DNR) to handle the fish.

"Are you going to tear up the pond?" Larry asked.

"I don't see the need to, at this point, but I can't be sure," Hoyle said.

As they went by the exit that led to the jail, Larry gave police directions to the place he dumped Barbara Williams's body. He said he drove by the jail and down Taylor Road with her body in the front seat of his Blazer. He intended to dump her in a different spot, but again, he said, he got spooked when a cop followed him down the road. So when the cop turned in to Wildlife Prairie State Park, he freaked out and dumped her body as soon as he could. He didn't realize at the time that he had dumped her so close to the house where the parents of his ex-girlfriend lived. After dumping Barbara's body, Larry did what he did every time he disposed of one of his victims—he went home and drank a fifth of Canadian Superior whiskey.

Before they got to the dump site, Larry asked Hoyle if he could make a videotape for his mother so he could apologize to her for what he had done.

Hoyle said he didn't think it would be a problem, but he had to check with his supervisor first.

They arrived at the dump site and Larry pointed out the location where he left Barbara's body. When Hoyle told him he was about a hundred yards away from where her body was discovered, he said he had been really drunk that night. Larry was again asked to give a videotaped statement. He agreed but asked that his face not be shown.

"When I dumped her, I was driving my Blazer, and she was in the front passenger seat," Larry said, adding that he transported all the bodies in his Blazer.

Blaming her death on the drugs, Larry said he never would have done any of the things he did without the drugs. He said he had oral and vaginal sex with her before he killed her.

"The drugs made me want to kill her," he said. "I never would've done these things without the drugs. I heard the voices in my head, but I never acted on them until I was using drugs. When I killed the first one, it was an accident. But after her, I'd plan to hunt and kill a girl. I could control the voices, except when I used drugs."

Larry next took the detectives to Taggert Road, where he disposed of the body of Brenda Erving. On the way he told them about being a member of Threw's Fishing Club in the early 1990s. Actually, he said he gained access to the club on his mother's boyfriend's membership. The fishing club, which had since shut down, had been located about three miles south of the area where Brenda's body had been discovered. He also shared his love for fishing for bass at the Banner Marsh State Fish & Wildlife Area, about twenty-five miles southwest of Peoria. And he talked about falling through the ice on the Mackinaw River, near Tremont, when he was about fifteen.

Soon the conversation took a more gruesome turn, and Larry talked about cleaning his bathroom twenty times with bleach and a scrub brush to get rid of the blood. He said there was a lot of blood from one of the girls that he put facedown on the bathroom floor. He used to leave them in his bathroom until he burned them or dumped their bodies.

When they arrived at the site, Wilson got into the car with Taylor, Hoyle, and Larry. Once again, Larry described on videotape what happened. Larry told police that Brenda was the girl who stabbed him in the chest. Although he didn't remember her injuries, he said his DNA was probably under her fingernails because she scratched him on the chest. He wasn't sure how she got the injury to her head, but he said he probably hit her with his fists.

Right after she was dead, he got her out of his house and into his Blazer. When he dumped her body, Larry said, he dropped some lottery tickets on the ground, but he picked them up. He was familiar with the area, which was the Zone, because he used to party there. He later burned Brenda's clothes, but he had a hard time burning her red raincoat.

* * *

The police left the Taggert Road site and headed to the Kickapoo Creek Road dump site. The detectives stopped at McDonald's on the way and bought Larry two double cheeseburgers and a Coke. As they drove to the location, Larry talked about a trip he took to Jamaica with a friend in the early 1980s. He spent about five days there, and on the trip home, he swallowed eight balloons of cocaine and smuggled them back into the United States.

The group arrived at the site a little after one-thirty. It was located on a bend in the creek across from the old Aspen Skil Hill, between Farmington and Pottstown Roads. Again, when they arrived at the scene, Wilson got in the car with Larry so he could videotape his statements.

Larry went to this location on three separate occasions in the late summer or early fall to dump the remains of three of the girls that he had burned. He went to the creek where there was a concrete pad and dumped the bones and ashes of two of them in the river. He sprinkled the remains of the third victim along a trail to the right of the spot where he disposed of the first two. He carried their remains in six of his mom's white frosting buckets, which he threw into the creek.

"Can we identify any of the girls from their remains?" one of the detectives asked.

"No. I made sure of that," Larry said. "The biggest pieces would be pieces of vertebrae, because they were too hard to burn and I couldn't crush them."

After Taylor and O'Neill videotaped the scene, they all left the Kickapoo Creek Road site for Larry's house. On the way to his house, Larry was very quiet and didn't really speak at all. The only thing he asked was that police keep trying to keep the media away. So Hoyle called Lieutenant Greskoviak to relay Larry's request.

When they arrived at the Bright residence, Larry pointed out the side of his mom's yard where he threw some of his victims' jewelry. He also showed police the metal cauldron that he had used to burn their clothing, as well as the two burn pits on the west side of the house.

Inside his house Larry showed police the hole in the wall that one of the girls made trying to escape. Then he showed them the window that another girl broke during a struggle for her life. He indicated he kept the bodies of the dead girls in his bathroom, sometimes for up to one day. One time his mom came into his house to talk to him and she had no idea there was a dead body in his bathroom.

Once outside again, Larry was concerned about the media, so he asked police if they could cover his face. So one of them went back inside and brought out a small blue tarp that he put over Larry's face. Larry then directed police to the area next to a shed where he filled in some tire tracks with victims' bone fragments and ashes. Then he took them to the garage, where he left the shovel he used to remove the ashes and bones from the fire pits.

After they finished up at Larry's house, the police drove him back to the Kickapoo Creek Road site so they could get a better idea of where he dumped the remains of the three women. On the way Larry said that there were two other dump sites that he had not mentioned to them.

When they arrived at the Kickapoo Creek site, police had Larry get out of the car and lead them down the path to where he dumped the remains, while O'Neill videotaped the area. Larry described walking down the creek and onto a concrete slab that was typically used for erosion control. He again explained that was where he dumped the remains of two of the women he burned. Then he pointed out the area on the ground where he threw the remains of the other woman.

When they finished up at that location, police went to the dump site in Norwood. On the way Larry told them he dumped the remains when he was babysitting an Alzheimer's patient for a woman named Sharon. The remains he dumped at Sharon's, as well as at his grandmother's house, were bones and ashes he had missed or dropped when he made the initial dumps.

At Sharon's house Larry got out of the car and pointed out where he had dumped the cremated remains. O'Neill videotaped the scene, and police could actually see the bits of burned bones and ashes on the ground.

The next stop was Larry's grandmother's house. When the group arrived, Larry's mother, grandmother, aunt, and uncle were there. Larry said he didn't want to see any of them, so one of the detectives explained the situation to Shirley. She agreed to leave until police were finished. After she left, Larry pointed out where he had dumped the remains. The police again could actually see the pieces of charred bone.

Wrapping up at his grandmother's, the detectives took Larry back to the Peoria County Jail, where they took photos and video of the stab marks and scratches on his chest. When they finished, they took him back to the Tazewell County Jail, where he was being held.

12

When they got back to the jail, Hoyle and Taylor escorted Larry to the interview room to continue talking to him.

After reminding him that his Miranda rights were still in effect, Hoyle told Larry that he was going to show him the photographs of the dead and missing women so he could identify them. For Larry, this was the worst part of the process.

Hoyle first showed Larry pictures of the four missing women. Larry said he tried to block them from his mind, but he thought he recognized one of them. He said he thought her name was Tammy. Then Hoyle showed him pictures of all the dead and missing women. When he came to the photo of Frederickia Brown, whose body was dumped outside Hanna City, Larry said she wasn't one of his.

Hoyle then started going through the photos, one by one. He showed Larry the picture of Frederickia Brown again.

"Not mine," Larry repeated.

The next picture Hoyle showed Larry was of Brenda Erving. Hoyle reminded Larry where she had been dumped.

"Yes," Larry said.

He said he didn't kill Wanda Jackson. But after seeing the photos of three of the four missing women—Tammy Walls, Laura Lollar, and Shaconda Thomas—he admitted to murdering them. The only missing woman he did not recognize was Shirley Trapp-Carpenter.

"Based on the information we have on these girls, do you think you're responsible for Shirley Trapp?" Hoyle asked.

"Yeah, probably if she was reported missing," he said. "I just didn't recognize that picture at all."

Hoyle showed Larry a picture of Sabrina Payne and said she was the woman found in the cornfield. Larry remembered her from the dump site, but he added she looked different in her photo. He also remembered Linda Neal from her dump site, not from her photo.

"Did you ever see anything on the news about the missing girls?" Hoyle asked.

"When the news came on, I changed the channel."

"Did you change it because you had done it?"

"Yeah, sure."

Toward the end of the interview, Larry told them that he had buried part of a victim's arm behind his grandmother's house, but he hadn't told them about it earlier. He said they'd have a hard time finding it because he tried to cover it up.

As the interview wound down, Larry told the

detectives he wanted to speak with them the next day to give them more details. He also asked again if he could make a video for his mother. The detectives agreed and left the room so Larry could speak to his mom on the tape.

"Mom, I just wanted to say I'm sorry. I had to tell them what I did to save you from more sorrow. You're tearing yourself up, Mom. I'm so sorry to the families of the girls that I killed. I want them to know I'm so sorry. And I pray every day for their daughters' souls. Mom, I love you with all my heart," he said, sobbing. "I'm so sorry that I turned out to be such a bad son. I just wanted to say I love you, Mom. And I told Mr. Borsberry I didn't want him to represent me anymore, to save you the money, Mom. You don't need to spend that. You got more important things to do. I just hope you forgive me, Mom. And I love you with all my heart. And I'm so sorry, Mom."

Sobbing even harder, Larry yelled out to the detectives that he was finished. Before they left the interview room, Larry asked for a new pair of shoes because his had gotten muddy during the day. When Hoyle turned Larry back over to the COs, he asked them to give Larry some new shoes. They agreed to do so.

The next morning, around nine-thirty, Hoyle and Taylor met with Larry again. Larry waived his right to have an attorney present and signed a waiver saying he wanted to talk to police despite his attorney's advice to the contrary.

With the formalities out of the way, Hoyle asked

Larry if there was anything else he had neglected to tell them about the murders. Larry said he remembered two more spots where he dumped some remains. He said there were more remains at a dump site at a house in Tremont, as well as at his grandmother's house. He said he buried the partial arm on a hillside near an old refrigerator behind her house.

He described throwing jewelry and small pieces of bones from the side of his mom's house on Starr Court onto the baseball diamond at the Knights of Columbus hall. He said the bones didn't even make it to the infield. He added that the grass had been mowed several times since he tossed the bones.

"Was anyone around when you burned the bodies?" Hoyle asked.

"One time there were workers from a fence company working on a fence in my side yard while I was burning," he said.

The conversation then turned to Larry's previous claim that he had AIDS. Despite telling police during an earlier interview that he had been infected with the virus, he now said he wasn't sure and he didn't want to know. He also declined to allow police access to his medical records so they could determine the truth about his health.

When police asked him about using his Blazer to pick up all the girls, as he told them earlier, he changed his story again. This time he said he picked up the last two, who had been identified as Linda Neal and Brenda Erving, in his Dodge Dakota truck. Larry told police he sold his Blazer because he wanted to get rid of it because of what he did. However, he wasn't looking to sell it until some guy approached him about buying it and offered him $500, he said.

Changing the subject, Hoyle asked why the women were nude when he dumped them.

"It was hard to put their clothes back on them. And I freaked out," he said, getting upset. "For the record, to the families, I'm so sorry for what I've done."

The interview focused on a number of areas, including Larry's proclivity for renting porn.

"Can you explain why you rented porn when you did?" Hoyle asked. "Because it seems that you weren't renting movies when you killed the girls."

"I guess I got a sexual addiction. I don't know."

Hoyle also asked Larry about the sex toys that he had, because investigators had taken large dildos from his house during two separate searches. Larry said he used sex toys on the girls before he killed them, but he burned them after the girls were dead. That meant there wouldn't be any DNA on the ones the police had found in his house. He explained that he bought a new dildo for each girl at Swingers World, a store that sold adult novelty items. Larry said he also burned about ten sex tapes, none of which was homemade.

"I didn't use the dildos on the girls after they were dead. I never did anything to them after they were dead," he said. "Someone told me the papers said I did something after they were dead, but that's not true."

As the interview continued, Larry again explained the process he used to burn the bodies. This time he said that as the fire burned, he used a shovel to chop at the wood and bodies. He added that he might have used a little gasoline on the fire to get it started, but he never used an accelerant on the bodies.

Hoyle then asked Larry whether any of the girls defecated, because it was common for people to defecate while they were being strangled. Larry said Tammy did. He knew it was Tammy, because, for some reason, her head didn't burn.

"She was looking right at me," he said, crying.

"Do you remember that another girl also defecated?" Hoyle asked, referring to Brenda Erving.

"Yeah, I remember. She got a little on the seat of my Blazer, but I cleaned it up really good."

Larry was then asked to look at more photos of the women. When he saw the photo of Linda Neal, he said she might be one of his victims, but he just couldn't be sure because he tried to block it all out of his mind. As he had done previously, he denied murdering Wanda Jackson. And he said he didn't remember Frederickia Brown, although earlier he said she wasn't one of his.

Again he remembered Sabrina Payne, not from her photo, but from the place where he had dumped her. And he didn't remember Shirley Trapp-Carpenter, Brenda Erving, or Shaconda Thomas. He did recognize Laura Lollar and said she was the second to the last girl he killed. He recalled that he felt sorry for her because she told him about her kids as she was dying.

When Hoyle showed Larry a picture of Tammy Walls, Larry said, "That's Tammy."

"Why do you know her name and not the names of the other girls?" Hoyle asked.

"I had her driver's license, and I burned it," he said.

"She was the one whose head was looking at you," Hoyle said. "What did you do with the head?"

"I prayed . . . and then I built another fire."

The detectives then asked Larry if he had any questions for them, and he brought up the subject of Cathy Bishop's baby, Suzanna. He said he didn't kill her, but he'd say he did if it meant her body wouldn't have to be exhumed. He told police he tried to save her life by performing CPR. Hoyle said he didn't want Larry to confess to something he didn't do. Hoyle then asked him about the baby Marie Waters lost. It happened when Larry and Marie were living together in Canton, Illinois.

"Were you scared you caused the baby's death?" Hoyle asked.

"Yeah," he said.

"Do you think you caused her death?" After a few seconds, Larry said, "She was hitting me, and I was defending myself."

"Where did you hit Marie?"

"I hit her one time in the chest by the shoulder," he said. "She hit me a few times. When I went to the hospital and found out she lost the baby, I freaked out. I know I didn't cause the death of the baby, it was cocaine. I was just defending myself. If I didn't do it directly, I did it indirectly by getting the cocaine."

However, Larry explained, he didn't get the cocaine for Marie, he got it for himself and she smoked it. Then she called one of her friends, who brought over a lot of cocaine that night. They also did a lot of mushrooms the night she lost the baby. Neither he nor Marie was ever questioned by the police about the baby's death.

The questioning then turned to the unlawful restraint case, and Hoyle asked Larry how much of it was true. Larry said Vickie Bomar's account of what happened was pretty accurate, and he was going to plead guilty to the charge. He said he ultimately let her go because he just didn't feel like killing her, and he'd hoped she'd tell police about him.

Finally Hoyle asked Larry what he had been planning to do when he and Wilson arrived at his house to arrest him.

"I was in my mom's kitchen and I had a knife. I was just going to come at you and make you do something, but then I heard my mom's car pull up," he said. "And I knew she'd jump in front of me and I didn't want her to do that."

As they were questioning Larry, Taylor and Hoyle were notified that Larry's lawyer, Joseph Borsberry, had arrived to see him. They left the interview room. When they reentered the room, they told Larry that his attorney was there to talk to him. Larry didn't want to see him, though, because he didn't want his mother to have to pay any additional charges. The detectives relayed Larry's message to Borsberry, who agreed to talk to him for free. After speaking with Larry, Borsberry told police his client would continue to speak with them.

When Taylor and Hoyle went back into the interview room, Larry first asked for some Tylenol, which he received. Then Hoyle told him that as the search went on, the detectives might have more questions for him. Larry wanted to know if they were going to be able to find the bones on the property in Tremont. He suggested police take him to the location so he could show them exactly where he threw the remains. He explained that he disposed of a leg bone and pieces of vertebrae, which were about eight or ten inches long, at that location.

A little before twelve-thirty, Hoyle and Taylor took Larry to the Tremont property so he could show them where the bones were. On the way Larry pointed out various places where he had spent time as a child, like the hills outside Tremont where he went sledding. He also told police how he used to get high with his friends across from Tremont High School.

As they got closer to the property, Larry told police it was his "thinking place," where he would go to just sit and think. When they arrived, Larry said that when he dumped the bones, he had walked down by the river to find just the right spot. But he said it would be easier to get there through the gate. However, the gate was locked, so the group walked around it. At one point they had to cross about thirty yards of frozen water. Larry finally directed them to a spot by a tree where, he said, he set the bones down. But a search of the area turned up nothing.

As police were trying to find the remains of the missing women, the coroner's inquest into Linda Neal's death was being held. A jury had been impaneled to determine the cause and manner of her death.

When the inquest got under way, Deputy Sergeant Darryl Stoecker, a detective with the Tazewell County Sheriff's Office, was questioned by Tazewell County coroner Dennis Conover.

Stoecker told the jury that on September 25, 2004, he was called to a secluded wooded area at the end of King Road, off Wildlife Road, in rural Hopedale. Two campers had found a body after ten that night and had immediately called police. When Stoecker arrived, he discovered the nude body of a black woman lying faceup in the grass, just off the road. The minute he saw her body, he said, he knew she had been murdered.

The sergeant said that a suspect had been charged with her murder a few hours before the inquest began.

Conover then told the jury that the medical examiner had determined that Linda, who had a small amount of alcohol, as well as cocaine in her system when she died, had been strangled to death.

After hearing the evidence, the jury reached a verdict of homicide. Linda's father, stepmother, sister, and other family members, who had attended the hearing, were glad that the man who took her life was behind bars. They praised authorities for swiftly solving her murder and apparently ending the nightmare for the families of the other murdered and missing women.

Just as police completed the search in Tremont, Hoyle got a cell phone call notifying him that

Larry had to be at the Peoria County Jail by five for video court. So they wrapped things up and took Larry back to jail.

During his court appearance, Larry tried to plead guilty to murdering Linda Neal, the only woman he had been charged with murdering. But Peoria County judge Albert Purham rejected his plea and appointed a public defender to represent him. Purham warned Larry that whatever he said could be used against him.

During the hearing Purham asked Larry if he wanted a public defender.

"No, I would just like to plead guilty, sir," Larry responded.

Purham asked Larry two more times if he wanted an attorney, but each time Larry said he wanted to plead guilty. Finally the judge appointed John Riddle, a public defender, to represent Larry during the hearing.

SA Kevin Lyons told the judge that Larry had confessed to murdering eight women, and had told police where they could find the remains of the four women who were still missing. Larry had only been charged with killing Linda, because his DNA matched DNA found on her body. Lyons said he planned to seek indictments against Larry in the future for murdering seven other women. Police didn't believe Larry had anything to do with the murders of Wanda Jackson and Frederickia Brown.

Before the judge ruled on bond for Larry, Lyons detailed some of what investigators thought had happened to Linda before she was murdered. Lyons told the court that Larry picked her up near the southern edge of Peoria; then he took her to get some drugs for a friend. After she got the drugs, Larry drove her to a local bar to deliver the drugs. Then he took Linda back to his place, where they drank and had sex.

When they finished, Larry grabbed her by the throat and, using a technique he knew, strangled her until she was dead, Lyons said. Larry then took one of his leather shoelaces, tied it around Linda's neck, dragged her body to his vehicle, and drove to a deserted levee near the Mackinaw River, close to Hopedale. He dumped some of Linda's belongings a mile or two away, then later burned both his shoelaces so he wouldn't be caught. Lyons said semen found on Linda matched a hair sample provided by Larry.

Lyons told the court that Larry had some connection to each of the places where a body was discovered. For example, Lyons said, Brenda Erving's body was found a few miles north of Farmington, close to a spot where Larry used to party when he was younger. And Sabrina Payne's body was dumped close to where Larry used to live.

Lyons said investigators were still trying to piece together some human remains found on the Brights' property, as well as on some five other locations around the area. He told the judge that Larry led police to the places where he dumped the women's remains. During his statement Lyons never gave a motive for the murders, although he said they weren't racially motivated.

After Lyons gave his statement, the judge granted his motion to hold Bright without bond.

"No amount of bond would protect the safety of the people of the state of Illinois," Purham said.

Because Larry had only been charged with one murder, prosecutors couldn't seek the death penalty against him at that point. But that could change if more murder charges were filed against him. Prosecutors were planning to take the case to a grand jury as soon as possible.

At a press conference after the hearing, Lyons said that some of Larry's friends said he had some kind of attraction to African-American women. He was also watching a lot of pornography that involved African-American women.

Lyons also told reporters that Larry killed the eight women at his home, and burned four of them in a pit in his backyard. Lyons explained that Bright burned the bodies for up to two days, crushed the bones, shoveled them into a bucket, and dumped them in various places in Peoria and Tazewell Counties.

"All the body parts are without tissue, and they are mostly in pieces and charred," Lyons said at the press conference. "Perhaps we can find some mitochondrial DNA, if it is something more than calcified bone."

Shirley Bright was heartbroken, not to mention incredulous, that her son was responsible for murdering eight women. She just couldn't believe that Larry had committed such horrific crimes. The son she knew could never have killed anyone, and she placed the blame on the drugs and painkillers he was taking for his back injury.

Shirley and her husband, Gary, separated because he abused alcohol and marijuana, and in 1981, she filed for divorce in Tazewell County on the grounds of "extreme and repeated mental cruelty." At that point he disappeared from Larry's life. But as Larry got older, Gary started seeing Larry again because he wanted a pal. It was Gary who had turned Larry on to marijuana.

Then, several years before he was charged with murder, Larry injured his back and had to have two surgeries. Because he was in constant pain, Larry abused Vicodin and other painkillers, Shirley said. And when Gary died of cancer in 1998, Larry used alcohol and cocaine to dull the pain of his dad's death.

After visiting Larry in jail, Shirley told the local media that her son was very sorry that he had killed eight women, but he didn't tell her why he did it. And Shirley didn't want to ask him. Shirley added that she didn't think the murders were motivated by race, even though Larry was white and the women were black.

Shirley said she and her family were deeply sorry for what her son had done, and they were praying for the families of the victims.

Several days after the court hearing, Hoyle got word that Larry wanted to talk to the detectives again. He and Taylor met with him at the Tazewell County Jail. Hoyle began the interview by telling Larry that the investigators had to dig under his mom's pond to make sure there was nothing there. Larry expressed concern about the fish and

Hoyle said they were being cared for by the state's Department of Natural Resources. Larry was also worried about the tractor that was being used to excavate an area near his shed. He was concerned that it was being driven across his mother's yard, but Hoyle told him it wasn't. Larry said he just wanted to make it easy on his mom.

During the interview Larry started to describe an area behind Dick Wolf's lumberyard in Morton where he dumped some of the belongings of one of his victims. Wolf was Larry's former employer. He said he threw some clothing, a pair of white high-top tennis shoes, and some jewelry on top of the building. He put them there because he had to work that day.

"I have something else to tell you guys, but I was hoping to watch the Super Bowl first," he said.

"We have to ask about that," Hoyle said.

"I didn't even want to mention it, because it's such a petty request."

What he wanted to tell them was that he put Tammy Walls's skull in a rural pond outside Tremont. Although he couldn't give them directions, he'd be able to take them to the pond, he said. Larry put the skull in the pond because it didn't burn, and when he put it in the water, it still had meat, hair, part of the neck, and a few vertebrae attached to it. He said he carried the head to the pond in a large shoe box, which he tossed out onto the road when he left.

Hoyle then questioned Larry about some unsolved homicides in Decatur and Rockford, Illinois, but Larry said he didn't have anything to do with them. He said he had gone to concerts in

Rockford and partied at bars afterward, but he didn't know anyone there. He only murdered the eight girls he already told them about.

"I put all my cards on the table, because I couldn't live with what I done," he said.

At one point in his life, Larry tried to commit suicide, and Hoyle wanted to know why. He said it was because of his ex-wife Cathy's son. Seven years after they were divorced, Larry said, Cathy told him he was the father of her son. He liked the idea of being a dad and started doing things with the kid. But then they did a DNA test and Larry found out the boy really wasn't his. That's when he became suicidal.

"Did you ever try to commit suicide after killing one of the girls or during the time you were killing them?" Hoyle asked.

"I wanted to, but I didn't," he said. "I knew God would forgive me for killing the girls, but he wouldn't forgive me for killing myself."

Hoyle then began questioning Larry about the murder of Linda Fields in Racine, Wisconsin. The circumstances surrounding her death were strikingly similar to what happened to the girls Larry admitted he killed. And he had lived near the place where her body was dumped. Larry said he had heard a little about it, but he really didn't know much. He said his friend George Jamison had mentioned it to him, because they had partied with her. When Hoyle told Larry that the police in Racine had found DNA on her body, he said that was good, because then they'd know it wasn't him when the tests were done.

"Killing ten girls isn't a lot worse than killing eight," Hoyle said.

Larry agreed, but he said it was tearing him up that police thought he had killed Cathy's baby.

"That's totally not true," he said.

"You have to admit, there were strange circumstances around the baby's death," Hoyle said. "And why didn't you show up to take the polygraph tests that were scheduled during the investigation?"

"I talked to an attorney and he said not to take the tests. He told me to call him if I was arrested," he said. "I know if I killed thirty girls, it wouldn't be any different than killing the eight."

"The same is true for the baby," Hoyle explained. "If you killed eight girls and a baby, it isn't a big difference."

But it was a big difference to Larry.

"I loved that little girl," he said. "She had health problems and wouldn't eat right. Cathy was the last one with the baby. She put her to bed. Then I heard a choking sound ten minutes later. The only thing I might have done was blowing too hard in her mouth."

Larry never once used the baby's name when he talked about her.

"Is there anything else you remember that you haven't told us?" Hoyle asked.

"On the second girl I told you about, Harry was there. I should have told you that at the beginning."

"Why didn't you?"

"Because he didn't do anything. The only thing he didn't do was call the cops," Larry said. "He told me to leave him out of it, and he gave me quite a bit of cocaine to keep me quiet."

"Did you ever use that against Harry to get more cocaine?"

"Yeah, twice. And he asked me why I was doing that to him, because he didn't do anything."

Explaining the death of the second girl, who was Barbara Williams, Larry said they were all doing some heavy crack when she started having a seizure or something. He and Harry thought she was dead, but then she started to come out of it. Harry told Larry he had to do something, which, in Larry's mind, meant "kill her." Although he was sure now Harry meant "help her."

"Harry denied ever being in your house," Hoyle said.

"Well, he was a few times."

"Was Harry in your house with any other girls?"

"I remember he was there with a girl who went by the name 'Sweet Chocolate,'" he said. "She was a black girl, slim, maybe five feet two or so, and about twenty-five years old. She had big tits and a gold tooth and a purple hair weave. She hung out along the north end of Peoria, along Madison."

"Do you remember talking to her about herself?"

Larry said he never talked to any of the girls about their personal lives. All he remembered about his time with Sweet Chocolate was that they smoked a lot of dope and had sex. Then he took her back to Madison. Coincidentally, Linda Neal's street name was "Chocolate."

* * *

As the questioning continued, Larry told police that he never brought any white prostitutes to his house. He did pick up white women at bars, but they weren't prostitutes. When he said he was always alone when he picked up the black prostitutes, Hoyle asked him about his earlier allegation that George Jamison was with him when he picked up Linda Neal.

"That's not true," Larry said, adding that he wouldn't mind hanging George out to dry. "I lied to hang him, because I hated him, but now I'm trying to clear my conscience with God."

Curious about why Larry called in a tip on himself to the Crime Stoppers line, Hoyle asked him to talk about the events leading up to the call. Larry explained that he had let a few girls go, hoping they would go to the police and he'd get caught. But that didn't happen. So he made the call before killing the last two women.

That's why Larry let Tiffany Hughes go. Tiffany was the woman who told her story to the *Peoria Journal Star.* Larry said her story was bascially true. He said he started strangling her and she got away and locked herself in his bathroom. When she came out, he had a gun.

"Where's the gun now?" Hoyle asked.

According to Larry, it was at the bottom of the Illinois River. Larry got the gun, a Smith & Wesson .357, with a six-inch barrel and walnutlike handgrips, from a guy who also sold him cocaine. He refused to give the police the guy's name, because he had a family and didn't need any trouble.

Although Larry fired a box of shells down by the river, he never fired the gun in his house, and he never shot any of his victims. He finally got rid of the weapon because he was going to kill himself with it. In fact, a few times he put the barrel of the gun in his mouth with the hammer cocked. He couldn't bring himself to do it, though, because he was afraid of going to hell. He knew if he didn't get rid of the gun, something bad was going to happen, so he ditched it.

"I threw it in the Mackinaw River, off the west side of the bridge by the grove where I grew up," he said, apparently forgetting he just told police he threw it in the Illinois River.

Then Larry went back to his story about his encounter with Tiffany. While she was in the bathroom, he was in a fit of rage and kicked the door in. He later took the door off its hinges and burned it. Then he took the door off his closet and put it in the bathroom.

"You guys should have found the doorknob in the burn pile," he said.

Although he wanted to kill Tiffany, he let her go; he wanted it all to end.

"I struggled with myself when I was out looking for girls. I tried to talk myself out of it," he said. "But when I saw a girl, my mind changed, and the good guy was gone."

"Why did you start killing the girls?" Hoyle asked.

He said he wasn't exactly sure why he was doing the killings. Initially he thought it was because he found out he had AIDS. But then he said the people at the blood bank never really told him he had AIDS, he just assumed he did, because they wouldn't take his plasma anymore.

"Did all of this happen because Ernestine gave you AIDS?" Hoyle asked.

"I'm not sure."

"Why did you only kill black girls?"

"I did pick up some white prostitutes, but I had a fascination with black girls," he said.

Then Larry began telling the detectives that he had been sexually abused when he was young by a guy named Dave and a guy named Kenny, who lived in a trailer park in Morton, Illinois. Larry was also pretty sure Dave abused his brother, Jerry. It happened when Larry was in the fourth or fifth grade, and Dave was in his twenties. At first, Dave started giving Larry things; then Dave humped him when they were fully dressed. It got worse, and Dave finally penetrated him. Larry tried to block it all out of his mind, but he remembered the abuse when he was trying to figure out why he started murdering the women.

"The voice I hear in my head is Dave's voice," he said. "I wish I could remember his name, because something needs to happen to him."

During that time Larry said his mom worked a lot, and he was left alone to take care of Jerry. He said his mother worked at a Laundromat, and not at the truck stop in Tremont. Shirley was also unemployed for some time, and they stayed on public aid because she couldn't afford his asthma medication without it.

"Did you talk to anyone about what you [have done] since you talked to the police?" Hoyle asked.

Larry said he talked to his sister and his mother,

and he told them about being molested when he was a boy and about being gang-raped in prison.

"None of this happened because I couldn't get a girl," he said. "I never had a problem getting a girl to go out with. But I did have a problem with relationships, mostly because of the drugs. My relationship with Marie Waters ended because of the drugs. She was the one girl I was in love with, and I still love her."

At that point Hoyle and Taylor stepped out of the interview room for about fifteen minutes. When they returned, Larry started telling them again about Racine and Linda Fields. He said he and George had partied with a black girl and had sex with her. Then George left with her in his truck for quite a while. She was really wasted, and George had to help her to the truck.

"While we were with her, we basically raped her," he said. "When George left, he was only supposed to be gone for about thirty minutes to get more crack, but he didn't come back for a good two hours. Two days later is when I heard what happened to her, but I don't think George did it."

According to Larry, George always showed up at his house on Larry's payday with a little crack and a black prostitute. That's because George knew that once Larry took a hit, he wanted more, and then he'd spend his check on the crack.

Larry stayed in Racine for about three or four months. He left because he and George ripped a guy off for drugs and shot him in the process. He either sold the gun he used, a nine-millimeter

Beretta pistol, to another crack dealer or traded it for more crack. Then one day someone broke into Larry's house. When his neighbor, who witnessed the break-in, described the burglar to Larry, he thought it was the guy he ripped off. So he packed up everything he owned and got the hell out of Racine.

With the interview concluded, Hoyle told Larry they wanted him to take them to the dump sites in Tremont and Morton. On the way they stopped at a McDonald's and bought Larry two double cheeseburgers, fries, and a Coke. As they drove to Morton, Larry told police they'd find some of his victims' clothing there.

Again he asked about the welfare of the fish that had been in his pond. He wanted to know if the fish could be put in the pond at Swan Lake Cemetery, if his pond wasn't put back together. Hoyle said he'd have to ask someone higher up about that.

During the ride Larry said one of the reasons he wanted to get caught was that he believed he had ghosts living in his house. He said after he killed the first couple of girls, things started moving around his house on their own. He was so freaked out, he wanted to have his mother tear the house down.

"Did that have anything to do with you deciding to confess?" Hoyle asked.

"I decided to confess as soon as you told me about the bones you found at my house," Larry said. "I knew the jig was up."

When they got to Morton, Hoyle contacted the

owner of the property, who gave police permission to search the area and retrieve any evidence that might be there. Larry then showed the detectives where he had thrown the tennis shoes. Police were able to see what appeared to be her tennis shoes on the roof in the gutter. Larry said he had also thrown a bracelet and two rings on top of the roof. He got scared someone would find them; so a couple days later, he went back to get them. He climbed out onto the roof, but realizing it was too flimsy, he got down without retrieving them.

As they waited for the crime scene technician to arrive, Larry talked about his grandmother and how he felt bad for her because of what he did. He said he had always been there for her whenever she needed anything. Then Larry thanked Taylor and Hoyle for treating him with respect, which was more than he expected for what he had done.

Despite an extensive search, the investigators only recovered the size-8 Nike athletic shoe in the gutter on the roof. The search completed, the detectives loaded Larry back into the squad car and headed for the pond in which he had dumped the head of Tammy Walls. Larry wasn't quite sure how to get to the site, because he had been high on crack and drunk on whiskey when he made the trip the first time.

As they drove down Augustin Road in Tazewell, Larry thought they were in the right area, although he couldn't quite remember the location of the pond. He did remember that a friend took him there when Larry was looking for lily pads for his mother's pond. They approached one pond that Larry thought might be the one, but then he changed his mind and said he didn't think it was.

Hoyle explained to Larry how important it was for him to try and find the right pond, because his bosses were concerned that he was just playing games with them so he could drive around and smoke cigarettes.

"I'm not jerking you guys around," he said. "I'll know it when I see it."

Taylor then called Ronnie to see if he could provide better directions, but they still couldn't find the pond. So Taylor called Ronnie back and he agreed to meet them and lead them to the pond. When he arrived, he directed the police to the pond on Allentown Road. He told them that this pond and the pond on Augustin Road were the only two ponds he showed Larry when he was looking for lily pads. Police left the area without searching for the head.

On the way back to the Tazewell County Jail, Larry explained that when he got to the pond, he went for a swim before he threw Tammy's head in it. He said he wanted to check and make sure the pond was deep enough so the skull would never be found. Larry said he swam to the middle of the pond and dove down to touch the bottom. He estimated that it was about twenty feet deep.

After stopping at a Hardee's restaurant in Pekin, where they got Larry a combo meal for dinner, the detectives brought him back to the jail.

13

As news of Larry's arrest in connection with the murders hit the press, a thankful community began to wonder exactly how one man was able to murder and get rid of eight women right in the middle of a residential neighborhood.

Maybe it was because one side of the Brights' property on West Starr Court was hidden behind some trees, while the rest of the property sat behind a six-foot wooden privacy fence. Not only that, but there was very little light in the neighborhood at night, making it relatively easy for Larry to pretty much do whatever he wanted without being seen. And since Larry and his mom were always doing yard work, neighbors—if they saw him at all—probably thought he was lugging dirt from one place to another.

And if Shirley had no idea what her beloved son was up to, it was no surprise that his neighbors were oblivious to Larry's heinous acts. Although some said it defied logic that no one in the area ever smelled burning flesh, maybe it was because no one really cared enough to notice. After all, it wasn't like Larry was a known psychopath.

Like area residents, authorities also wanted to know how Larry had been able to literally get away with murder for so long. So they began talking to Larry's neighbors to see if they had seen or heard anyone at the Bright residence digging, burning, or doing anything else out of the ordinary.

One neighbor, Allan, said although he had lived in his home for forty years, he had only seen Larry on a couple occasions. Recently Allan had seen him with a wheelbarrow near some large evergreen trees, but he never saw Larry or anyone else digging or burning anything on the Bright property.

Another neighbor told police neither he nor his wife knew the Bright family, and they had never seen anything ususual going on at their place. However, he did remember seeing Larry working near his privacy fence in the fall of 2004.

Police also talked to the Brights' next-door neighbor Ray, who said Larry and Shirley had moved to the neighborhood about a year and a half earlier. Ray's recollection seemed to differ from Jennifer's; she thought the Brights had moved in four years earlier.

Ray said the previous owners had lived in the house on West Starr Court for thirty-seven years. Ray had visited those people on numerous occasions and said they had an electric fireplace in the house. He told police over the years they had burned brush on their property and they had installed the privacy fence and the barn-shaped shed in the backyard.

Ray explained that Shirley knew the previous owners—she worked with one member of the family—and bought the house from them in July or August 2003. Soon after moving in, Larry dug a pond behind the house for the fish he brought with him from the McClure residence.

In July or August of 2004, Ray and Shirley agreed to split the cost of having a tree removed that was straddling both properties. After the tree removal company cut down the tree, they stacked the wood near the back of the Brights' fence and they chipped the limbs into mulch. Then Larry spread the mulch around the trees and the bushes in his yard. The Brights also had a load of rock delivered, which Larry distributed around the bushes on the west side of the house.

Ray told police for a time Larry drove a dark gray Chevrolet Blazer, but he bought a light blue Dodge pickup truck in the spring of 2004. He said the Blazer disappeared in the fall of 2004, and he hadn't seen it since. According to Ray, Larry would leave the house in the truck several times a day for short periods of time. But Ray and his wife were sound sleepers and they never had any idea who came and went at night.

Next police talked to John, whose wife, Joyce, helped Vickie get away from Larry. John told police that he usually left for work around seven-thirty in the morning and got home between six and nine at night. His wife left for work a little after six in the morning and got home between six-thirty and eight-thirty in the evening.

John said after the news of the murders had been reported in the media, he and Joyce tried to remember whether they had observed anything ususual at the Brights' house. They said they never saw Larry burning anything or digging up the yard. But there was the incident of the black woman running away from Larry's house in July 2004. He said the woman asked Joyce for help, but she didn't want her to call the police, so Joyce drove her home.

Investigators also wanted to talk to Matthew, who was the sixteen-year-old grandson of John and Joyce. Matthew called police to tell them he saw Larry dump some kind of material near the pine trees next to his grandparents' house. Police went to his house in Pekin to speak with him.

Matthew said he lived with his grandparents during the summer of 2004, and beginning August 19, he spent the weekends with them after school started. Matthew told police he had spoken to Larry a number of times, and Larry even offered him a summer job digging fishponds. But when Larry told him it took six to eight hours to dig a pond, Matthew said he wasn't interested.

During the summer that he lived with his grandparents, Matthew saw Larry and Shirley regularly working in the yard. During the week and on the weekends, Larry did some landscaping, including spreading dirt and mulch under the pine trees on his property—all of the work was done during the day. Matthew said that from June to August 2004, Larry almost always had a fire burning from about noon to eight at night. It seemed Larry burned a lot of leaves and brush he collected from his property.

* * *

With Larry in custody, authorities heaped praise on the women who had been lucky enough to meet up with Larry and escape with their lives. If it hadn't been for the information they provided, catching Larry might have been more difficult.

State's Attorney Kevin Lyons said Larry's name surfaced many times in the more than one thousand tips the task force received. Because of those tips, investigators were able to locate about a half-dozen prostitutes who told them about their harrowing experiences at the hands of Larry Bright, Lyons said.

And when Larry's name came up in connection with the murder of Linda Neal, customers at a bar that Linda often frequented identified Larry as the man who was with her the night she disappeared.

Although the families of the eight women Larry admitted to killing were glad that he had confessed, the families of Wanda Jackson and Frederickia Brown were left to wonder what had happened to their loved ones.

Time and again Larry denied having anything to do with the deaths of those two women. Peoria County sheriff Mike McCoy, who admitted there was a chance that Larry was lying, said the task force was continuing to develop evidence to solve those murders.

On the last day of January, Detective Taylor got word that Larry wanted to talk to police again. So he and Hoyle went to the Tazewell County Jail to meet with him.

Larry wanted to clarify his previous statements about what had happened in Racine regarding George Jamison and the black prostitute who partied with them. Although Larry had implied that he had never seen the woman again after she left with George, he changed his story and said he saw her a week later. Larry said the woman, whose name was Jackay, showed up the next week and partied with him and another woman.

"Two days after George left with the woman, I heard that a black prostitute had been found dead, but I didn't know who she was, or if George was involved," he said.

Larry next told police he also remembered where he put the last little bit of bones—pieces that had popped out of the pit when he was burning the victims—as well as some clothing. The bones he left out by West Jersey Township in Stark County, near the cemetery where his father was buried. After visting his father's grave to tell him what he had done, Larry left and drove to a little stand of trees on a street close to the cemetery, where he dumped the remains.

The clothes—pants, a pair of pink panties, and shoes—he disposed of near a creek in Knox County. He was driving toward Galesburg when he took the Knoxville exit and stopped on a nearby county road. He got out of the Blazer, walked a little way, and threw the clothes down by a creek. He said he put the panties in one of the shoes and wrapped the pants around both shoes.

The clothes belonged to the last girl he burned. He found them in the burn pile out by the tree when he was cleaning things up after he was first questioned by police. He wasn't sure why they didn't burn.

"We found a blond hair on a chain that we found in a burn pile at your house, and that's why we want to know about Bonnie Fife," Hoyle said.

"I didn't do anything to Bonnie. If I did, I'd tell ya."

"Did you ever throw any of the victims' stuff at any other work sites?"

"Yeah, I did. I threw some jewelry out at a barn I was tearing down with Dick Wolf's son, but I can't remember where," he said. "I remember I found a small bracelet on the ground by an evergreen, next to the pond. I don't know if it was one of theirs or whose it was. I put it in my mom's bathroom in a holder that holds brushes and things. I asked her about it, and she said it wasn't hers, but she thought it was a friend's."

Hoyle then asked Larry about throwing Tamara Walls's head in the pond. Larry had told police that he stood on the end of the diving board and threw the head out into the water. Larry thought he threw it underhanded and straight out in front of him. But he said he wasn't quite sure, because he had been really, really trashed.

Earlier that day, before talking to Larry, the detectives had driven to the pond off Allentown Road, where they saw the regulation fiberglass diving board and the dock that Larry had described. Larry asked if there was a wooden outhouse there, but Hoyle said there wasn't. That confused Larry because he was sure he had seen an outhouse by the pond. He was also pretty positive the pond was on Augustin Road, not Allentown Road, although he admitted the pond he showed police on Augustin looked too big. He remembered it was a smaller pond, and the dock sat up, off the water. There was also a lot of moss growing all around the pond.

The detectives then began questioning Larry about his blue Dodge Dakota truck. Hoyle asked how many girls he had picked up in it. Larry said possibly one, but he didn't think any, because he tried to keep it as clean as possible in case he ever got stopped by police. Then he added that he had picked up girls in the Dakota—just not any of the girls that he ultimately killed. In an earlier interview, Larry said he picked up a victim by Woody's Bar in the Dakota, but he never transported a body in it.

"What about the girl who got away?" Hoyle asked. "Was she in the blue truck?"

"Yeah, that might be one of the reasons I let her go," he said. "I'm really glad you caught me, because I don't think I would ever be able to stop unless I got rid of the drugs."

Then Larry began talking about the dead woman in Racine. He told the detectives that they'd be able to clear him if they compared his DNA to any DNA that was found on her body. However, Hoyle explained that just because his DNA wasn't there, it didn't mean he didn't do it. Larry understood just what they meant.

As far as Larry knew, police would only find his DNA on the one girl, meaning Linda Neal. He told the detectives they wouldn't even find his DNA on the girl who scratched him (Brenda Erving) because he cleaned under her fingernails with rubbing alcohol and a little knife.

"Did you move her after she was on the ground?" Hoyle asked.

He said he did, because some of his lottery tickets fell out with her, so he "kinda scooted her over" to get them.

"I remembered a show when a man got busted because of his lottery tickets, and I always played the same lucky number, three sixty-one," he said. "My lottery tickets were stuck to her torso, and her head moved when I moved her torso to get them."

"Was there any reason you left her socks on?" Hoyle asked.

"Because she left them on," he said. "The only way I would change their appearance was to put on clothes. I wouldn't take off their clothes."

"Was there any particular television show that you watched that helped you know how to cover up the evidence?"

"Mainly, Court TV, which I watched a lot. I also watched the History Channel and the Discovery Channel."

"Do you remember anything you ever did that you learned from Court TV?"

"Just cleaning up the bodies."

When Hoyle asked Larry if he was one of those serial killers who got off on the media attention, he said he was just the opposite. Larry didn't want the media attention, because it tortured his mom and his family. He said when he was first arrested and interviewed, before he asked for his attorney, he had planned on "spilling the beans." He figured he'd just tell them what he did, but then he chickened out and decided they'd have to prove it.

He explained that the day the detectives went to talk to him at his cell, he didn't want to say anything. He wanted to protect his mom because she was going through hell. But he decided to talk when he heard they were going to dig up her house. Larry tried to tell his mother what he had done, but he stopped when she became hysterical.

When the interviewed ended, Larry offered to take the detectives to a couple other sites at some point, if they wanted.

The detectives were notified two days later that Larry wanted to talk to them again. When they met with him, he explained that he had received a letter from a friend and wanted to know if he could write back to him. Hoyle told Larry he had to clear it through the jail personnel first.

After giving Larry a Pepsi and some smokes, and going over his Miranda rights again, Hoyle showed him a photo of a woman named Sherrik, who had been missing from Peoria. Larry said he didn't know her, and again said the only women he killed were the ones he already told them about.

During the questioning Larry asked Hoyle why the police wanted to know if his mom had ever worked at a truck stop. He wondered why they didn't ask about any of her other jobs. Hoyle told Larry they were just trying to tie various locations together. (He didn't want Larry to be upset because they thought his mother was once a prostitute.)

Larry again told police that once they found the

charred remains of his victims, he knew the jig was up. He said the main reason he was helping police find the girls' remains was because he wanted to be buried with his family, and he was sure their families wanted to be able to bury their loved ones.

Then Hoyle told Larry that the plan for the day was to first go and try to find the pond where he threw Tammy Walls's skull, then locate the spot in Stark County where he dumped teeth and a few vertebrae, and finally find the clothes he discarded in Knox County.

"It's going to be hard to get DNA from the burned remains," Hoyle said. "So it might speed up the identification process if we can find the victims' clothing."

"Is that the reason I haven't been charged with the others yet?"

"I don't know, and I don't want to answer the question because I don't want to misinform you."

"I just want to get this over with," Larry said. "I'm going to say I did it every time I go to court. My lawyer wants me to say I'm 'mental.' Mental problems might have been in it, but I knew what I was doing was wrong. There's no doubt about that. I fought with myself."

At that point Larry went into more detail about the influence Court TV had on his ability to hide his crimes. He told police he used to watch a lot of Court TV before he decided to kill anyone. Then after he killed the women, he remembered watching Court TV shows that explained how people who committed murders covered up their crimes.

Larry said he went to great lengths to cover up his killings. He washed and wiped down anything he thought might have a fingerprint or a stain on it. And he also vacuumed the carpet.

"Do you remember the Court TV show that showed you how to cover up and burn the bodies?" Hoyle asked.

Larry didn't know the name of the show, but he remembered it was about murders in the state of Washington.

"He was a serial killer, too," he said. "That's where I got the idea to dispose of the bodies in that way. I guess I'm a serial killer."

"What do you remember about that case in Washington?"

"The guy got caught because a girl got away, and the guy basically told on himself," Larry said.

"That sounds like what happened to you," Hoyle said.

"Yeah."

"When did you realize that you were a serial killer?"

"When I saw it on TV," he said. "One night I was watching *Monday Night Football,* and I saw something about a serial killer. So, after the game I switched the channel before the news came on. I never looked at the newspapers. I'd try to throw them away before my mom saw them."

"If you wanted to get caught, why did you try to cover it up?" Hoyle asked.

"When I was sober, I tried to get caught," he said. "After I killed someone, I'd stay up all night long, cleaning and burning. I'd vacuum and wipe things down in case there was a fingerprint somewhere. Then the next day, I'd get up and hope it was a bad dream, but I'd go behind the house and see the burned body and realize I was doing this."

When asked if he ever had to decide between two girls, Larry said sometimes, but when they were on opposite sides of the street, not when they were together. He never talked to two girls at once.

Larry often drove by a girl four or five times to see if she was being watched, or if she was a police decoy. He knew that police used decoys, because that's what they did on Court TV. The night he picked up the last girl he burned, Laura Lollar, he saw the cops down the street talking to two prostitutes. He drove by again and they were still talking to the girls, so he went to a different location and picked Laura up.

He usually picked up girls who were "geeking" already, which meant they were already high on crack and looking for more. A couple girls got into his Blazer—at different times—but then changed their minds. He didn't know why. He just knew that he would have killed those girls if they hadn't decided to get out.

After the interview ended, the police loaded Larry into a squad car and took off for the various dump sites, stopping at McDonald's to get Larry two cheeseburgers and a Coke. Then they went to the pond where he said he had thrown Tammy's head, videotaped the scene, then drove to Knox County.

On the way Larry told police more about himself. As a kid he remembered standing outside watching a neighbor girl as she walked around her house naked. Then he'd go home and masturbate while thinking about raping her. He used to mow her lawn and estimated he watched her fifty or sixty times. However, he never approached her sexually. He didn't remember her full name, but he thought her first name might be Kathy. Sometimes when he watched her, he had a .410-gauge shotgun with him.

Larry had a fascination with black women and anal sex. After he was gang-raped in prison, he liked having the girls he was with use a dildo on him anally. But he never had any of the girls he killed use it on him—only the girls he didn't kill.

As they talked, Larry again asked why the police wanted to know if his mom had worked at the truck stop. This time Hoyle told him the truth.

"The reason I asked might hurt your feelings," Hoyle said, "and I don't want to ask if it's not true."

"Go ahead, ask the question."

"During our investigation it was alleged that your mom worked as a prostitute in either Tremont or Morton. Is it true?"

"Yeah, I knew that she worked as a prostitute. I never talked to her about it, but I knew. She only did it because she needed money to raise me and my brother. She never brought any men to the house, though. I used to stay up late waiting for her to come home, because I was afraid something might happen to her."

When they got to the location where Larry said he hid the clothes, Hoyle got out and searched the area, but he didn't find anything. So they left for the next location in Stark County. As they drove, Larry talked about his relationship with his dad, and how Gary wasn't a good dad when Larry was growing up. But they became good friends when Larry was an adult. As they drove by the West Jersey cemetery, Larry asked Hoyle to be quiet so he could say something to his father, who was buried there.

"Dad, I'm sorry I let you down," he said. "I love you."

As they approached the first road north of West Jersey, Larry said, "This is it."

He said he had gone over a little hill and dumped a few teeth, some vertebrae, as well as the bucket, near a small grove of trees, although he wasn't quite sure where. A search of the area turned up nothing.

On the way back to the jail, Hoyle again asked Larry what he thought had happened to Bonnie Fife.

"Something like this, I guess. But it wasn't me," he said. "There are some sick motherfuckers out there. I guess I'm one."

"You know there's going to be some questions about your honesty, because we didn't find anything today," Hoyle said.

"Everything was the way I described it. I don't have any reason to bullshit you. But the pieces I dumped were very small, and would be hard to find."

"Maybe you did have a reason, if you used us to make one last visit to your father's grave."

On Friday, February 4, 2005, Taylor was notified that Larry wanted to talk to him and Hoyle again, so the detectives went to the jail to meet with him.

Before beginning the interview, Taylor told Larry he had bumped into his mom the previous night at the Peoria Civic Center, and she seemed like she was doing okay. She was grateful that the task force members were being nice to her and her family during the investigation. What Taylor didn't tell Larry was that his mother was seeking counseling.

Then it was Larry's turn to talk. He said the previous night he had had a vivid dream about the pond where he threw Tammy's skull. And he didn't think the pond he took the detectives to was the right one. The pond in his dream had a dock that was shaped like a *T,* and there was a diving board. Not only that, there was also a green outhouse with a crescent moon carved into the door. In his dream he dumped some of his victims' teeth out of a baby food jar and down the hole in the outhouse. Then he threw the jar away in a metal garbage can, with holes, next to the outhouse, which was filled with beer bottles and cans.

The dream was like watching himself in a movie. Finally he woke up in a sweat. He said he didn't know if his dream was just a dream or a memory. The part of the dream that stood out the most was the peeling green paint and the crescent moon on the outhouse.

"When you first told us about the pond, you said Ronnie showed you where it was," Taylor said.

"I thought he did, but I got lost, and the pond in my dream wasn't either of the ones I showed you," he said. "Maybe it was just a dream."

As happened in the other interviews, the topics of conversation changed very quickly. Hoyle moved the discussion away from the pond and back to Larry's house. He wanted to know about a little blue dress that police found in the rafters of the garage. Larry said he remembered throwing something from one of the women up into the rafters, but he didn't remember what it was. Hoyle said it looked like some kind of prom dress, but Larry said he thought it was a little blue sundress. So Hoyle made a call to the PCSO lab and was told it was, in fact, a blue sundress. Larry couldn't remember which of his victims was wearing it, but he did know it was one of the women that he burned.

The questioning then turned back to the teeth that Larry really kept in the baby food jar.

"How did you get the teeth you dumped?" Hoyle asked.

"They were in the ashes after I cleaned up," he said. "The jawbones were gone, but the teeth were still there. I remember seeing on Court TV that teeth are a good way to identify people. They don't really burn up, and they hold DNA better than anything else."

Hoyle told Larry that police hadn't found the gun he tossed in the Mackinaw River, and asked if he could give them any better directions. Larry explained that he had flipped the gun over the edge of the top of the bridge, but he wasn't sure if it hit water or land. He had it with him when he was getting rid of some buckets. He said he threw it away because he kept putting it in his mouth. He said it should be on the west side of the levee, where he had dumped some bones.

"Did you ever dismember any parts of the bodies before you burned them?" Taylor asked.

"No, I let the fire do the work. I wasn't about to cut bodies up, because I have a weak stomach, and I'd probably end up puking on myself if I did something like that."

When asked why he never killed any white girls, Larry thought for a few seconds, then said, "I don't know." He said he had never even picked up a white prostitute. Even if he had seen a white prostitute, he wouldn't have picked her up because she wasn't what he was looking for. He preferred black prostitutes because they were his "fantasy-type thing." He reminded the detectives that most of the women in the porn videos he rented were black.

"I have no idea why," he said. "Even my sister asked me why the victims were all black."

As they talked, Larry told Taylor and Hoyle that he was being contacted by people who wanted to write books about him.

"There are a lot of vultures out there," he said. "One of them told me I could be famous and make money. The *Journal Star* wrote to me a few times. They want me to do an interview and tell it in my words. I don't want to be famous, 'cause if I'm famous, then my mom's going to go through shit."

Thinking it over, Larry said maybe he'd write something someday and have the money go to the victims' families. Some of them had kids, and he thought it would be nice if they could go to college on him.

"Maybe they can forgive me somehow, but I don't think they will," he said, getting choked up. "I did it, and that's what I want more than anything in the world—forgiveness. I know it ain't gonna happen. I know I'd never forgive [me]."

Larry was genuinely overwhelmed when the detectives told him that family members of one of the victims said they would pray for him.

"That felt good," he said.

Larry started talking about the ponds again, and said although he didn't think it was either of the ponds he showed them, the larger pond off Augustin Road would be the best bet if it had an outhouse with a moon cut out of the door.

Hoyle explained that the ponds were important because the skull would be one of the largest pieces of the missing women that they'd have, and it would help bring closure to at least one of the families. Like the police, Larry wanted to help the families get closure more than anything.

As the investigation into Larry Bright continued, two experts talked to the *Peoria Journal Star* about serial killers.

Although not speaking specifically about Larry, retired FBI agent Clinton Van Zandt said statistics indicated that typically serial killers were white men in their early thirties—although there had been older serial killers, as well as serial killers from all racial groups.

And according to Dr. Jeffrey Walsh, assistant professor of criminal justice sciences at Illinois State University, serial killers usually targeted victims of their same race, although that wasn't always the case.

For example, Jeffrey Dahmer strangled and

dismembered boys and men of all races. And Derrick Todd Lee, the Baton Rouge serial killer, who was convicted of two murders but linked to the murders of seven women between 1992 to 2003, was black, while the women were white.

Like other serial killers who targeted prostitutes, Larry's victims were victims of opportunity because they were easy prey. And those serial killers knew that because of their lifestyle, it would take some time—if at all—before anyone even reported them missing.

Infamous serial killers, such as Jack the Ripper and Gary Leon Ridgway, the "Green River Killer," murdered prostitutes. And Joseph Miller killed at least two prostitutes in Chicago in the 1970s before he was paroled, only to murder three more prostitutes in Peoria.

While Larry admitted to murdering eight women, he continued to claim he did not murder Frederickia Brown and Wanda Jackson. That wasn't at all unusual, according to Van Zandt. Serial killers often held back information on certain murders, while some admitted to murders they didn't commit.

And sometimes serial killers might look to exchange information in return for a favorable deal from authorities, or to prolong the inevitable.

Walsh said Ted Bundy provided new information on his murders as his execution date neared, hoping to get a stay while investigators followed up on the information, Walsh said.

When asked why serial killers might alter their methods of disposing of their victims, both Walsh and Van Zandt said serial killers often evolved and learned how to be better killers.

However, what the public didn't know at the time was that Larry's reason for dumping some of the bodies of his victims intact and burning the bodies of his other victims had less to do with evolution and more to do with opportunity. Larry told police he sometimes had to get rid of a body quickly because his grandmother was coming to visit or it was raining. In those cases he wasn't able to burn them.

Van Zandt also said that some serial killers admitted to learning new ways of disposing of their victims from television programs. That's exactly where Larry said he got the idea to burn his victims. Larry said he was watching a program on the History Channel and saw something about Hitler's body being burned. That's when he had the idea to burn his victims' bodies.

Walsh called serial killers, like Larry, who killed their victims in the same place, "place specific offenders." Larry killed seven of his eight victims in his house on West Starr Court, while he killed one at his house on West McClure Avenue, where he and his mother were living at the time.

And why did Larry let some of his intended victims go? Well, Walsh said, it could be that the victim just wasn't right, or maybe a victim made the killer think of her as a real person, not just as an object, by mentioning her children or other family members.

But Larry's reason for letting some of his potential victims go was much simpler—he wanted to get caught.

Walsh said investigations into serial murders often go on for years, and sometimes are never solved. However, task forces formed to investigate two serial murderers in Peoria made quick work of those investigations.

The task force working in 1993 caught serial killer Joseph Miller in less than a month, and the task force investigating the murders and disappearances of the ten Peoria women had Larry in custody in about three months. He confessed to the murders a month later.

14

Hoyle and Taylor went back to the jail to meet with Larry again, on February 7. He had had "visions" about the pond and wanted to talk to the detectives about them. Larry said his mind kept going back to the pond, and he could see a very large oak tree next to it. Hoyle reminded Larry that there was a big oak tree by the pond on Augustin Road, and asked if he could recall anything about the land leading back to the pond. Larry said he thought the grass was high, and he remembered there was a white toilet seat inside the outhouse.

Then he remembered that he had dumped some remains in the corner of his yard by his privacy fence, and the fence around the baseball diamond. It was in the same place where he dumped waste from his toilet because it wasn't working. He also put a two-inch piece of bone in the mulch by the pine tree, although he had no idea why he did that.

"Is there anything else you need to ask me?"

Hoyle asked if he had any more details about the missing girls that would help identify them.

Thinking for a minute, Larry said he kept at his house, for about a day, the first girl he burned. After he decided to burn her body, he built a fire. But it didn't work right the first time, because he didn't let it get hot enough, and there was "a lot of stuff left." That's when he realized that he had to really heat the fire up. He took her ashes to Tremont.

"Is there anything about her that could help us figure out who she was?" Hoyle asked.

"I remember she was wearing a blue dress."

He said the second girl freaked out right before he strangled her, because she knew what was up. He thought she was wearing the capri pants that he dumped in Knox County. He torched her, and the first girl that he burned, in the spot where he later installed the small pond. Then he dug a pit next to the pond, where he burned the bodies of the other two. He dumped the remains of his second victim at his grandma's house and at the Kickapoo Creek area. He wasn't sure why he spread her remains out the way he did. He didn't remember her name, though. He only remembered Tammy Walls's name because he had her driver's license. He thought Tammy was the third girl he burned.

After picking Tammy up in the north end of Peoria, he took her back to his place, where they started using coke. She was drinking, and she had said she was an alcoholic. After they had sex, he strangled her. Then he put her body in the bathroom, and he got the fire going really good. He let it burn for three or four hours, until it was white-hot. Then he dragged her body out of the bathroom, dropped it on top of the fire, and covered it with wood.

As the fire was doing its dirty work, Larry went back inside and started scrubbing to remove any trace of Tammy from his apartment. He stayed up all night wiping everything down. At times he'd return to the fire, stoking it up real good.

Confused, Larry stopped talking for a minute. Then he asked, "Which girl am I explaining?"

"The third [missing girl]," Hoyle said.

"That would have been Tammy," he said.

By the time the fire was pretty much dead, Larry said, everything was gone, except for her head and a little piece of her neck. So he put her head in a shoe box and took it to the pond, along with the baby food jar, containing about ten teeth.

"If a girl had a purse, what did you do with what was in it?" Taylor asked.

"I'm pretty sure I would have burned it," he said. "I looked through them to see if there was any identification or anything. And I guess I was looking for money, too. I saved some jewelry, but I knew if I took it to a pawnshop, I'd get caught. If I threw a purse out, I made sure it was empty, and I wiped it clean of fingerprints."

When Hoyle asked Larry what mistakes he made, Larry responded, "Killing them, in the first place."

"I meant, what mistakes did you make to get caught?"

"The rubber breaking. That's what got me caught," he said, referring to his DNA that was found in Linda Neal. "When that happened, I

thought about pouring bleach inside of her, but I
didn't have any bleach. I knew that's how I'd get
caught. I would've kept going."

The detectives also wanted to know whether
Larry had some kind of fascination with fire. He
said, when he was a kid, he and a friend acciden-
tally burned down three barns when they were
smoking cigarettes. He emphasized that they were
accidents. Once, when they were teenagers, they
were partying by the Mackinaw River and burned
down an old cabin. He didn't say whether that was
an accident.

He admitted he enjoyed fires and watching
them burn. Even when he was burning the girls,
he liked to watch the fire—but he didn't watch
until he was done cleaning. Sometimes he stayed
up all night watching the fire burn.

Next on the detectives' agenda was the death of
Cathy Bishop's baby, Suzanna. As he had stated
previously, Larry said he had nothing to do with
her death. Again he said that Cathy took the baby
and laid her down in the playpen. About fifteen
minutes later, he heard Suzanna gurgling. He ran
to her and tried to give her CPR. When Hoyle
asked why he didn't take a polygraph to prove he
wasn't lying, Larry once more said his attorney advised him not to. Larry also admitted that every
time he had been in trouble, he had always followed his lawyers' advice. But this time was different. This time he knew he couldn't live with
himself anymore. And he knew once the police
found the women's bones, he was done.

* * *

Hoyle and Taylor went back to the jail a couple days later because Larry had asked to see them. He said he had been thinking and remembered some things, like throwing a gray sweatshirt out the window of his truck as he was driving to Mackinaw to get drugs. He described taking Broadway Road to the end, turning right, then left onto a gravel road that led into Dee-Mack Road in Tazewell County. He threw the sweatshirt, which he thought belonged to one of the women he burned, out on a dirt road.

As the interview progressed, Taylor asked Larry about one of the girls he let go when he lived on McClure. He was talking about Teracita, but he didn't tell Larry her name. He explained that it was clear the woman had been there because she knew exactly what it looked like inside. And they found evidence that further corroborated her story. Still referring to that woman, Taylor asked if Larry remembered shaving the pubic hair off a girl he brought home because he told her she was too hairy. Larry said he remembered.

"Did you insert pleasure balls inside her?"

"I could have. I had some plastic balls with string on them that you can put in vaginally or anally," he said, adding that he thought he picked that girl up in the north end of Peoria.

"Was she wearing a tampon because she just had a baby?" Taylor asked. "Did she leave the tampon on the floor?"

Larry said he didn't remember the tampon. He said it was hard to remember the details because there were so many women he let go, and he was always so messed up.

"I knew I never should have let none of them go," he said jokingly, "but I'm glad I did."

Just about a week later, Hoyle and Taylor got word that Larry wanted to talk to them again. During that interview he told police he had lied to them about three things, and now he wanted to come clean. He said he lied about setting fires when he was younger. He actually set a lot of fires when he was a kid and burned down three or four cabins and a couple corn bins. But he never set any houses on fire. The last fire he set was in 1988 or 1989, when he set a cabin on fire.

And he lied when he said Harry Cannon was with him when he killed Barbara Williams.

"Harry wasn't there. I blamed him because he was my supplier. When I was trying to get clean, he'd give me a little crack for free. I was hoping you guys would arrest him and he'd have dope on him," he said. "I know why I did these things— because I was raped while I was in prison."

"Why are you changing your story about Harry?" Hoyle asked.

All Larry said was "It was just me."

Larry explained that he struggled with being raped for years. Then something just snapped and he wanted to get even for what had happened to him.

"But if it was black men who raped you, why did you target black females?" Taylor asked.

"Because I'm not gay."

"Do you know the names of any of the guys who raped you?" Hoyle asked.

"No. It was while I was in Joliet," he said. "Our cellblock was taken to the showers. The first guy came at me and punched me in the face. Then a bunch of guys held me down and took turns on me. I know the guard heard the screams, but he didn't do anything."

"So [that] was the reason you killed blacks, to get even?" Taylor asked.

"Yeah," he said. "After holding something in for so long, something snaps and then ya act on it."

But Larry said he wasn't sure why he killed certain women. Maybe they struck him wrong or something. Again he said the first two women he killed were "accidents."

"After that, it's like when you go into the woods to hunt an animal," he said.

Hoyle then asked Larry about the shoelace found on Linda Neal's neck.

"There was another female's DNA on it. Did you use it on anyone else?"

"Yeah. I used it on one of the girls I burned. I think it was the second one. After I choked her, she started to come back to, so I put the lace on her and tightened it up. I left it on to make sure."

"Why did you take it off?" Hoyle asked. "Why didn't you just burn it?"

"I thought I did, but I'm not one hundred percent sure."

"What time of year did you burn the girls?" Hoyle asked.

Larry said it was either late spring or early summer. His mother was having the house painted, so he covered up the remains with dirt until the painters had finished. Then he dug up the remains and disposed of them.

For the next several days, police continued their investigation, trying to uncover more evidence to link Larry to the murders. They didn't find anything in the Benson Road area, south of the Mackinaw River in Tazewell County, where Larry said he dumped some bones. But they did find what looked like a human bone under some heavy brush next to the fence behind Larry's house.

At eight in the morning on February 17, Hoyle and Taylor picked Larry up at the jail and drove him to court to be arraigned on two of the eight murders. A Peoria County grand jury had returned indictments against Larry a week earlier, charging him with first-degree murder in the deaths of Linda Neal and Brenda Erving.

In court Larry again tried to plead guilty to murder, but Circuit Judge James Shadid said, "Today is not the day." At an earlier hearing, Bright had tried three times to plead guilty to murdering Linda Kay Neal, but the judge in that case also refused to accept his plea.

Larry said nothing as Judge Shadid read the charges: two counts of first-degree murder for the choking deaths of Linda and Brenda. When Shadid asked Larry if he understood the charges, he said, "I really want to plead guilty." But Shadid wouldn't accept his plea. Shadid told Larry he faced either a mandatory life sentence or possibly the death penalty if he was convicted in the deaths of both women. If he was convicted of killing only one woman, he faced from twenty years to sixty years in prison. Shadid said he wouldn't accept Larry's guilty plea because of the seriousness of the case.

"I understand, but today is not the day to do that. Your rights are going to be protected. We are acting in your best interests," the judge said.

Even though the public defender's office had been appointed to represent Larry, Shadid also appointed the capital defender's office to the case because the death penalty might come into play. However, at that point the Peoria County State's Attorney's Office hadn't made a decision about seeking the death penalty. Assistant State's Attorney Nancy Mermelstein said that decision would be made before Larry's next court appearance, which was set for March 15.

On the way back to the jail, Larry told Hoyle and Taylor that he remembered where he put a necklace that belonged to one of the victims. It was in Morton, inside a smashed-up brown Ford Ranger pickup truck that was owned by Dick Wolf's business. The truck was at the same place where police recovered the sneaker Larry had thrown on top of a building. Larry said it belonged to the same girl as the sneaker had, which, he said previously, belonged to Barbara Williams. And he said that he put a Hampton's Electric T-shirt that belonged to one of his victims in his dresser drawer with his shirts.

"Why did you keep it?" Hoyle asked.

"It was nice and it fit me."

* * *

In a follow-up interview, Larry told Hoyle and Taylor that he had been having more dreams about the pond, and he kept picturing Heritage Road. He described two posts and a cable that went across the road on the ground. And there was a NO TRESPASSING sign that was also on the ground. He again mentioned the big oak tree.

Hoyle then told Larry they were going to take him to a couple places, but they didn't tell him exactly where they were going. The conversation during the drive consisted of how to build koi fishponds and landscaping in general. After about half an hour, they arrived at the site where the body of Frederickia Brown had been discovered. As they approached the section, Hoyle asked Larry if he was familiar with the area. Larry asked if they were outside of Hanna City, and Hoyle said they were.

"I'm sure I didn't dump anything here," Larry said.

"This is where one of the bodies was dumped," Hoyle said.

"Not one of mine."

Police then drove to a vacant lot by a bar in Pottstown, where Wanda Jackson's body had been found in March 2001. When asked if he was familiar with the area, Larry said no.

"Is this where one of the bodies was found?" Larry asked.

"Yes," Hoyle said.

"That was dumb of them," Larry responded.

"Why do you think it was dumb?"

"There are too many houses close by, and there's a chance to be seen by someone," he said. "That's why I dumped the bodies of the girls I killed in rural areas."

When police next talked to Larry, he told them that vacant lot in Pottstown looked familiar for some reason. It was almost like he had been there at some point. He didn't remember "that girl," meaning Wanda, but he did remember the vacant lot.

"I don't know if I may have done that, too, and not remember it, or what's going on," he said. "I don't know if my mind blocked it out, but I kept thinking about it and seeing the scene over and over."

Larry said he kept seeing the side of the church, the parking lot, the vacant lot, and a white building, which was the bar.

Hoyle told Larry he didn't want him confessing to killing someone he didn't kill, but he did want him to try and remember if he did, in fact, kill Wanda Jackson.

"I understand," he said. "If I did it, I don't want you out looking for somebody else. I don't remember doing it, but I just keep seeing the scene."

When asked if he ever picked up any girls with anybody else at the Kings Park Estates, Larry said yes, a big black guy named David who was about forty-five and drove a black Cadillac Escalade. Sometimes when he couldn't reach Harry, he'd meet David in the Kings Park area, where David sold drugs. Larry met David through Ernestine. Larry also partied with a girl named Jessica, who lived in Kings Park. Jessica was a white woman in her late twenties or early thirties who had two children.

Then Hoyle asked Larry if he ever picked up girls around Bradley Park, near Western Avenue and Main Street. He said he did, but he didn't remember who they were.

"Do you remember anything about the girls you picked up there? Like maybe a birthmark on someone's neck?"

Larry didn't recall a birthmark, but he asked to see a picture of the girl Hoyle was talking about. Taylor left the room to get some photographs, including one of Wanda Jackson, the woman with the birthmark.

After looking at Wanda's picture, Larry said, "I might have picked her up. I think I might have dated her. I remember seeing her somewhere, but I don't think I did it. All the other girls, I remember doing it."

Then he brought up the "scene" again—the Pottstown bar where Wanda's body had been found. Something about the vacant lot was sticking in his head. Studying her picture, Larry said she was really pretty and she looked familiar.

"I see the scene with the church through the trees, then the vacant lot and the building. I might have gone into the bar and asked if there was a meat store in the area that I could take a deer to."

Taylor then brought up a subject none of the detectives had ever talked to Larry about previously—the possibility that Larry had murdered women in other parts of the country and even the world. Taylor first asked Larry if he had lived in Australia for a year after he got the settlement for hurting his back at Heinz Masonry in Kickapoo. He said he wanted to, but he never did. However, he did travel around the United States sightseeing by himself for about three months, going to Alaska, Florida, and California. He took about $10,000 in cash and some credit cards with him.

"Did you ever kill anyone while you were traveling?" Hoyle asked.

"No."

"Did you ever come close?"

"Yeah, when I was in California, I thought about it, but I never did anything," he said. "The first girl I killed was in July [2003], right after my birthday."

"Did you ever pick up any black prostitutes when you were traveling?"

"I picked up a couple blacks, a couple Mexicans. I got ripped off a couple of times."

Larry then brought the interview back to the picture of Pottstown he kept seeing in his head. He said if he did it, he just wanted to get it all out, but he really didn't think he did it. He said he thought the area looked familiar because he took the deer to the butcher shop in town, or maybe he had met David at the bar. Still, Wanda looked really familiar. Maybe he did it, but he just blocked it out.

"I wish there was some machine that you could just hook up to my head and get all these memories out," he said. "I'm really sorry for what I did, and I just want to take it like a man, whether it's life in prison or the death penalty."

Larry said he was right with God and he just wanted to plead guilty when he was arraigned on the other six victims. He didn't want his family or the families of the victims to hear the details about what he did to the women.

"The families may think they want to hear what happened, but they won't really want to hear it," he said. "I did it, and I'm willing to, you know, I want to take responsibility for what I've done."

On February 24, Hoyle and Taylor got a message that Larry wanted to speak with them again.

Hoyle began the interview by asking Larry why he wanted to talk to them.

"There's another victim."

It was another girl from Peoria. A skinny black girl. Another prostitute. He picked her up around July or August 1997 and strangled her. She was the first.

"Why did you just remember now?" Hoyle asked.

It wasn't that he just remembered, but rather that no one ever asked him about her. He figured he might as well get it out at that point. He didn't remember her name, but he did remember picking her up in the north end of the city and taking her back to his house on McClure. They were partying and something went wrong, although he wasn't sure what. Then he ended up strangling her.

After he killed her, he put her naked body in his Isuzu truck and drove it to a place along the Mackinaw River near Tremont. It was near a spot with a sandbar, where a creek went into the river. He put logs and a lot of small brush on top of her body. He struggled with the logs because some of them weighed about a hundred pounds. He threw her clothes in the garbage.

Hoyle explained to Larry how important it was to figure out who the girl was; then he asked Larry to go over it again. Larry told the same story, adding a couple extra details, like the fact that when he arrived at the dump site, he drove down a levee and parked. He dragged her out of his truck and carried her across the river. At that time of year, the river was generally low, so it would have been possible for Larry to walk across it. He said he put her on the same side of the river as a grove of white trees.

"You know some of the investigators might be a little skeptical and think you're not telling the truth," Hoyle said. "Can you show us exactly where you buried her?"

Saying he had no reason to lie, Larry said that he could take them to the general location, but he didn't think he could find the precise spot. After all, it had been eight years.

"If you saw a picture of her, would you be able to recognize her?"

"Yeah. I remember she had a gold tooth on the right side," he said. "It wasn't her front tooth, but her fang tooth."

After spending some two weeks questioning Larry, Hoyle and Taylor had a feeling Larry was hiding something else. They were right. Larry said there was another victim in Arizona. It happened basically the same way as all the others. The only difference was that she was Hispanic, not black. He met her at a truck stop outside of Phoenix, sometime in 1999. He took her to a Motel 6, about thirty or forty miles outside Phoenix, where he strangled her. He dumped her in the desert. He said he used an atlas during his trip and highlighted the places he visited in yellow Magic Marker.

"I can't believe I done all this shit," he said.

"At this point there's no difference if you killed fourteen or eight," Hoyle said. "I just don't want you telling me something you didn't do."

"There's just ten of them," Larry said.

Taylor then pointed out that there were similarities between the murder of Linda Fields and the murders Larry committed.

"It wasn't me," he said. "They got DNA from that one."

"But you told us before that you always wore a condom, and the only time you left DNA was when the rubber broke," Taylor said.

Hoyle then gave Larry a lesson about serial killers. He explained that studies showed that once a serial killer started, he couldn't stop. So it didn't make sense that Larry killed in 1997 and 1999, then not again until 2003.

Larry said during those four years he was fighting with himself not to kill again. And even though he always had those feelings after the first one, he felt better about himself and was able to fight them.

"Maybe there's more that I blocked out," he said.

"What made you remember these?" Hoyle asked.

Changing his story some, Larry said one of the detectives from Racine had told him to come clean and admit—to himself, his God, and someone else—what he had done. He said he was thinking in his cell after that and decided to tell the detectives.

Then he went back to his first story and said he didn't tell them about the others because they didn't question him about them.

"Did you kill any girls anywhere else that you didn't tell us [about], because we didn't ask you?" Hoyle asked.

"Not purposely," he said. "In my mind I didn't think I did more than eight, until last night. Then I started thinking about it and I was scared about being sent somewhere else."

Hoyle told Larry to talk to his lawyer about being sent out of state because he thought the lawyer would tell Larry not to worry about it.

"I don't know, my mind blocks things out."

"Are we going to get another request tomorrow that you want to talk to us and then hear about additional victims?"

"I don't know," Larry said.

The next day the detectives met with Larry again. He told them he left the atlas from his cross-country trip in his apartment in Racine. He had packed the atlas and a few other things in a box, which he ultimately forgot to take with him. He was halfway to Peoria when he remembered it, so he didn't go back to get it. He said he didn't think his landlord had thrown it away, because it was a large atlas in a zippered leather case. Larry wanted the detectives to get the atlas back so he could show them where he dumped the victim in Arizona. He wasn't sure he could remember the route he took without it.

"And there are some other things on the map," Larry said.

"Like what?" Hoyle asked.

"Two other victims in other states."

"Where are they?"

"I'm not sure. That's why I want my map, because I put a little red highlight pen mark where they are. I marked my trip in yellow, but there [are] red marks where I put the bodies."

Hoyle told Larry the chances of getting the atlas were slim to none. But Larry said his landlord wouldn't have thrown it out, because it cost about a hundred bucks.

"Do you remember what states the other two victims are in?" Hoyle asked.

"One's in Oklahoma. I was there trying to find my dad's cousin Simon in the little town where my dad used to live. But I couldn't find him."

"Why did you go to Arizona?"

Larry said it was mainly to see the London Bridge, which had been transported to Arizona. While in Arizona he also visited Meteor Crater, where a meteor hit the earth, as well as touring the Painted Desert and the Grand Canyon. While he was in California, he saw the giant sequoia trees, and he also tried to find the pier at a beach in Burbank, near where he used to live when he was a kid. His dad had found a big starfish there and had given it to him. Larry carried some of his dad's ashes with him on the trip and sprinkled them into the ocean.

"Tell us about the victim in Oklahoma," Hoyle said.

Larry said after a night of drinking and drugging, he and a "young black gal" went to a motel, where they had sex. She was about twenty-five, slim but with large breasts. After they finished, he strangled her with his hands. Before he dumped her body, he put her jeans and T-shirt back on her. Then he drove her to a big lake in a little town where his dad had grown up. His dad had taken Larry there to visit his grandmother. He didn't remember the name of the town, but he said his mom, his uncle, and his dad's second wife knew where it was.

Larry disposed of her body about three or four hundred feet off a dirt road that ran along the side of the lake. He estimated it was about a quarter mile above a dam, and there was a small dock for boats, with some fishing boats tied up to it. Before he left the area, Larry threw the victim's socks, shoes, and underwear in a garbage can there. He didn't really remember why he killed her.

"Where's the other victim?" Hoyle asked.

"I can't remember, that's why I want the map, because it was marked on it."

He couldn't even remember what state it was for sure. It might have been Washington.

"Are there just the three victims?"

"I'm pretty sure."

In addition to the women he killed, Larry probably picked up along the way five or six others who didn't suffer the same fate. Although, he came close one other time. He had an argument with a prostitute in California and was getting ready to kill her, but she got away.

After hearing about these other victims, Hoyle again asked Larry about the murder of Linda Fields in Racine. He figured maybe he had blocked it out. Larry said maybe he did it, but he didn't think so, because he wouldn't have dumped her so close to where he lived. He was trying to be careful about things like that. He would have dumped her in a more remote area.

Then Hoyle asked about the victim in Davenport.

"I don't think that was me," he said. "I just don't remember. But the Davenport detectives told me there was a car like my Blazer seen near where the body was found. But I wasn't driving the Blazer then."

"That vehicle might not have been involved," Hoyle said.

"I really don't remember it. It could have been me. I'm not sure. I couldn't say a hundred percent no."

"Why after originally telling us you only killed eight girls, you're now remembering more?" Hoyle asked. "What's helping you remember?"

Larry explained that he was finally coming to terms with what he had done, and he just wanted to get it over with. He didn't want to have to go through all the "bullshit" again. He just wanted it done. Then he told the detectives they really should try to get the map, because there might actually be more victims.

"Have you told your mom about these other girls yet?"

When Larry said he hadn't told her, Hoyle said it would be better if she heard it from him rather than from the police or the media. Taylor told Larry he'd try to arrange for him to call his mother before police went to talk to her that night.

* * *

Taylor and Hoyle left the interview room, leaving Larry alone for about fifteen minutes. When they returned, Hoyle asked him what else he remembered about the woman he killed in Washington. He said she was black, about six feet tall, with short hair and green contacts. He said they must have been contacts, because there aren't too many black women with green eyes. Although he didn't remember where he picked her up, he dumped her in a rocky area with a lot of pine trees.

"Why do you think it was Washington?" Hoyle asked.

"It was after I left California, heading toward Alaska, so I think it was in the state of Washington. But it could have been in Northern California."

"Did you kill her in your blue Dakota truck?"

"I don't think I ever killed anyone in the truck," he said. "I'm not sure, but I probably killed that one in a motel room."

"Were you ever scared taking the victims out of a hotel room and putting them in the truck?"

"Hell yes," he said, adding that he always parked right in front of the door.

Taylor asked Larry if he could put the victims from his trip in order. Larry said he wasn't sure, because he had been trying to block it out of his mind, and the harder he tried, the fuzzier it all became. He said it usually came back to him when he was walking in his cell.

"Maybe I done so many, that I just don't want to remember."

* * *

A few days later, Larry sent for the detectives again. When they got settled in the interview room, Larry asked to see a picture of Barbara Williams. He wanted to know who she was. He said her cousin had written to him, saying she had forgiven him, and asked if she could visit him in jail. Larry said he wasn't going to do that. Hoyle said he didn't have a picture of her, but he reminded Larry where he had dumped her body. Larry remembered who she was and said he didn't need to see her photo.

Larry had some notes with him that he had written in his cell about the girl he killed in the Northwest. He said she had a scar on her knee, like from an operation or something. Trying to narrow down the area where he picked her up, he said it was about a week after he drove through the redwood forest. He dumped her body next to a flat rock that was about the size of an airplane. He hid her by throwing things over her. To get to the dump spot, which was about ten miles from the Pacific Ocean, he drove down a dirt road surrounded by pine trees.

Hoyle asked Larry if he could tell them a bit more about the Oklahoma kill. He said he couldn't remember the name of the town, but it was near a big, gigantic lake with a marina, surrounded by woods. There were about ten boats in the marina.

After some further thought, Larry said he didn't think he killed Linda Fields in Racine. However, he admitted to killing another woman in the area sometime around May 2000. She was about thirty years old, his height, slender, with short hair. She also had two missing teeth on the top right. *And* she was white.

"Why a white girl?" Hoyle asked, obviously surprised.

"I don't know. I think that's the only white girl I ever did."

Larry killed her in his apartment and dumped her body near a place where he used to go fishing with friends. It was about twenty miles outside of Racine. He again denied having anything to do with the death of Linda Fields, because he wouldn't have put her body in such a public location because it was dumb.

But Taylor reminded Larry that he did some pretty dumb things, too, like dumping the body of Linda Neal and driving around with dead black women in his truck. Taylor figured if Larry was high and drunk, Larry might have done something stupid.

"If you killed a girl in Wisconsin, it won't really change things much," Hoyle said.

"I really might have," he said.

Hoyle told Larry there were a lot of similarities between his murders and the murder of Linda Fields.

After hearing that, Larry said, "It very well could have been me, but I must have been spooked real bad to dump her there. I think I would remember getting spooked. If it was done [the way you said], then it could very well have been me."

The conversation then turned to the Tremont dump site. He talked about the levee that was between the sandbar and the body. He put the woman there because he thought the levee would protect the body from being washed away by the high water of the river. Larry asked if police had gone back to the area. He was told investigators had gone out there, but they hadn't found anything, and they'd probably wait until it was warmer to go back out. Taylor said he went there, but he thought he might have been on the wrong side of the river. Larry said he went back there to go fishing with a friend, although he didn't even look at the spot where he dumped the body.

Taylor and Hoyle met with Larry again, about a week later. The first thing they talked about was the murder he did in Oklahoma. While they were in the interview room, Hoyle received a call from Oklahoma state trooper Bruce Smith. Hoyle had asked Smith to call so they could discuss the place where Larry dumped the body, which was near a dam in a town called Vinita.

Smith listened as Larry described to him the area near Vinita; then he asked for more detailed information about the dam and the surrounding vicinity. After he finished talking to Larry, Smith said the directions Larry gave didn't match up with the area near Vinita. He said he'd check the surrounding areas and call back later.

When the call with Smith ended, Hoyle asked Larry if he could remember anything else about the girl that he said he had killed in Racine. Hoyle said the police had just received information that Racine police had discovered the body of a white female around the time that Larry said he had done the murder. But the woman in question had been beaten, and there were bite marks on her breasts.

"Did you do anything different to the girl in Racine?" Hoyle asked.

"No, just strangled her."

"Do you remember anything more specific?"

Larry recalled going about fifteen or twenty miles out of town in the direction of Milwaukee and dumping her body at a campground. He said the campground was by a stream that sturgeon swam in during a certain time of year.

"Was she ever found?" Larry asked.

"I'm not sure."

Larry said he rented a place in Racine from February to June 2000. Before that, he had lived with George Jamison. After he moved back to Peoria, he went back to Racine a couple times to visit his half sister.

"Could you be wrong about when you lived in Racine?" Hoyle asked.

"Yeah, but you can verify it using my work records from when I was working at Holton Brothers."

As the interview continued, Hoyle told Larry he was concerned that Larry was lying to them just so he could get out of his cell and have a cigarette and a soda. He told him it was okay to put in a request to talk to them even if he had no information and just wanted a cigarette.

Larry then asked about his court date on March 15. He wanted to know if he was going to be charged with the other murders before he went to court. He wondered if they were going to ask for the death penalty. Hoyle said that decision was up to State's Attorney Kevin Lyons.

Hoyle left the room for a few minutes, and Taylor asked Larry about his settlement money. Larry said he got the money in January 1999 and had spent it all by July of that year. He said he took his trip after he got the money but before he moved to Racine. Taylor said that couldn't be right, because the dates didn't match up with his previous statements.

Larry didn't say a word.

A few days later, Larry filled out another request to talk with Hoyle and Taylor. So the detectives went to the Tazewell County Jail to meet with him.

"I wussed out on my mom," Larry said.

"How did you wuss out?" Hoyle asked.

"I couldn't tell her," Larry said, meaning he couldn't tell her about the girls he killed in the other states. "I started to tell her and she started crying, so I told her I was lying to you guys, so she'd quit crying."

"So have you lied to us?" Hoyle asked.

"No. I just want to get this over with because my mom can't take it."

"You're the only reason this is getting stretched out," Hoyle said. "If these last victims are a lie, it's not going to help your mom deal with it."

When Larry told the detectives he remembered more "on kind of where" in Oklahoma, Hoyle called the sheriff's office in Mayes County, Oklahoma, and gave them the information Larry was providing.

Larry said he picked up the victim in Vinita, the town where his dad grew up. It was in the spring of 1999. He picked her up in a run-down neighborhood where he bought crack from a black man.

He killed her at a small, cheap hotel. Although he didn't know the name of the hotel, he thought it was in Vinita. He registered at the hotel using his real name.

After she was dead, he put her T-shirt and jeans back on her, then took her body to a lake near a dam, about two miles away. On one side of the lake, there were boats moored at a little dock. He drove across the top of the dam, turned left on a dirt road, and dumped her body in the lake.

"How did you know where to take the body?" Hoyle asked.

"Some years before, when my dad took me to the town to visit one of his cousins, some neighborhood kids showed me all around the area."

The Oklahoma detective said the information Larry provided didn't match up to any area he was familiar with, so he was going to do more checking and ended the call.

Hoyle told Larry the investigators wanted to believe what he was telling them, but they needed to confirm some of the information. They asked if he could remember the names of any of the towns he visited while traveling. Larry said no, adding that the atlas was the key to everything.

Over the next few days, law enforcement officials from other states visited Larry to talk to him about unsolved murders in their jurisdictions. Investigators Mark Sorenson and Brenda Guillien, of the Racine Police Department (RPD), who were looking into the death of Linda Fields, arrived to talk to Larry. After Larry told Hoyle and Taylor about the woman he killed in Racine, they had contacted the investigators to give them the information.

While the Racine investigators were at the jail, members of the task force shared information about Larry with them. They also gave the Racine police photocopies of an address book that belonged to Larry. The book contained the name and phone number of Theresa, a woman Larry used to live with in Racine, as well as the names and phone numbers of a couple other women and a man named Richard Harper.

Guillien and Sorenson went to see Richard Harper to ask if he knew Theresa's last name. Harper said he thought it was Sykes. He said at one time she had a white boyfriend who lived on Main Street. Harper immediately recognized Larry from a photo the police showed him, although he said Larry had a beard when he knew him.

After talking with Harper, Sorenson called Taylor to tell him Larry's former landlord's records indicated that Larry rented the apartment on Main Street in April 1999. He left town on June 14. He said he threw away whatever belongings Larry left behind.

Sorenson told Taylor that because Linda Fields's death occurred in 2000, the timeline didn't match up, unless Larry went back to Racine. Sorenson said although the dump site was in a residential area, it was under a big pine tree with very low-hanging branches that would have provided some cover. Larry was probably familiar with the area because he had lived nearby.

Guillien and Sorenson also located Theresa.

She was at the Racine County Jail, where they proceeded to interviewed her. Theresa told them she had lived with a white guy in a house on Main Street for about a month. She denied being a "true" prostitute, because she never had sex with Larry. In fact, they didn't even sleep in the same bed. She slept on the couch in the living room, and Larry slept in the bedroom. They were both heavy into drugs. Theresa became very concerned when the investigators told her why they were looking into Larry's past.

According to Theresa, all she and Larry ever did together was get high. He always supplied the drugs, mainly crack. He often bought a couple hundred bucks' worth at a shot. He also liked his beer and bought it by the case. Sometimes Theresa would get some valium for him from one of her connections.

Sorenson and Guillien were curious about why Larry took care of her, making sure she had food, drugs, alcohol, and cigarettes—if she wasn't giving him sex in return. Theresa said the only thing she ever did for him was shove a big dildo up his butt over and over when he wanted it. He demanded she shove it in harder and harder. She vividly remembered doing it because she thought it was so nasty.

Theresa was introduced to Larry by one of her friends.

She said Larry left Racine abruptly in the summer of 1999. She went to the house one day and found all her belongings in boxes in the hallway outside his apartment door. When she went into the apartment, she saw that all his stuff was gone. There was nothing left, not even one box. His bedroom set was gone, the fish tanks were gone, and the cat was gone. She never heard from him again.

When asked if she had ever traveled to any park outside of Racine with Larry, she said she didn't remember going anywhere out of the city with him. She also said she didn't know anything about him shooting a drug dealer, and she never saw him with a gun.

After the investigators left the jail, they got a message from one of the deputies that Theresa remembered going to Island Park in the center of Racine with Larry. But Sorenson said, as far as he knew, no human remains had ever been found at that park, which was not located twenty miles outside of the city.

15

Handcuffed and shackled, Larry Bright was led into the Peoria County Courthouse in mid-March. Bright didn't try to plead guilty as he had done in the past, choosing, instead, to sit quietly during the six-minute hearing. He remained silent as Circuit Judge James Shadid told him that prosecutors were planning to seek the death penalty against him for the murders of Linda Neal and Brenda Erving.

After SA Kevin Lyons decided to seek the death penalty, Circuit Judge Shadid appointed Springfield attorneys James Elmore and Jeffrey "Jeff" Page to represent him in the deaths of Linda Neal and Brenda Erving. When he filed the death penalty motion, Lyons told the *Peoria Journal Star* that his decision didn't "involve any hand-wringing." Lyons told the newspaper what Larry did was "deliberate, premeditated, repeated—brutal murders."

Shadid appointed the pair because not enough attorneys in Peoria were certified to try cases dealing with the death penalty.

The judge also let the public defender's office withdraw from the case, although Peoria attorney Hugh Toner, who was also a part-time public defender, stayed on the case. According to the regulations of the Capital Litigation Trial Bar, attorneys on both sides had to have the necessary experience to try a case involving the death penalty. Although Toner had applied to try capital murder cases, his application had not been accepted at that point.

Even though Larry had admitted to killing eight women, he had only been charged with two, because authorities hadn't been able to tie him to the other murders. Although investigators had recovered more than one hundred burned pieces of bone from Larry's victims, DNA testing on the remains of the women probably wouldn't be ready for three or four months. And even then, the intense heat the bones had been subjected to could have destroyed the DNA. Lyons, though, was committed to charging Larry with as many of the murders as possible.

But despite the fact that Larry was willing to plead guilty to the murders, if the case went to trial, it could possibly end up costing taxpayers as much as $500,000. For one thing, Larry's attorneys would have access to the Capital Litigation Trust Fund of Illinois to defray some of the costs associated with a death penalty case. Each year, money for the fund is appropriated by the Illinois General Assembly, and expenditures for each case are approved by the trial judge.

* * *

In a telephone conversation several days after the hearing, Larry told Phil Luciano, a reporter with the Copley News Service, that he'd tell him in exchange for a couple hundred bucks why he committed the murders. If not, Larry said he'd keep his mouth shut until he could write a tell-all book and give the proceeds to the victims' families.

During the call Larry said he prayed for his victims every night. He said they didn't deserve what he did to them. In a published report, Luciano said he kept pushing Larry to reveal his real motives for killing. Larry, however, was having none of it and ended the call after five minutes.

But during their conversation, Larry said it wasn't just one thing that made him kill, it was many things that had happened to him throughout his life. However, he denied race had anything to do with the murders.

He told Luciano that he would tell him the whole story, but he wanted to make a little cash for coffee and other toiletries in jail. Larry also told Luciano that his attorneys wanted him to plead insanity, but he was going to enter a guilty plea, even if it meant the death penalty. He said he was prepared to take it like a man.

But while Larry was preparing to take his punishment like a man, his mother was already being punished for her son's crimes. Although police had said Shirley had no idea what her son was doing, people in the community still accused her of somehow being complicit. Shirley even told police that two African-American men had followed her after one of her weekly visits with Larry at the Tazewell County Jail, but she managed to

lose them. Her life had been turned inside out—
so much so that she had taken to staying with a
friend, afraid of what might happen to her if she
stayed at her house on West Starr Court.

At another hearing the first week in April,
Judge Shadid ruled that Larry would be examined
within sixty days to determine if he was fit to stand
trial. If he was deemed fit, his trial most likely
wouldn't get under way for at least six months.
The judge also approved a request by the defense
for a DNA expert, who would monitor the tests on
the blood and semen that investigators found in
Larry's house. Authorities believed that the
stained sheets and comforters taken from his
room could link him to some of the murdered and
missing women. Before the hearing ended, Shadid
set Larry's next court date as May 6.

About the same time, the twelve-member task
force, which had been working around the clock
to investigate the deaths and disappearances of
ten African-American women, had been reduced
to just two full-time investigators, who were tying
up loose ends. But no sooner had the task force
been cut, when a human skeleton was found behind the Peoria & Pekin Union Railroad offices,
along the banks of the Illinois River in Creve
Coeur, Tazewell County. Authorities turned the remains over to a forensic anthropologist for testing.
DNA results were expected three weeks later.

Police in Canton were anxious to know if the
skeleton was that of Bonnie Fife, the thirty-seven-
year-old woman who was last seen on July 26 by a

friend who dropped her off at a South Peoria house.
Task force members had already determined her
disappearance wasn't connected to Larry.

There was also speculation that the remains
could be those of Karen Hobdy-Cage, who had disappeared about a year and a half earlier. The
skeleton had been found about six blocks from
the house where Karen's boyfriend lived at the
time she vanished. But police in Creve Coeur refused to comment on that case.

Several weeks later, the bones were identified as
belonging to a female who was approximately fifty
years old. Authorities were planning to compare
DNA from Karen to the skeleton's femur. Ultimately the remains were identified as Karen's, but
she was not one of Larry's victims. Police didn't
find any evidence of foul play at the scene. After
an inquest the cause of Karen's death was ruled
"undetermined," and the case remained open.

Larry was back in court May 6. At the five-
minute hearing, Judge James Shadid approved a
motion by the defense to have Larry examined by
Springfield psychiatrist Dr. Terry Killian to determine if Larry was fit to stand trial. The mental
exam was set for sometime in mid- to late June and
the results could be known by Larry's next court
date, which was set for July 22. Shadid also agreed
to a defense request to have a DNA expert observe
investigators when they processed evidence for
DNA and conducted other forensic tests.

While sorting the hundreds of skull and bone fragments to send for DNA testing, an anthropologist

determined that they came from at least two women. After getting that information, Lyons said he would review the tests and decide whether to charge Larry with any additional murders.

The next time Larry met with Detectives Dave Hoyle and Cy Taylor, he wasn't too thrilled with what they asked him to do.

"Since the last time I talked to you, they have another request to have you tested for HIV. I don't know why," Hoyle said. "You got a problem with that?"

"Yeah, if I get tested, they're going to make me take the medication."

"I imagine you could refuse the medication," Taylor said.

"If you say no, they might be able to get a court order to have you tested. Whether they can or not, I don't know," Hoyle said. "Let's face [it], if you have it, you probably should take the medication."

Taylor said he wasn't sure if they could force him, because he had certain rights, and one of those rights was probably the right to refuse medication.

"Here's the other thing," Hoyle said. "You've been in here a while and you've gotten to know all these guys, and if, for some unknown reason, you fell down in the shower and you cracked your head open and you started bleeding like a stuck hog, those guys probably should know that, so they didn't get exposed."

"I know, but I'd tell them that I think I have it, if that happened," Larry said.

Finally Larry agreed and signed a waiver to let the jail nurse draw his blood. While they waited for the nurse to arrive, Hoyle asked Larry about a rumor that was flying around that he wasn't going to plead guilty anymore. Larry said a lot of people were telling him not to plead guilty, but he was still planning to do so, because he just wanted to get everything over with.

Hoyle said if Larry's case went to trial, it would be one of the biggest trials the county had ever seen. Larry said again he had no intention of changing his plea.

"Did anyone ever tell you what it's like on death row?" Hoyle asked.

Larry said it was basically the same as the jail. "You can have television, commissary, cigarettes—except it's dirtier and noisier," he said.

"Why would it be dirtier?" Hoyle asked.

"Because it's a hundred-year-old prison," Larry said. "I don't want to die, but either way, that's going to be the end result."

"So you think if you go to general population, somebody's going to get you?"

"Oh, yeah. Oh, yeah."

At that point the nurse came in to draw Larry's blood, and the interview ended.

The next time Larry met with the detectives, he got the results of his HIV test.

"Well, your HIV test came back and it's negative," Hoyle said.

"It's negative? What's that mean?"

"I guess it means you're not positive for HIV right now. I guess you could be positive a year from now, but I don't know. As of last week, you were negative for HIV."

During the interview Larry halfheartedly admitted to killing the girl in Racine, although he never said he was talking about Linda Fields.

"There's some cigarette burns on the black girl," Larry told Hoyle and Taylor.

"You remember putting cigarette burns on her, but you don't remember killing her?" Hoyle asked.

Larry said the reason he didn't mention killing her before was because he didn't want to be sent to face the music in Wisconsin.

"But if you killed her, Wisconsin isn't going to take you away from us," Hoyle said. "If you killed her, you've got to tell us. The only way you're getting out of here is in a box. So if they want to take your dead body and try it, let them."

"I know, but I have plans for my dead body," Larry said.

"If you killed eight girls in Wisconsin and one in Illinois, it might be different," Hoyle said. "If you didn't kill her, don't say you did. But if you did kill her and dump her there, you have to tell us."

"Yeah."

"Tell us about how you killed her," Hoyle said.

"By strangulation. I was up visiting Monica, and I picked her up and we partied in a motel."

"Which one?"

"I know where it is, but I don't know the name," Larry said as he described the location of the motel for Hoyle and Taylor.

"Do you remember her name?"

"No."

"Did she have her clothes on?"

"On. I re-dressed her."

"What were you driving when that happened?"

"I'm not sure what I was driving. I tried so hard to forget. Probably was the Dakota."

"Anybody see you with this girl?"

"The guy we got dope off of did."

"Did you remember this the whole time?" Hoyle asked, more than a little skeptical about Larry's story.

"It's just been coming back to me. I'm just so ashamed of what I done. It's just sounding worse and worse. I try not to think of myself as that person, but it was me."

"How did you strangle her? Did you use a rope?"

"No my hands."

"Did you kill her in the hotel room or in the truck?"

"In the hotel."

"Why do you remember the cigarette burns?"

Larry explained that the Racine police mentioned that something had been done to the woman's body; there were either bite marks or cigarette burns on her.

"I just keep seeing cigarettes," he said, adding that he put cigarettes out on her, under her breasts, while she was still alive.

"Did she fight with you?"

"Yeah."

"Why did you do that?"

"I know you don't believe me," Larry said, "but I'm not one hundred percent sure I did it. I don't know if it's my mind messing with me. I just remember bits and pieces."

"You're not one hundred percent sure you killed her?" Hoyle asked.

"No, I keep seeing it, but I don't know if I did it."

"Well, only two people know if you did it or not, and one of them can't talk to us," Hoyle said.

"I have a recollection of going into a motel, and I see burning her, but I don't know if it's because of what they told me happened," Larry said.

"Those guys from Racine are going to want to talk to you again," Hoyle said.

"I don't know if I'll be any help to them."

"Either you did, or you didn't," Hoyle said. "Not a lot of things will change, if you did or you didn't."

"I know that. I wish I could say one way or another whether I did or didn't," Larry said. "I think I did. I've been trying to remember. I don't remember the deed, but I remember other things. But I don't know if it's what they told me, or it comes to me in a dream, or I actually did it."

"Well, we'll have to see if you remember something they didn't tell you."

"If there's two cigarette burns on the lower chest, then I probably did it."

"They told you about that, didn't they?"

"No," Larry said, meaning they didn't tell him the location of the burns.

"Well, we'll get ahold of them and find out."

"'Cause I have a lot of nightmares, and I don't know if it's what they said, because they said something was done to her body, like biting or burning or something. And they asked me about biting or burning," Larry said. "And I remember two cigarette burns."

"We'll talk to them and find out," Hoyle said.

"But I don't want to get too deep into it, because it's their investigation, not ours."

"It's terrible what I've done. I just want to get this whole damn thing over with."

The next time Larry was interviewed, he wanted to know if the Racine police were coming back to talk to him.

"Last time we talked, you said you didn't have much to tell them," said Cy Taylor, who met with Larry alone.

"I don't remember doing it. Just certain things stuck in my head. I don't know if it's 'cause of what they said, but I had a dream several times, and I remember cigarette burns. I don't know if I did that, or if it's 'cause of what they said or what's going on," Larry said.

"Did they say something about cigarette burns?" Taylor asked.

"Yeah, they said something about cigarette burns," Larry said. "And I was wondering if they found the white girl?"

"On the cigarette burns, was that the white girl or the black girl?"

"The black girl."

"If you want to talk to them . . . Last time we talked, I was pretty sure you said you didn't have anything else to say," Taylor said.

"If there were cigarette burns on the lower chest, maybe there's something to talk about. I don't know if I just dreamed it or what, but I just want to get it over with now."

(Subsequently Larry admitted to police that he

didn't do any of the other murders he confessed to. He said that he made it all up, and that the only ones he did were in Illinois.)

When Larry met with Hoyle and Taylor again, he explained that he wanted to be sentenced to life in prison because he wanted to be able to give his mom a hug when she came to see him. Apparently, there was no physical contact on death row.

"You asked me why I did it," Larry said. "I told you some things but not everything. A lot of why I did it was the sex and the power. After I got going, it was basically another drug. I ain't proud of it. For everybody involved, I want to get this over with. What I'm scared of is, if I get a life sentence for the two they charged me with, and then they charge me with the others, and I get the penalty."

Hoyle then asked Larry about a couple keys the investigators had found when they were sorting the bones and ashes of the victims. Larry said one of the girls had two keys, but he didn't know which girl. He said that when he was burning the clothes, he put the keys with the ashes and took them to his grandma's house.

"I remember it was a house key and a padlock key," he said. "I think they might have been on a thin key chain and it melted, but I'm not sure."

"You know the keys might help us positively identify one of the victims if they opened her door," Hoyle said.

"I remembered the keys," Larry said during his next interview. "I kept a key from all the victims, except one. I think where they were [was] in a cabinet in my house. They're on a key ring, but the ones in the ashes, I don't know if they belong to them or not. I just kept one and got rid of the rest of the keys. I don't know why I kept a key. It was just something I did. The extra keys I dumped."

"Why did you keep them?" Taylor asked.

"A souvenir, I guess. You can tell a lot about somebody by their keys."

"What can you tell about people?" Taylor asked.

"Some people keep their keys nice and shiny, even though they're old," Larry said.

"What can you tell about me?" Hoyle asked, handing Larry his keys.

"You're not very neat. I always shined my keys and used a toothbrush to clean them. When I was a kid, I used to collect them and keep them clean," Larry said. "It seemed some of the girls did that, too. Even if they had old keys, they were shiny. I went for the odd-shaped keys. There should be nine keys on there."

"You took one from the girl in Wisconsin, too?" Hoyle asked.

"Yeah. And one of the last ones didn't have any keys."

"My first instinct is that you're full of shit, and you just wanted to [get out] to have a cigarette," Hoyle said. "I don't know why you didn't tell us before."

"I wanted to keep them, but you can have them," Larry said. "You always asked me if I kept anything from the girls. I did. It was something that didn't mean anything to anyone except the person who owned the keys. I told my mom in a letter, you guys would probably be coming for the keys."

* * *

On July 22, Judge Shadid ruled that Larry was indeed fit to stand trial. The judge based his ruling on the fifty-five-page report written by Killian, who determined that Larry understood that he had been charged with first-degree murder and could assist in his own defense. Although Larry's attorneys didn't contest the report, they said they would request a more comprehensive psychological test if the case went to trial.

Several weeks after the hearing, employees of the Keystone Steel & Wire Co. in Bartonville, a village in Peoria County, uncovered human bones as they were draining a shallow canal behind the plant. When police arrived, they also found a pair of shorts in the area. The Peoria County Coroner's Office used dental records to identify the remains as those of Bonnie Fife, who was last seen at a crack house in Peoria on July 26, 2004.

Investigators had previously questioned Larry about Bonnie because they knew each other, but Larry adamantly denied any involvement in her disappearance. Hoyle and Taylor met with Larry after Bonnie's body was discovered to determine if he had anything to do with her death.

But before they questioned him about Bonnie, Larry said he had something else to talk to them about.

"I remember I put some underwear and makeup in a hole under a concrete slab on our neighbor's property," Larry said. "What reminded me is that when I was getting my hair cut, the haircut lady bent over and I saw her drawers, and they were purple, the same color as the panties I hid. They're in, like, a little plastic bag."

"How far in the hole did you stick them?" Taylor asked.

"Well, I was afraid there was something in there, so I didn't put them in too far."

"I don't want to get bit by no groundhog," Hoyle said, figuring he was going to have to look for them. "Do you remember which girl?"

"I'm not sure."

"One that got burned, or one that got dumped?"

"I'm not sure."

"Which one you leaning to, though?"

"One of the girls that got dumped," Larry said. "After the first time you questioned me, I still had those in my house. Then I waited until real late one night and I stuck them under there."

Hoyle then decided it was time to talk to Larry about Bonnie.

"They found Bonnie's body. You know anything about that?"

"No, I took a lie detector test."

"You didn't pass it all the way. You just passed it on some things," Hoyle said. "So the guy who's doing the investigation . . . guess who's his main suspect right off the bat?"

"Me."

"Yeah. There's just certain things about it that are pointing the finger toward you."

"I can imagine."

"Why do you think that?"

"Because I killed other people, and I had a grudge

against Bonnie. But I haven't seen her for ten or twelve years. The last time I saw her was when me and Marie were still together. I had nothing to do with it. Where was she found?"

"I'm not going to tell you that, because I'm not the one who's leading the investigation," Hoyle said. "The last time you saw her was when you and Marie broke up. Where was that? Do you remember?"

"When me and Marie were still together was the last time I saw her. We were partying at Bonnie's house in Canton."

"When you were with Marie, you brought other people into the relationship sexually and had three-ways. Was Bonnie one of those?" Hoyle asked.

"No, no. I disliked her. Marie said something about it, and I said, 'Not with Bonnie.' I didn't like her at all. I may have threatened her back then, but I didn't do anything to her."

"What didn't you like about her?"

"Her and Marie would go out and they'd do drugs, and they'd be gone for a couple days. It pissed me off."

"Did you have a confrontation with her about it?"

"I told her exactly how I felt. I wasn't keeping no secrets from her."

"Did you ever threaten to kill her?"

"I may have said that."

"Did you ever slap her, hit her?"

"No, I never laid one hand on her."

"Did she ever threaten you?"

"Threaten me?"

"Yeah, you know Bonnie, she could kick most men's ass."

"No, she never threatened me," Larry said, chuckling. "We had a big argument, but no blows or anything like that."

"A lot of Bonnie's friends are pointing the finger at you because you already told us you killed eight, nine, ten people," Hoyle said, counting on his fingers.

"I can imagine what they're thinking, but that ain't so."

"Part of the reason we're even talking to you about it is because there are some similarities between the way Bonnie was found and the way some of the girls you said you killed were found. That's what we've got to get to the bottom of. What's concerning the investigators is the similarities, and Bonnie happens to be right in the middle [of the other murders]. So, did you kill Bonnie Fife?"

"No."

"The problem still remains about Bonnie," Hoyle said. "You flunked part of that lie detector test. I know one part you flunked. The question 'Are you holding anything back from the police?' So I know you're holding something back from me. And I want to know what it is. You know that if you did this, nothing's going to change."

"I didn't kill Bonnie. I disliked her, but I didn't want her dead."

(Larry was never charged in connection with the death of Bonnie Fife.)

Hoyle then switched gears and asked Larry if he had ever found any pins or screws in the bones and ashes of the women he burned. He said he had not.

Larry again said he hoped he'd be able to plead guilty at his next court date and get it all over with.

Before meeting with Larry again, Hoyle went to look for the panties but wasn't able to find them.

"There were some big-ass groundhogs there, but I didn't get bit," he told Larry. Hoyle drew a picture of the location of the concrete slab, where Larry supposedly hid the panties.

"When you put the panties in there, they were wrapped in a little white plastic bag?" Hoyle asked.

"Yeah, a hole on the side of the slab."

"Next time I'm going down there with a car jack and jack the whole slab up," Hoyle said. "Did you tell anyone else about them, like your mom?"

"No, I didn't tell anyone but you."

"They should still be there, then," Hoyle said.

"Maybe the groundhogs got them."

(It's unclear if the detectives ever recovered the panties.)

Although Larry had initially tried to plead guilty to murdering eight women, he changed his tune and decided to fight for his life—despite having told Hoyle and Taylor he wasn't planning to change his mind. His attorney James Elmore said Larry's family convinced him not to give up. Shirley, especially, played a major part in her son's decision.

Elmore was also getting ready to file a motion requesting a psychological exam for Larry, because he truly believed that his client had some psychiatric problems. And he was preparing a motion to have Larry's trial moved out of Peoria

County due to the widespread media coverage about the case.

At a November 7 hearing in Peoria County Circuit Court that lasted only four minutes, Judge Shadid approved a defense request to hire Terry Killian to examine Larry Bright to determine if he was sane when he murdered the eight women. Six weeks later, Elmore filed the motion for a change of venue, arguing it would be impossible for Larry to get a fair trial in Peoria County because everyone knew who he was.

State's Attorney Kevin Lyons said he most likely wouldn't oppose the motion because of the extensive pretrial publicity. However, he had to take into consideration the added expenses of moving the trial, including transportation and hotels—expenses that could add tens of thousands of dollars to the cost of the trial. Lyons said the trial, which was expected to last about three weeks, would probably begin sometime in the middle of 2006.

In late January 2006, Lyons had announced that investigators had identified a jawbone found at one of Larry's dumping spots as Tamara "Tammy" Walls's. They used dental records to tie the bone to Tammy. Larry was then indicted for her murder. At a court hearing, Larry's attorneys entered a plea of not guilty on his behalf. And Judge Shadid postponed arguments on the defense's motion to move Larry's trial to another county, because the psychiatric exam to determine if he was sane when he committed his crimes hadn't yet been completed.

16

While Larry was languishing in the Tazewell County Jail at the beginning of 2006, authorities were looking into the disappearance of Jessica Curless, an eighteen-year-old Peoria woman. Jessica was last seen alive by her mother on January 9.

When they hadn't heard from her in five days, Jessica's parents called police. They were concerned because she hadn't picked up the insulin she needed to keep her diabetes under control.

Friends and family described Jessica for the *Peoria Journal Star* as a shy young woman who really didn't have many friends growing up. However, when she was a sophomore, she became more confident and began making new friends. They said she loved singing, and after she graduated, she remained active in the chorus at Richwoods High School. She was also taking classes to become a certified nurse's assistant.

Jessica moved out of her parents' house in November 2005, moved into the home of an East Bluff couple as a live-in babysitter—although she didn't

share information about her job or the family
with anyone—and started seeing less of her friends.
Jessica loved hanging out at the Lucky Lady and
Dave's Goodtime Billiards in West Peoria. However, she apparently didn't do drugs or drink.

Sometime in January, police called Jessica's parents to tell them that they had arrested two men in
South Peoria who were in possession of Jessica's
1997 Pontiac Sunfire. Their daughter, however,
was nowhere in sight. The men, thirty-three-year-
old Michael Hunter and fifty-one-year-old Carlos
Hobson, lived close to where Jessica had been
living.

When police searched the car, they noticed that
pieces of fabric from the vehicle's upholstery and
the driver's-side seat belt had been removed. That
material was later discovered in Jessica's blue
jacket, which was found weighted down by rocks
on the banks of the Illinois River.

Earlier, a passerby had found Jessica's wallet,
containing her driver's license and her Richwoods
High School student ID card, in the same area.
And investigators discovered a black plastic bag
filled with more of Jessica's belongings hidden
close by under a slab of concrete. Investigators
were able to get a fingerprint from it, although it
was never clear to whom that fingerprint belonged.

Hobson and Hunter were arrested for conceal-
ing a homicide. But the next day those charges
were reduced to obstruction of justice in connection with a theft or battery, since the two men had
some of the young woman's belongings.

Also in January, police arrested twenty-two-year-
old Hershel "Buddy" Morgan, of Peoria, in con-

nection with a number of home invasions, armed robberies and sexual assaults in Peoria, Woodford, and Tazewell Counties. And they believed Morgan was good for all of them.

After he was arrested, Morgan was held in the Tazewell County Jail, the jail where Larry was also being held. Morgan had been charged with four counts of home invasion, two counts of aggravated criminal sexual assault, and one count of residential burglary. Investigators also believed that Morgan pulled some of the jobs with an accomplice, who happened to be a woman.

When police interviewed Morgan on January 16, he denied knowing Jessica, although he said her name and face seemed familiar. But finally, when pressed by investigators, Morgan changed his story and admitted to knowing Jessica, but he said she probably ran off to Florida with a man she was seeing named Cody.

Police also believed that Morgan murdered Jessica, because they found traces of Jessica's blood in her Pontiac Sunfire, which Morgan admitted to driving. He had been driving her car when he was pulled over by the Illinois State Police for a seat belt violation. That's when Hunter and Hobson, who were also in the car, were arrested. Morgan, however, jumped out of the car and took off before police could question him, and he was never reported as the person who was fleeing from the police. Hunter ultimately cut a deal with prosecutors and fingered Morgan as the person who murdered Jessica.

While Hobson, Hunter, and Morgan were in custody, police continued searching for Jessica's body, although her family just couldn't bring themselves to believe she was dead. Jessica's family, however, didn't think their daughter was the woman who had been helping Morgan. They did think she might have been murdered because she knew too much about certain crimes, and someone feared she might go to the police.

Somehow, although it's not quite clear exactly how, Larry told the police he'd talk to Morgan to see if he would give up the location of Jessica's body. In exchange, he wanted to watch his beloved Pittsburgh Steelers play the Seattle Seahawks in the Super Bowl.

Investigators jumped at the chance, and over several days, beginning on the last day of January, Detective Dave Hoyle, of the Peoria County Sheriff's Office, and Detective Cy Taylor, of the Tazewell County Sheriff's Office, met with Larry to see what he had learned. Larry's involvement, though, was never made public.

The first interview began with police reading Larry his rights. Then Larry signed the paper indicating he understood those rights. He said he didn't have to write anything about his lawyer not wanting him to talk to police because he wasn't going to be talking about his case.

After small talk about Hoyle's kids buying him a watch and new handcuffs for Christmas, they got down to business.

"All right, what's up, buddy?" Hoyle asked.

"Well, I been talking to him. He's admitted to doing it, and he said that he has guns and money, and he puts them in a plastic bag and then puts them in a paper bag and then puts them in another plastic bag. And then he said something about bearer bonds and he has those hid right by where the girl is. And he said his girlfriend doesn't know where the girl is, but she [really] does. Because it's his favorite spot, but she don't know that the girl is there. So a good way to get to it might be through her," Larry said, hardly taking a breath. "I've been talking to him about religion and stuff, and I told him that he needs to come clean about it. And he says, 'I don't want to go to prison forever.' I know that this ain't going to get resolved by the Super Bowl, so I just want to do this . . ."

"Larry, you know what, if they go talk to his girlfriend and find out where his favorite spot is, and they go and find her, maybe we'll get it done for you," Hoyle said. "You know I can't make any promises. But I won't object to you watching the Super Bowl. You keep trying."

"I'll keep talking to him."

"We all knew, when we started talking, that it was a long shot that he'd say, 'Okay, you go to this dump, take thirteen steps to the east, fourteen steps to the right, and there she is.'"

"You know, she might be burned," Larry said.

"Really, how come?"

"He was asking me about burning, and he said that he tried it. He's told me he's committed two murders."

"Did he tell you where the other one was?" Hoyle asked.

"Just in the woods."

"What woods?"

"I don't know."

"Did he say when the other one was?" Taylor asked.

"He said that the two guys that you have in custody in Peoria weren't involved."

"Has he told you what his name is?"

"Hershel, but he goes by Buddy."

"So he didn't give you any details about anything, then, huh?" Taylor asked.

"No, he talks about his robberies a lot, and about how he slapped that girl's tittie in one of those home invasions. I guess he's got a sexual harassment charge against him because he slapped her tittie, or something."

"Did he tell you how he killed her?"

"He shot her."

"Did he tell you that?"

"Yeah, and I guess the reason is her license plates were called in or something, and then he thought that she was going to tell on him or something. She actually sold some of the bearer bonds. I don't know if this is a made-up thing. They don't even do bearer bonds anymore, do they?"

"I don't know anything about it. I don't know where somebody like her would know where to sell them at, anyhow," Hoyle said.

"Did he say where they were when it happened?"

"No. I'm scared to ask that type of question because that's like a cop question, you know what I mean? And I'm trying to be slick. He talks all night long. I wake up and he's like, 'I did it. I did it.' He's going for an insanity thing, he told me. And this guy is slick. I mean he can do a trick. He takes a piece of paper and he'll put it in his mouth and push it back. And in back of his tongue, in his throat, there's this little shelf and he can hide things behind his tongue and open his mouth, stick out his tongue, lift up his tongue, and then it comes back out."

"So he said he's going for an insanity plea, huh?"

"Yeah, 'cause he's had injuries."

"Did he ever tell you what this girl's name was?"

"No, he didn't."

"Did he ever refer to her by a first name or by somebody's girlfriend, or something like that?"

"She was the getaway driver, evidently. He never did tell me her name."

"[Did he ever say why he killed her?]"

"Because he heard that you had got her license plates and were going to talk to her, and he got all scared, and that's why it happened."

"Did you talk about the sketches at all?"

"No, he didn't say nothing about sketches."

"What else did you guys talk about, besides her getting killed?" Hoyle asked.

"You know, just normal, next-door neighbor—type shit."

"Like your hobby and his hobby and fishing?"

"Yeah, he likes fishing. And he always goes fishing by the river, and I was going at it from that angle."

"Did he say where he goes at by the river?"

"Yeah, all over by the side of Peoria, but I wouldn't think he'd put a body there or else it'd be found. That's what I was trying to get at, and the places he told me were, like, under the bridges, and a place, like, that a body wouldn't be found—unless it was buried or hid good, you know."

"And he didn't say what he did with her?"

"She's buried. He asked me one time about how I burned bodies and I told him, and he said, 'That didn't work for me.' And I said, 'What, you tried it?' And he said, 'Yeah, but it didn't work.' So I don't know if this girl's burned, or he was talking about the other one. And he seems like he's full of shit."

"Do you think he's lying to you to impress you?" Hoyle asked. "Which part do you think he's full of shit about, the burning or the other?"

"Yeah, the burning. He could be telling the truth, but it just seems like he was trying to impress somebody."

"So this guy didn't talk about where he might have buried her, or how he might have buried her, or if somebody helped him bury her, or anything like that?"

"I think he did it by himself. He told me, when he tried to burn someone, he dug a pit and he used tires and wood, but I don't know, 'cause then he asked me how I did it."

"So what'd he do when it didn't work for him?"

"He just buried 'em," Larry said. "If you can, after this is all done, I'd appreciate you guys moving him back. Because I knew something was up, because he was in cell eight, and all of a sudden, they moved him right next to me two days before you guys talked to me, that's why I knew. I know what you want."

"We need to find her, though, the family, you know how it is?"

"Especially a nineteen-year-old girl," Larry said.

"How do you think we're going to find her, Larry?" Hoyle asked.

"His girlfriend, that's your best bet. And he might confess."

"Did he say anything to give you an idea what his favorite spot might be? What kind of a place it might be?" Hoyle asked.

"It's along the river."

"What are you basing that on?"

"He told me he likes to fish, and he buried all his stuff in the woods or by the river, as far as all the money he's got. And he has quite a selection of guns, automatic weapons."

"Maybe if you just talk to him about your favorite spot, whatever it might be, and describe it to him, maybe he'll do the same to you. Just say some bullshit, 'You know, I really wish I could go back down to my thinking spot. Just go down there and sit for an hour.' And describe it to him."

"I think other than him confessing, I think the girl," Larry said. "If there's some way you can get to her. Maybe not even let her know what you're after. Just ask about his favorite spots and stuff."

"Did he say anything more about the car?"

"No, he never talked too much about the car. He said they did a DNA test on him, because there was some blood in the car. I'll try it and we can hook up again Friday or something."

"Maybe you should do it Thursday, so it will give us time to get your shit set up for you?"

"I'm not too worried about that," Larry said.

"I know, but if we told you we were going to do something, I'd like to be able to get it done for you," Hoyle said. "Another thing you can use with him is to say, 'You should use this shit to your advantage. You know they've got you. Cut a deal with them saying that "I'll give you the body for this."' Tell him [to] cut a deal. Tell him, 'You've got the upper hand right now. Try and work something out.'"

"What does he think about his situation?" Taylor asked.

"He's hopeful that he'll get bailed out, even though he's got a seven-hundred-and-fifty-thousand-dollar bail."

"Who's going to bail him out?" Hoyle asked. "He ain't got anybody to bail him out."

"From what he says, his uncle's got a cattle ranch. I don't know."

"Does he think he's looking at a bunch?" Taylor asked.

"He thinks he's looking at, like, fifteen years for the home invasions and the residential burglaries," Larry said.

"He's looking at more than that for just one of them, and there's several of them."

"That girl just needs to be found," Larry said.

"I understand they've had her mom on TV saying, 'Help find our daughter.' She needs her back," Hoyle said.

"So her mom still thinks . . ."

"I think her mom is holding out hope," Hoyle said. "If they're missing, you still hope and pray to God that somewhere, somehow, they're still alive. But people like that they know, but they're just not ready to admit it to themselves until there's a body."

"You said something the other day, Larry, that I was going to ask you about," Taylor said. "He talked about doing them in the larger area, and he's been doing them for a while."

"Yeah."

"The burglaries or home invasions or both or what?"

"He told me he liked doing it when people were home. He preferred it when they were home. He said he'd make them get their safe and all kinds of stuff. If I'm doing a robbery, I would want them to be gone, and you get what you get and you get out. Just for the fact that sooner or later, you're going to have to kill somebody."

"Either that, or somebody's going to kill you," Hoyle said. "I guarantee he showed up at my house, he wouldn't make it out."

"Did he talk about hurting anybody at any of them?" Taylor asked.

"Just slapping that one gal. He was real proud of that."

"Did he tell you there was some kind of radius around where he did them?" Taylor asked.

"He said in the thirty-mile radius is what they usually did."

"He said 'they'? Was he telling you about somebody else?"

"Well, these two [guys] you got in custody, I guess, mainly did everything with him."

"Did he say that?"

"Yeah. You got two guys in custody in Peoria, I guess, from what he told me."

"And he said they helped him do a lot of the stuff?" Taylor asked.

"Yeah."

"We still got a few more days to talk to him, right?" Taylor asked.

"Yeah, and I'll keep an ear open, because I'd feel better about myself if I could help," Larry said.

"Well, yeah, who wouldn't? Especially when you hear about the mom and the dad and what they're going through right now, and you're kind of familiar with some of that, anyway. And you know how it made you feel and you can help us find somebody."

"If he did it, I can't speak for anybody else, but it was like the weight of the world was off of me once I told on myself. I know I screwed myself, but it was worth it just to get that constant pressure [off]," Larry said. "People don't believe in ghosts, but there are ghosts. And when they're on your trail, it's no good."

"And when he said he shot her, did he give you any details about that? Did he say where he shot her, or what he shot her with?"

"No, I wanted to ask him, but it's like don't ask him too many questions, because whenever you start asking him a bunch of questions, he clams up. But if you just let him run his mouth, he'll sit there and talk and talk," Larry said. ". . . He point-blank told me that he killed her."

"Do you remember when he first told you? How long ago it was?" Hoyle asked.

"It was like the second day that he moved next to me."

"You think it was, like, the twenty-fifth? That was Wednesday."

"Yeah."

"I was really kind of hoping he told you more," Hoyle said as they concluded the interview.

A couple days later, Hoyle and Taylor were again interviewing Larry about Hershel Morgan.

"I might have something for you," Larry said after Hoyle read him his rights. "I found out where his two favorite spots are."

"How'd you do that?"

"Well, I talked to him about fishing. Dave's idea," Larry said. "You know where Willow Knolls is? Not Willow Knolls, Charter Oak. You know how they got that fancy horse farm on one side of it? A big white fence that goes all around the side. There are two roads, one that goes in and one that goes out. The one that goes out, there's a lane that goes back, and there's a little pond back there. Go into that pond. You know where I'm talking about?"

"It's next to the horse pond?" Hoyle asked.

"No, no, no, no," Larry said.

"Oh, I know what you're talking about, Charter Oak and Orange Prairie Road."

"Well, the Charter Oak subdivision."

"Yeah, and it's got the fence that goes on for about two miles."

"Yeah, yeah," Larry said. "Well, the road coming out, there's a pond by the road. That's not it. Before you get to that pond, there's a lane that goes back there, and there's another pond back there. And he liked going back there. And the other spot, I don't [know] exactly where that is, but it's back by the dump. There's [a] strip mine lake, and he said there's all kinds of old refrigerators and all kinds of shit back there, actually in the water. And he said he stood on a car that was in the water, fishing."

"A dump with strip mine lakes?" Taylor asked.

"No, it's a strip mine lake, but they dumped all kinds of shit in the water," Larry said. "Those are the two places he told me about. That first place by Charter Oak, he really liked, though."

"What did he tell you about it?" Hoyle asked.

"I told him about my favorite spot, going back there, and he was telling me about his favorite spot. He liked going back there because it was all secluded. I don't know if anything's back there or not. It's definitely worth a look, though."

"So you can drive all the way down this lane?" Hoyle asked. "They got it gated off?"

"Way back when, they didn't have it gated off, but I don't know about now. It's been ten years since I been back there fishing."

"And this is the place he goes to?"

"Yeah, when I worked for Custom Builders, we built a lot of houses back there, and sometimes during the day, it was too hot for work, it was never too hot for fishing and drinking."

"So that's what he claimed, he went to each of these places to fish or just to go there?" Taylor asked.

"To fish and to think."

"Did he ever talk any more about her, though?" Hoyle asked.

"Yeah, somewhat. Her name's Jamie, right?"

"No," Hoyle said.

"He was talking about a Jamie."

"What did he say about Jamie?" Hoyle asked.

"I don't know if it's an act. In the middle of the night, he'll start talking to himself, and he kept talking about a Jamie. So I wrote down Jamie. Then he'd say, 'Buddy's a bad, little dude. Nobody messes with Buddy.' He's little, but he's bad," Larry said, laughing.

"So Buddy's a bad dude, huh?"

"Yeah, that's his nickname."

"Oh, yeah, that's right."

"But I'd say Charter Oak would be a good one to check," Larry said. "But that other, I don't know exactly where it is. But I think I was even there swimming with Eddie, because I remember we went somewhere out by the dump. I think it was somewhere off of Trigger Road, and we were diving off a car that was in the water. So I don't know if that was the same spot he was talking about or not. He keeps talking about the money and the bonds. Every time someone's in there, he brags about what he's in there for."

"What's he tell them he's in there for?" Hoyle asked.

"He says he's in there for all these robberies and murder."

"He tells other people that shit?" Taylor asked.

"Yeah."

"So you told Buddy about your favorite spots, that's how you got him talking about it?"

"Yeah, the Mackinaw River right by the grove."

"And then you asked him what his favorite spot was?"

"Then we were talking fishing."

"He didn't say anything else?" Taylor asked.

"No, just gibberish."

"Nothing about the girl?"

"No, because they keep beeping us," Larry said. "You know how when they listen to us, they beep. Well, he's all paranoid about that. 'They're listening, they're listening. Shut up. They're listening.'"

"Did he call one of these places a frog pond?" Taylor asked.

"No, that would be the place he was talking about behind Willow Knolls, behind where the big barn is. There's a little pond back there. But he told me the only way to get there was you had to walk. He talked about that place, too. But I don't think that would be a place he would want to carry a body in. I wouldn't want to, anyway, especially if there's blood all over it. I'd want to be able to drive back," Larry said. "If that don't pan out, I'd say that girl is your best bet, if you can get to her. And they've been arguing on the phone, so that might be possible."

"They have?" Taylor asked.

"What were they arguing about?" Taylor asked.

"Well, she's saying she don't know if she can stick with him if it's true about what he did. I guess she's pregnant, and you know how women are when they're pregnant," Larry said. "I wish I could do more. I don't really care about seeing the game, I just want this girl found."

"Well, we've been looking, but, obviously, we haven't found her," Hoyle said.

"Where did you come up with the frog pond? From one of his friends?" Larry asked.

"I don't know," Hoyle said. "I just know he's talked about a frog pond before."

"That could be the one behind that teen club that closed down a while ago."

"The one that closed down about ten years ago, Second Chance," Hoyle said.

"Yeah, that big barn. There's a trail that goes back behind there, I guess. There's a house there, and you gotta go through the field and there's a gate and a pond back there he always went fishing to, too. And it had a lot of frogs and shit in it."

After talking about his own case for several minutes, Larry asked Hoyle if State's Attorney Kevin Lyons listened to the recordings of his police interviews. After Hoyle said he thought someone in the prosecutor's office listened, Larry offered up his own plea deal.

"I'll plead guilty to life with no parole, no possibility of appeals. I'll sign all that over, you know just a heads-up," Larry said into the camera as Hoyle and Taylor laughed.

Several days later, Hoyle and Taylor again talked to Larry about Morgan.

"That place that I told you out by the dump, did you find that lake?" Larry asked.

"Nope," Hoyle said.

"From what he tells me, there're little pine trees. She's out there at the lake."

"When did he tell you this?" Hoyle asked.

"Saturday, he was talking."

"Okay, tell me exactly what he said," Hoyle said.

"Well, we were talking about frog ponds, and I was talking about where I put bodies and such, and he said he put her out there."

"He said he put her out by the dump? Did he tell you how to get there?" Hoyle asked.

"He don't know the roads."

"That's all he said was a lake with pine trees?"

"The small ones. He said there were small pine trees out by the lake."

"Did you talk about if he dragged her very far, or if he pulled right up next to it?"

"You can drive right up there," Larry said. "I think I was there once, but I'm not sure where it is. All the kids used to go swimming there, I guess. He said he swam there and fished there."

"How'd he tell you again that's where the body was?" Taylor asked.

"We were talking, and he told me that the place by where the car was in the water, and he said the body was there."

"Is that the words he used, 'the body'?" Taylor asked.

"He said 'she' was there."

"How did this whole conversation initiate? How did it first start?" Hoyle asked.

"We were just talking bullshit, like we always do, through the wall."

"And in the middle of this bullshitting, he just said, 'She's by the lake, with the pine trees on it'?" Hoyle asked.

"Yeah, he's been bragging about it to everybody down there," Larry said. "He says, 'Larry's down there for a bunch of murders, and I'm there for murder, too.' All cocky about it. In his cell he's made some handcuff keys out of plastic and he has a razor blade."

"He does?"

"Did you see it?"

"Yeah," Larry answered.

"Did you tell the COs about it?"

"No."

"When did you see it?'

"Saturday. He took the razor blade out of the razor and cut a fake razor blade out of a plastic shampoo bottle and put it back in the shaver, because the [COs] look at them to make sure the blade's still in them, and he had the razor blade."

"He showed you the razor blade?"

"Yeah. I don't know where it's hid or where he has it."

"You know they're going to have to go in and look for it," Hoyle said.

"I know it, but if you find it, you gotta move the guy, you can't leave him next to me," Larry said. "I don't want him getting to me."

"Not if they search your cell, too," Hoyle said. "They'll just have to wake him out of his sleep and say, 'Shake down.'"

"Okay, so how are we going to find this lake?" Hoyle asked.

"As far as the lake, that's all I know about it, what he told me," Larry said.

"Well, where's all this big information that you told us that you're supposed to have?" Hoyle asked. "You know the information you're going to trade for the Whopper and [onion] rings."

"I decided not to trade. . . ."

"A lake out by the Peoria dump that you can drive to with pine trees by it," Hoyle said.

"The main thing is there's a car in the water," Larry said.

"Well, I don't know where that's at. Car's half in the water? All the way in the water?" Hoyle asked.

"It's in the water. You can stand on it. It's half-way covered up."

"Did he tell you about the car?"

"Yeah, he told me he used to stand on the car and fish."

"Buddy told you about the car? He said the car was still there?"

"Yeah."

"Did they drive her in the lake?"

"No, she's buried by those little pine trees."

"Do you think you're going to find out any more, or do you think you should ask him directly?" Hoyle asked. "Do you think maybe it's time you just asked, 'Where the fuck'd you put her?'"

Larry didn't answer the question.

"Anything else?"

"No, that's all I know," Larry replied.

17

Finally investigators found Jessica's body on March 3, behind an abandoned house and barn north of Spring Bay, in Woodford County, but it's not clear if Larry was instrumental in the discovery. Her body was found fully clothed and lying next to a wooded area. There were bruises on her hands, and her body showed signs of decomposition.

Police interviewed Hershel "Buddy" Morgan about Jessica again, on March 6, at the Tazewell County Jail and showed him a picture of her body. Morgan cried and feigned disgust, begging investigators to believe him when he said he had nothing to do with her death.

In fact, he said his friend Carlos Hobson murdered Jessica in her car. Morgan said he was sitting behind Jessica, who was in the driver's seat, when she was killed. He said when Hobson hit her on the head with a hammer, her blood splattered across his face.

He said he, Hobson, Jessica, and a guy named Danny White hid out from the police near the abandoned farmhouse. But the detectives weren't buying it. They believed that Morgan killed Jessica so she wouldn't inform on him.

Despite their best efforts to get him to confess, Morgan contined to deny he murdered Jessica. But in July, Morgan was charged with murdering Jessica by hitting her in the head with a ball-peen hammer. The hammer, which was covered with traces of her blood, was found in the grass near her body. Authorities said Morgan killed Jessica because he didn't want her to help police with their investigation against him for the home invasions, sexual assault, and burglary, which was just what Larry had told police.

Morgan pleaded not guilty to murdering Jessica. The state's attorney decided not to pursue the death penalty in the case.

Morgan's murder trial began in March 2008. During the trial, Kevin Zeeb, a forensic scientist with the Illinois State Police said the only DNA evidence that could potentially connect Morgan to Jessica's murder was a pair of his pants.

After the six-day trial, the jury of nine men and three women took about four hours to find Hershel "Buddy" Morgan guilty of murdering eighteen-year-old Jessica Curless by hitting her in the head with a hammer and dumping her body in a patch of weeds near a vacant farmhouse, north of Spring Bay. He is serving a life sentence without parole in the Stateville Correctional Center. It's unclear if Morgan ever knew that Larry snitched on him.

18

On May 8, 2006, Larry Bright's attorneys and the state's attorney's office received the 116-page evaluation done by Dr. Terry Killian, which, according to the prosecution, did not indicate that Bright was insane. Around the same time, Lyons was contemplating a plea deal for Bright that would spare his life. Lyons said he would agree to a sentence of life in prison without parole if the victims' families supported it. He believed the wishes of the families were particularly important because the murders had affected so many people. But if he agreed to a plea bargain, it meant Bright would have to admit to murdering all the women, so the families of the victims who had not been identified could get closure.

The judge gave both sides three weeks to work out a plea deal, and he set another hearing date for May 30. If a deal wasn't negotiated by then, he said, he would set a trial date and rule on the defense motion for a change of venue.

After the hearing Lyons filed a motion with the

Illinois Supreme Court asking for permission to have a single video camera in the courtroom to capture the plea hearing—something he had never done in his eighteen years as the state's attorney for Peoria County. Lyons thought Larry Bright's case was so unusual and affected the entire community that it warranted having a camera in court.

Although the supreme court was almost at the end of its session when he filed the motion, Lyons hoped the esteemed body would still rule on it. That, however, did not happen.

Finally, on May 31, 2006, Larry Bright pleaded guilty to murdering eight women. He was sentenced to life in prison without the possiblity of parole. As part of the plea agreement, Bright admitted to strangling seven of the women to death and causing the death of another woman who died of an overdose of cocaine.

Under the agreement Bright admitted that from July 2003 until late 2004, he strangled to death Linda Neal, forty, Brenda Erving, forty-one, Shirley Ann Trapp-Carpenter, forty-five, Shaconda Thomas, thirty-two, Laura Lollar, thirty-three, Tamara "Tammy" Walls, twenty-nine, and Sabrina Payne, thirty-six. He also admitted that he caused the death of Barbara Williams, thirty-six, by giving her cocaine. A picture of each woman appeared on television monitors in the courtroom as Lyons recounted the evidence against Larry Bright. And each time Judge Shadid asked Bright if he was guilty of killing the women, he answered yes.

Bright was sentenced to seven life sentences to be

served concurrently. He also received a thirty-year sentence, to run concurrently with the life sentences, for causing the cocaine death of Barbara Williams. As part of the deal, Bright waived his right to any appeals.

William Young Jr., Brenda Erving's stepfather, didn't think Larry would last all that long in prison.

"When I first found out that Larry Bright had murdered Brenda, the first thing I thought about was what I could do to the man who killed my daughter. I felt really bad, but I knew I couldn't do that," William said. "I think life in prison will do more than putting a needle in his arm and killing him. But I don't think he'll last that long."

When police finally determined that Larry Bright had killed Mark's sister Linda and the other women, Mark Neal was incensed. And, like William Young Jr., he wanted to do to Bright the same thing that Larry had done to his beloved sister.

"I wanted to kill Larry," he said. "I wanted to go to Peoria and commit a crime to get to him in jail and kill him. Period. I've changed my life and I've been in church for a while now, and to say that is wrong. But that's how I felt at the time. I do believe in an eye for an eye, but now I don't want to kill him personally. They say you're supposed to forgive, but you don't have to forget. Do I forgive him, as of today? No, I still don't. I haven't gotten that far in my religion to look him in the face and tell him I forgive him. I can't say I'll ever be that religious.

"I agreed to life in prison. I been to prison. I was a gangbanger and I know what they get people for in prison. I hoped then and, I'm sad to say, I still hope somebody will kill him in there before he dies an old man."

Even though Larry Bright pleaded guilty to murdering the eight women, no one was really quite sure why he killed them in the first place. As police determined during their investigation, Bright was far from a hardened criminal. Sure, when he was nineteen, he went to prison for two years for burglary—an event that changed him. When he got out of prison, he started using cocaine and he drank heavily. After he hurt his back at work, he became addicted to painkillers. He couldn't hold a job and soon became depressed and started turning to black prostitutes for sex. But murder?

Larry Bright didn't start out to kill anyone—the first couple deaths were accidents—but then something happened. He started hearing voices that he couldn't control when he was high on crack. It was then that Bright began hunting for his prey.

At the hearing Jeffrey Page, one of Bright's attorneys, read a short statement written by his client: *I know that I have committed some horrific and unthinkable acts. I am very sorry for the grief and the heartache that I have caused.*

Members of the task force, as well as the victims' friends and families, were in the courtroom to hear Larry Bright admit to murdering the eight women. Bright's family, however, chose not to be present.

The victims' families weren't convinced Larry Bright felt any remorse for his crimes. But one of Bright's other attorneys disagreed. After the hearing

Hugh Toner told the *Peoria Journal Star* that in his twenty-five-year career as an attorney, not many of his clients wanted to plead guilty from the outset.

"When was the last time you saw someone who was charged with murder, and on day one, wanted to plead guilty. It is not like he changed his mind," Toner told the newspaper. "Before death was off the table, before anyone had said anything about anything, he wanted to plead guilty. So I think that shows he has accepted responsibility. Is he remorseful? Yes."

Because Larry Bright pleaded guilty, the total cost of his case was only $221,515, instead of the $500,000 to $700,000 it could have cost the state, had it gone to trial. But that was just for the trial phase of the case. The four local police agencies involved, the Peoria and Tazewell County Sheriff's Offices, the Peoria Police Department, and the Bloomington Police Department spent a total of $350,000 on the investigation, while the Illinois State Police were on the hook for about $200,000. Those costs included more than a dozen detectives, several crime scene investigators, a couple analysts, and even an anthropologist, who worked a total of 18,600 hours over six months to find out what had happened to the ten murdered and missing African-American women from Peoria.

But authorities weren't going to have to shell out the $20,000 reward that had been put up for information leading to the arrest and conviction of the person responsible for the murders. And that didn't make Vickie Bomar very happy.

Throughout the investigation police received

more than one thousand tips regarding the deaths of the ten women. But none of the people who called the tip line named Larry Bright as a suspect in any of the murders.

But Vickie thought she was entitled to the money because she testified in front of the grand jury about her harrowing experience being held against her will by Bright. It was that testimony that led to Larry Bright's indictment on the charges of unlawful restraint. Vickie said she would be happy to share the reward money with any other woman who helped lead police to Bright.

The problem was that Vickie didn't contact police on her own after escaping Larry Bright's clutches—because there were two outstanding warrants for her arrest—even though she knew that police were looking for a potential serial killer who was murdering prostitutes. She only agreed to talk to police after acquaintances told police about her.

While Sheriff McCoy acknowledged that Vickie Bomar helped police nail Larry Bright, he said she didn't go to them with the information. They went to her. And that's why the Peoria County sheriff didn't pay out the reward money to her or anyone else.

When the dust had settled, Sheriff McCoy was glad that the murders of the eight women had been solved, but he still wanted to find out what had happened to Frederickia Brown and Wanda Jackson. If Larry Bright had been telling the truth when he said he had nothing to do with the murders of those women, that meant that whoever killed them was still out there.

So their deaths remained opened, and investigators continued to work with members of the black community to solve their murders. Even though Bright repeatedly denied killing them, McCoy wasn't convinced. He thought Bright probably murdered Frederickia but not Wanda, because her body was found two years before Larry Bright's killing spree began.

Although both women were black, used drugs, turned to prostitution to feed their habits, and were strangled, Frederickia, unlike Wanda, was murdered right in the middle of Bright's other killings. But Larry Bright's attorneys claimed he had no reason to lie about their murders. His life sentence—he is serving it at the Menard Correctional Center—would be the same, no matter if he murdered eight women or ten women.

Some of the investigators on Larry Bright's case agreed that he had no reason to lie about Frederickia's murder. And they thought that she might have been the victim of a copycat killer. But still Bright and others remained "persons of interest" in the deaths of Frederickia and Wanda, but police just didn't have enough evidence to make an arrest.

Like the police, the families of Frederickia Brown and Wanda Jackson are still looking for closure as well. It's hard to move on without the answers they so desperately seek: who killed their loved ones and why? Although many of Frederickia and Wanda's family members believe Larry Bright killed them, they want nothing more than to know for certain.

* * *

And in Racine, Wisconsin, Linda Fields's daughter still believed that Larry Bright murdered her mother. Larry, however, has always denied killing her. And even though investigators have worked hard to solve her murder, they have never been able to tie anyone to her death.

Like the families of Frederickia and Wanda, Linda Fields's family still holds out hope that one day someone will provide investigators with the information the police need to solve her murder.

Even though the authorities, the families, and the Peoria community know the answers they want might never come, they know some good has come out of the Larry Bright case. For one thing, the City of Refuge Worship Center has opened a substance abuse center to help people stay off drugs. And authorities said the investigation has helped improve cooperation between police and Peoria's large African-American community.

As for Larry Bright, he's spending the rest of his natural life in a cell in the Menard Correctional Center, a maximum-security prison in Menard, Illinois.

And for the families of Larry's known victims—Linda Neal, Brenda Erving, Shirley Ann Trapp-Carpenter, Shaconda Thomas, Laura Lollar, Tamara "Tammy" Walls, Barbara Williams, and Sabrina Payne—their loved ones may be gone, but they will never be forgotten.